MW01258100

CURAGGIA

Curaggia

WRITING BY WOMEN OF ITALIAN DESCENT

edited by
Nzula Angelina Ciatu, Domenica Dileo
and Gabriella Micallef

CANADIAN CATALOGUING IN PUBLICATION DATA
Main entry under title:
Curaggia: writing by women of Italian descent
ISBN 0-88961-231-5

1. Canadian literature (English) — Women authors.* 2. Canadian literature (English) —
Italian-Canadian authors.* 3. American literature — Women authors. 4. American
literature — Italian American authors. I. Ciatu, Nzula Angelina. II. Dileo, Domenica. III.
Micallef, Gabriella.

PS8235.W7C87 1998   C810.8'09287   C98-932635-7
PR9194.5.W6C87 1998

Copyright © 1998 the editors: Nzula Angelina Ciatu, Domenica Dileo & Gabriella Micallef
Individual pieces copyright © 1998 the authors

Cover design and internal layout: Heather Guylar
Editor: Ann Decter
Copy editor: Leslie Thielen-Wilson

ACKNOWLEDGEMENTS
"Blending Literary Discourses" was reprinted in *Beyond the Margin: Readings in Italian
Americana*. Eds. Paolo Giordana and Athony Julian Tamburri. Madison, NJ: Fairleigh
Dickinson University Press, 1998.
"Bottled Roses" by Darlene Madott is reprinted from *Bottled Roses* by permission of
Oberon Press.
"Dancing the Tarantula" by Francesca Roccaforte will also appear in *Mary Loves Angie,
Vinnie Loves Sal: Writings by Italian Descended Lesbians and Gays*, edited by Giovanna
Capone, Tommi Avocoli Mecca, Denise Leto (Toronto: Guernica Editions, forthcoming).
"Domestic Affairs" by Diane Raptosh first appeared in the cultural and historical review
Italian Americana.
"Looking at the Tree and not the Forest," by Domenica Dileo, was published in *Diva*,
January, 1990.

All rights reserved. No part of this book may be used or reproduced in any manner
whatsoever without written permission except in the case of brief quotations embodied in
critical articles and reviews. For information address Women's Press.

This book was produced by the collective effort of Women's Press.
Women's Press gratefully acknowledges the support of the Ontario Arts Council and the
Canada Council for the Arts for our publishing program.

Published by Women's Press, Suite 302, 517 College Street,
Toronto, Ontario, Canada M6G 4A2.

Printed and bound in Canada.
1 2 3 4 5 2003 2001 2000 1999 1998

THE CANADA COUNCIL | LE CONSEIL DES ARTS
FOR THE ARTS | DU CANADA
SINCE 1957 | DEPUIS 1957

Contents

DIMI, When are the Lesbians Coming for Coffee? (Laura)

What if Someone Found Out We Wash Dandelions, Cook them in Olive Oil and Garlic, Eat Them with Thick Crusty Bread? (Mary Russo Demetrick)

Her Tongue the Culprit (Carol Mottola Knox)

The Story in Her Bones (Anna Camilleri)

Her Garden Asks for Water (Francesca Gesualdi)

Life is Theatre (Mary di Michele)

Contributors

Editors'
Introductions

Understanding Oneself as Oppresser and Oppressed

"Class conscious is knowing what side of the fence you are on."
(Ontario Federation Of Labour — Poster)

In many ways this statement always speaks to the place with which I am familiar. My family migrated from southern Italy to Canada for a better economic livelihood. My father came to Canada in 1965, four years prior to my mother, my siblings and myself. He came first to see if Canada would provide a better place for him to be a 'good breadwinner.' When he arrived in Canada, he started working in the construction industry as a manual labourer. My mother had no choice but to come to Canada because she feared that if she did not migrate my father would not send money for us to survive in Southern Italy. There were no employment opportunities for her as there was no job market for women in southern Italy. The main paid employment for women in my mother's town of S. Onofrio was seasonal olive collection, which would bring some extra yearly cash but in no way provide a livelihood. In addition, as a woman my mother would not be socially accepted in a small so-called peasant southern town of 2000 people if she did not follow her husband's request to "bring the family to Canada."

Politics Of Location — Divide and Conquer Methods
Prior to migrating to Canada my father attempted to settle in Northern Italy. He worked in Milan in car factories but, because he experienced hardship finding housing, he returned to Southern Italy. It was common for northerners not to rent to southerners, based on the common sense racist assumption that Southerns, in particular "single" men, are criminals and delinquents. The unification of Italy in 1861 created conditions in which Southerners did not own their land. Land was primarily owned by Industrial Northerners; they spoke "Italian" not dialect, and were affiliated to Europeans in skin color and ancestry. My parents cultivated the land in exchange for a small percentage of produced value. I grew up conscious that my family would only get a certain percentage of goods produced and that the rest would go to the "big Barons living in Rome" who would come once a year to collect his goods. These social relations instilled in me a class conscious as far back as I can remember. At a very young age, I knew that whoever owned the means of production would control the conditions for our livelihood.

However, these power relations do not address other oppressive forms of power. Some men from my town of S. Onofrio, Calabria seasonally migrated to work in the mines of Ethiopia after the Italian capitalist state colonized Ethiopia in 1935. They came back talking about the many hours of hardship, then they would talk about the 'African Woman' as their "rewards." As a young child, I could not make much sense of what that meant. As an adult when I started reading feminist anti-colonial works about the rapes that 'African' women experienced at the hands of foreigners, I understood what was being said about the abusive practices of southern Italian working-class men towards Ethiopian women.

Recollections of what an Italian working-class adaptation to a new cold country was all about

Within the first month of arriving to Toronto, Canada, in 1969, I was enrolled in school and my mother started working in a chesterfield factory. She decided to cut her long braided hair to fit into the new social order. Everybody in the family would tease her that she would not go back to Calabria since it would be a long, long way back and costly. She was told that she needed to adapt to a "city" life to forget the rural life that she left behind. My mother kept the cut braids for the first five years that we were in Canada, even though the hair dresser wanted to buy them to make a wig.

The first major snowfall arrived within the first month that my mother went to work. We were not familiar with snow, let alone with walking on it. Leaving for work, my mother would often be the first to walk on the new fallen snow. It was difficult to see the patches of ice underneath. One morning, she slipped. She went to work for fear that if she returned home she would loose her job, a job that she knew would be hard to replace. A family cousin got her the job; the more family members who worked in the factory, the higher the promotion would be for my cousin. She spoke English and moved up to a supervisory position. My mother did not want to cause my cousin any embarrassment. That evening when she arrived home, her foot was swollen and blue. She put on an elastic band aid and went to work the next day, leaving a half hour earlier, so that she could walk slower and avoid the ice patch.

How stereotypes of Italian working class women filter into practices that locate them into a predetermined social location

I came to Canada when I was nine, and my older sisters were in their teens. Both sisters went to technical-vocational high schools. In no way was this their choice. One of my sisters always dreamed of going to University, but the teacher insisted that she would have better job opportunities going to a technical high school. Job opportunities meant secretaries rather then teachers. In some ways, my parents accepted this, because my sisters did not speak English well. When it was my turn to sign up for my high school of choice,

I wrote a collegiate on the application form. Collegiate was the route to university. The teacher asked me to stay behind after class, told me that I must have made a mistake, and steered me toward a technical high school. I remember not knowing what to say, since my family supported my choice to go to a collegiate. My parents believed, since I came to Canada younger then my sisters, I would have more time to learn English, thus I would be able to have a better academic education and hence better employment opportunities. Upon hearing what my teacher had instructed, my father threatened to come to school to tell the teacher that I will go where my parents tell me to go. Being new and young to a country, it was difficult to understand and make a political analysis of these experiences.

More recently, while working at Interval House reputed to be the first North American battered women's shelter,* during our regular "feminist collective" staff check-in, I checked in about possibly joining an Italian women's group. I mentioned that professional Italian women were a part of this group, including doctors, teachers, writers, etc., and said that I have to wait and see if I could join the group, because they have their own process. One co-worker responded by saying it sounds like a "Mafia" group. Although Italian men and women have achieved some upward mobility in Canada, the comment "Mafia" group, by my co-worker implies that even when we achieve economic privileges, it does not get measured by the merits of hard work or personal merits. Somehow we must have gotten where we are by "Mafia," or corrupt means. This counteracts how white middle-class anglos are viewed in similar situations; they are seen to be entitled to their achievements, the accepted outcomes of "their" hard work. Even within the context of middle-class achievements, being Italian, puts us in a different, "corrupt," "suspicious," category of otherness.

Being Oppressed and Oppressor:
Paradox relations of being one

The personal experience that I have shared thus far creates my point of reference as a social and political being, as a working-class feminist, as a marxist, as a lesbian. My Italian Canadian immigrant experience, my Southern Italian experience, are two different points of reference that are part of one same world. Trying to make sense of my own geographical transformation locates me in a privileged geographical land in which I am continuously faced with common sense assumptions of the Mafia. These common sense assumptions, whether in North America or in Italy, serve to maintain the status quo — the interest of the white, middle-class patriarchal/heterosexist social formation.

To speak of our experiences as Italian women is indeed the first step. By speaking, we challenge our own internalized assumptions of ourselves. In understanding our own resistance to classist, racist, patriarchal practices, we can make links to other forms of oppression. Thus we can work towards common political goals. We can work to eradicate the dominance of oppressive powers over all of us. Through an understanding of our history as working class people in Italy, we can understand our personal experiences so that we can eradicate the injustice being done to other social groups. Within this political frame this anthology breaks ground for Italian women.

Any introduction starts with how this anthology came about. In 1990 I had read an issue of Sinister Wisdom, a quarterly journal, on Italian women. Among the American authors, I came across a piece about being Sicilian/Italian from a Canadian Italian Lesbian, Nzula Angelina Ciatu. As soon as I read the piece I knew that one day I would look for her name in the Montreal phone book.

This started the initial, ongoing discussion between Nzula and I about growing up in Italian working-class families, trying to make sense of "identity" as Italian women. Even with this dialogue there were political differences between her and I. We talked about how issues of class, race, gender, sexuality or practices of incest/abuse affected our lives. In other words, we talked about things that were familiar to both of us as "Italian women," such as migrating from rural Southern Italy, speaking our own Southern dialect at home, attempting to learn English in elementary school in Canada. This was part of growing up Italian in Canada for both of us. How we were objectified by our teachers and the kids in our schools. We discussed our own families of choice that we have outside of our own biological families.

Somehow we wanted to reach out to other Italian women and see what they had to say about their experiences. We wanted to use our resources, our own experience of feminist organizing, to provide a space to represent the diversity of Italian women's experiences. I was on the Manuscript Assessment Committee at Women's Press and discussed the possibility of doing an anthology. The project would expand Women's Press's readership to a new "community." As well, the Press's mandate for inclusive representation of women would be strengthened. Nzula and I continued to have political discussions concerning issues of identity/colour politics/South and North differences and decided to have a working editorial group of three rather than two. I asked Gabriella to join the project since she and I had worked in "feminist" organizations in Toronto since 1986. She was also the first out Italian Feminist lesbian that I met.

With the anthology completed, the political meaning is left to the reader. It does raise the question of who the audience is. Is it the Italian community? Is it the feminist community? It the academic community? What in hell does an Italian anthology mean to the reader as an active part of the larger social political context?

Introductions are also a time for self-evaluation, for understanding what has been accomplished in completing the project. As editors, we had the privilege to dialogue, in limited ways, with most of the writers that we have chosen to publish. This anthology reflects the complex issues of its writers, issues that have affected all of us as "Italian" women in some form or another. Our personal experiences filter what we write. One Italian woman called to find out if she could submit to the anthology, since she was not abused, did not leave "home," was not disabled, but was happy with her "Italian family." My response was "yes" and started laughing to myself. I immediately realized that laughter is a sign of moving on. I laugh at the courage that we as Italian women have always had and continue to have, in all the forms that shape our lived experiences.

'Curaggia' to all women who submitted to our call for submissions.
Bocca a Lupo.

Domenica Dileo, Co-Editor

---

*   This is a common assumption among shelters workers, both in our oral history and written documentation. However, it was brought to my attention that Andayuhn shelter for Native Women in Toronto was established in 1972, one year prior to Interval House. This oversight raises the obvious racist reality.

The Moon Only Howls when Hands Leave Lips and Words Spread like Dew to Conspiring Minds

The first Italian lesbian and feminist that I met, contacted me after I'd published an article delineating some of the cultural, gender, and racial obstacles preventing Italian women from living to our fullest potential. Growing up, the contradiction had laid itself out like asphalt on an untread path, thick and unmoveable: in such a women-centred, women-lead, women-affectionate, women-speak culture, how could it be that my choices, my expansion as a being were so limited by my gender? Intense gender schisms rocked the ocean floor through steps we so cautiously place. Like many other Italian women, I left the mountain rock that cradled me lifeful, the scents that soothed my cell surface to the very deepest chambers of memory. I left my family home to become all that I could be, as if culture or race could be boxed away, stored, and left behind.

In the feminist community I could release my voice to endless boundaries in reach of all that it meant for me to be a woman, a working woman, a university student, with or without children, with or without a partner, a woman not conforming to sexually oppressive realms. This, when the most I was meant to do was to become a hairdresser, a secretary, marry a man, keep house, and have children, parameters that defined success within the culture and class in which I grew up. But the paradoxes continued, and the complexities of culture, race, and sexuality played out like divagating rhythms, rarely harmonizing. What I could never be in the feminist community, was Sicilian. What I could not be in my Sicilian community was lesbian and feminist. What I could rarely express, in either the Italian or feminist communities, were the complexities of my mixed-racial heritage. Divergent shells, personalities, parallel bridges that would only meet at some undignified crossing.

My involvement with this anthology has been forged out of my search, from a longing to fill empty space, to find places where I could exist without fragmentation. I found that others were searching as well. I learned, too, that their journeys as Italian women, like mine, were paid for at great expense. Not the visible scars, bitterly engraved in the mounds of our skins, that burnt copper into ore, but the marks on our breaths, at the tips of our spoken words that swayed peaks with glacier winds, and often stung a bitter and tasteless residue into all who heard.

With this anthology, I want to honour the survivors: those of us who are outcast, beaten, or threatened upon coming-out; the numerous Italian women whose families have severed contact because they chose to leave the home unmarried or because they did not conform to sexist dictates; I honour the women who have no choice but to stay, and those who stay out of choice, and who continue to confront and survive. It is the crescent moon of stories so cutting, I hold fire to tongue in words sweet-spoken. With this anthology, I honour the women treading new ground, funnelling life into existence at a gambler's bet, and hope to connect community with community, to encourage a dialogue within Italian circles about gender, race, class, and sexuality. Indeed, I honour Italian women growing up in supportive families without gender constraints. I join in celebration, the rooted and expansive pleasure of our Italianita.

A Feminist Historical Rationale

Feminism in North America has become a challenging force to many women's lives. It has given both practical and theoretical tools for us as women to make sense of our lives and to transform our conditions within a repressive society.

The women's movement and individual feminists have been addressing the question of "voice," who in society holds the power to speak and to be heard. While women in general have been ignored and hidden throughout history by a male-defined capitalist system, many women from white ethnic groups have also emulated the racism, elitism, and ethnicism inherent in a male-dominated society. In past years, voices from marginalized peoples have forced a traditionally white women's movement to re-examine its theories and practises according to class, race, sexuality, and disability. The voices of women of colour, lesbians, women with disabilities, working-class women, sex-trade workers, and others have all emerged to create movement for concrete change. Within this discourse, where are the lives and experiences of Italian women?

Certainly, Italian women within North America follow a forceful tradition of powerful daughters, mothers, and grandmothers. Our individual strengths as Italian women have indeed made historical and sociological marks within our surrounding communities. Why then have our voices been so muffled within literary traditions — both feminist and mainstream?

In *The Dream Book: An Anthology of Writings by Italian-American Women* (New York: Shocker Books, 1985), editor Helen Barolini explains how the very real threat of assimilation helped streamline children of Italian immigrants into the practical arts:

In America, schools were not always regarded as the road to a better future; more often they were seen as a threat to the family because they stressed assimilation.... When your frame of reference is a deep distrust of education because it is an attribute of the very classes who have exploited you...then you do not encourage a reverence for books among your children.

Threats and experiences of assimilation have contributed to the literary absence of Italian women, as have ethnocentric practises and stereotypes by both feminist and mainstream circles. Walking into a bookstore in search of Italian-American women authors, Edvige Giunta describes how she is steered by the bookseller to the cooking section: "Even bookstores...have managed to keep Italian women in the kitchen" ("Blending Literary Discourses"). Among the published journals, anthologies, and texts by Italian writers in North America, those by male writers greatly outnumber works by Italian women.

Nevertheless, Italian-Canadian/American women's voices have been making their mark on the mainstream. *The Dream Book* was among the first to begin to break the literary silence by bringing to the forefront writings by fifty-six Italian-American women. The journal *La Bella Figura* was another vehicle for Italian-American women writers to make themselves heard. *The Voices We Carry* (Montreal: Guernica, 1994), an anthology by Mary Jo Bona, focused on Italian-American women's fiction, and *Sinister Wisdom*, a lesbian feminist journal, had a special issue on Italian and Sicilian-American women. The fall 1996 issue of *Voices in Italian Americana*, edited by Anthony Tamburri et al (Purdue University), was on Italian/American women authors.

As Italian-North American women, we write in the context of this history. In speaking and writing our truths, we frame, clarify, demystify, and continuously redefine our roles as women. We defy the stereotype of the obedient wife and the selfless forever-giving mother. We dare to break cultural and familial codes of functioning, such as omertà — Southern Italian cultural silence which mandates, 'See no evil, hear no evil,' and certainly don't write about it to be published! Omertà, along with a distrust of mainstream services which have traditionally been discriminatory, are two of the reasons why issues of violence against women have rarely been addressed within our own Italian and Sicilian communities.

When Italian women write, we make public these experiences of violence, dictating resolutions on our terms. We bring forward the complexities of our realities, as well as the intricate richness and joys of our lives. In doing so, we begin to carve a wide, emanating space in patriarchal literary milieus.

Through all of this, our voices have begun to reach one another across geographical boundaries: momentum spins, gathers, and prospers. Community is forged with new invigorating boundaries on old familiar ground.

The Italian women's reality within North America with all of our diverse tongues, ethnicity, class statuses, skin colours, divergent historical origins, and sociological placements that fall under the umbrella "Italian" will only add depth to the ongoing and necessary discourses around racism and classism within feminist and mainstream communities.

Nzula Angelina Ciatu, Co-Editor

Curaggia, Writing by Women of Italian Descent

This anthology was conceived over three years ago. I joined my two co–editors in mid-conception, so to speak, to help carry her to term and through delivery. We have spent years in utero, each pregnant with our own struggles: fighting demons, chasing our dreams, working through this anthology, as we all faced fairly major life shifts. Pregnant at the time, in transition in many ways, emotions shook me, dislodged me, sent me on a rough trip. Our personal journeys, full of twists and turns, at times made it difficult to nurture this project, precisely because this anthology is about journeys, about movement, about letting go.

Through these shifts, we would meet to talk, dialogue, make decisions, talk some more. And it continued. Unlike my daughter, who was in a hurry to appear (she arrived well before her due date), this anthology remained in the womb, feeding off our loves and our losses. So much so that we wondered, at times, if we would give birth to her at all.

You see, we arrived here at this juncture, the three of us, each with our own road map. Courses set through our own aches and desires. How do you navigate while in motion, in two or three, at times, opposing directions? How do you share aches and pains, lusts and desires, the stories that make up our lives? How were we to do this?

Then the fervour of creation showed its hand, reminding us that this was a passionate process. We could not do this solely with our heads. We needed to explore. Explore the crevices and creases, the rifts and ruptures through our beliefs, values, and experiences. Know each other a little more. Take some chances. Not be so sure. Un po de "curaggia" is what we needed.

We asked other women who identified as Italian to send us their writings, to tell us about their isolation, violations, fascinations. In essence, to tell us about *their* aches and pains, lusts and desires: the stories, the journeys, their thoughts and reflections, their memories and aspirations. We asked them to speak about the least spoken, to say the least said.

Pieces arrived slowly at first, then, word of mouth spread the news, and our sorelli replied with intensity. We received over 1,000 pages of submissions. Many of us were prepared, needing to speak our truths. We have chosen poems, stories, journal entries, art work, essays, and prose that speak to our experiences: our desires, our sorrows, reflections of our lives. From a mother speaking about her response to her daughter's independence in Francesca

Schembri's "Meglio Morta che Disonarata," to a young Sicilian dyke speaking about her experiences on the street in Boa's "Young, Proud and Loud," they speak what is difficult to hear, forcing reflection on our own behaviour. Reminding us of our own rigidity. Toni Ellwand's "The Motorcycle," and Anna Camilleri's "The Red Dress," touch our own experiences of unnamed pains. These stories speak of broken trusts, abuse of power, and we are left for the most part, to make sense of it on our own. We struggled through issues of race and culture. What did we mean by Italian? Who do we mean? Birthplace, language, upbringing, first or second generations, and how does race play into it? Where does race intercept ethnicity? How does skin colour play into this? We struggled with the notion of differences, assimilation, and ethnic/social identity. In "On Naming" (Edvige Giunta), "Identity as Context" (Susan Raffo) and "Excerpts from a Letter" (Denise Leto) issues of identity — cultural and racial — are addressed.

It is important to mention that we only received one submission from a woman identifying a bi-racial heritage, that is women who are of both European and African, Asian or Aboriginal descent. Nor did we receive submissions from Black, Asian or other non–white women born/raised in Italy and/or Italian culture. Although we acknowledged the need for and conducted outreach to bi-racial and women of colour communities, we continued using mostly Italian networks and contacts, expecting maybe, a strong cultural identification would find a racially diverse Italian group.

That was naive on our part. For many of us with skin colour that is seen as desirable in the western world, we experience the benefits rather than the tyranny of racism, and issues of race continue to be a point of struggle. Racism continues to wash away the cultural experiences of Black and of colour peoples. Remember the objection to a Black woman recently crowned Miss Italia. The colour of your skin continues to matter, so much so that ethnic identity is second to race identity. The colour of our skin continues either to, override and ignore, or value and highlight our cultural identification. Cultural bonds across race lines continue to need our sustenance-we can't let go!

In this anthology we combine, like a risotto marinara, a little bit of this and a little bit of that. We have thrown together our laments, life's pains, our desires, yearnings, our joy and pleasure at the things that make us laugh, all drenched in our passion and drama for life.

We celebrate our relationships with mothers, daughters, lovers, and friends, the struggles and the blessings. In Laura's "La, Are You A Lesbian," a mother and daughter share reflections of their relationship. Michelle Alfano draws us into our own childhood, recalling our perspectives as kids in her lovely "In Which Music is a Dominant Factor," an operetta of a family in motion from the perspective of the children. Francescadi Cuore delivers the best sermon I have heard as she takes us on a journey, challenging our notions of Catholicism, challenging us to celebrate ourselves in "Leaving Home," a short prose piece full of profound and thoughtful dialogue. These stories, poems, essays and rants demand that we cry when needed, stand firm when necessary and always laugh with each other.

Curaggia sorelli, we will all get through.

Gabriella Micallef, Co–Editor

Editors' Note

The title for this anthology arose from the many submissions received from women of Italian descent all over North America. As we sat surrounded by these submissions we began to see the courage it took to write many of these pieces. We recognized the courage many of us have had to muster up, to find in ourselves. "Curaggia" is what we were told by our families when somebody was going through a hard time. Curaggia figlia mia... Curaggia figlio mio... Courage my daughter. Courage my son. We have used dialect and feminised the word to pay tribute to women's courage, to acknowledge our strength, our ability to survive, and to acknowledge our faith, that we will get through, we will get through it all.

Editors

The Spread of Air Between Us
(Denise Nico Leto)

Meglio Morta che Disonorata

Francesca Schembri

Mom, whether you like it or not
I'm going out tonight.
No figlia — non t'arrishchiare,
Di tuo padre ti vui fa' ammazzare.
Mom, I'm not a baby anymore
And soon he has to know
He ought to let me go.
Figlia, ti da' volta il cervello?
Finire voui in un bordello?
Stai muta! — vai a lavorare,
Stasera se ne puo' parlare.
No! Mother, you don't understand,
We're not in Italy anymore —
Girls here, go out and date
With their male prospects.
Zitta, sei ancora una bambina
E vuoi giocare a signorina.
Mom, I'm twenty and in love...
Zitta...zitta si sa poi la voce,
Sara' poi questo no' spiantato
Non se' neppure avvicinato!
Mother, you can't communicate
He's nglese! He's not 'uno di noi,
We don't want to be married.
Figlia, che disgrazia!
Ma come fai a guardami in faccia?
Mother, I'm spending the night out
Figlia sciagurata!
Mi vuoi fa cadere ammalata?
Mom, nothing will stop me
I'm going with him tonight.
Oh, figlia che rovina,
Meglio tu non torni viva!

Mother of A Priest

Rosette Capotorto

the mother of a priest
has high status
in an Irish neighborhood
in the Bronx
even if she is Italian
a bit dark, a bit loud
a bit flashy

her one true son is a priest
who works for the Archdiocese
liaison for the Cardinal
(the one who runs St. Patrick's)

the mother of a priest
is the mother of a priest
even if she is divorced
smokes Pall Malls
and wears plunging necklines
on her doorstep
the neighbor women leave flowers
from their gardens
fresh baked scones
brown bread wrapped in
white cloth and
rosary beads blessed
at St. Anne's
by one of their own

the mother of a priest
loves dark rooms
black lace
Sophia Loren
and long sheer nightgowns
from Alexander's

perhaps that is how her son
first came to love

the confessional
to crave time in the
dark corners of churches
among the men of golden
robes and soft hands

the mother of a priest
is given plenty of rope
(enough to hang herself)
but they will never hang her

they can't be sure
how she, whatever she seems,
ends up with this son
this lovely priest
who's been to Rome
and loves the Pope
and works for the Cardinal
but is not too proud
to say Mass on Sunday morning
in an obscure church
in Woodlawn
(a small town if ever there was one)

in soft notes of envy
touched with grace
the women wonder
(how did she do it)
little do they know
she laughs in my kitchen
smoke snaking from her nose
and cackles
I had nothing to do with it

she takes no credit
for this priest of a son
she simply stands in his shadow
quietly
even if her breasts show

she's lived in the Bronx
all her life
she knows how to hedge a bet

rations

Giovanna (Janet) Capone

At 72
my mother's heart
fibrillates
for no apparent reason.
My father is lying in a hospital bed
five days now
while they stabilize his insulin.

At home, my mother naps on the couch
An hour later she wakes up
with fibrillation.
Her heart is beating too fast
She panics, worrying about my father,
wondering what the hell is going on.

Months earlier, my brother was in a car accident
In a drunken stupor
he plowed his jalopy
into a tree
Christmas eve
and he comes home bloody.
My mother calls the doctor
puts him in a cab
sits with him in the hospital emergency room.

Christmas day
and all the cooking to do
a houseful of people about to arrive.
My mother, at 72, bends over a pot of sauce
It's the holiday
and everything has to be just right.
She cooks for eight people
with high blood pressure
and a wacky heart.

"Ma, sit down. I'll take care of that."
"Go in the livingroom," she yells.
"It's already done!"
Christmas night
and my mother's in the emergency room
her heart racing.

"It's fibrillation," the doctor says.
"Your heart rate is speeding up."
His years of knowledge tell him this.

So she undergoes stress tests.
She lies on a flat steel table
and rotates in a thousand different directions.
A blue dye seeps through her veins
while a machine makes photographs,
mapping her from head to toe,
like the Italy
she came from.

Then she walks on a treadmill
for thirty minutes
a rubberized belt moves her small, round body forward
and forward and forward.
A machine records her heart's response.
I ask her later,
"Ma, is this a test to measure your stress
or to wear you out even more?"
She laughs at the whole ordeal.

The doctor finds nothing wrong with her.
He's amazed.
"How do you handle your stress?" he says.
"I yell," she answers without hesitation.
A proven method,
it still works after all these years.

"Why can't she relax?" we complain,
four decades younger
and a generation removed from Italy.
"She needs to chill out.
She freaks out over everything.
If someone's having a crisis

she's having the crisis too!"
"She's enmeshed with her family."
"Women who love too much. It's co-dependent!"
my sister-in-law says.
"No it's not. It's Italian," I say,
"and it's none of your goddamned business."
Oh God! Here we go again,
till somebody yells
"Shaddup!"

My mother's heart
is a finely tuned instrument
capable of high speed vibrations.

Like an engine
whose job it is to love
she shifts into higher gear
when necessary.

Lucia's Garden

Adriana Suriano

Earth's flesh feeds me at six years old.
Tomatoes align themselves with zucchini
grape vines embrace both burgundy and golden
pear and peach trees conceal
your tired face
figs split open
eaten off their branch.

A shed shields your tools
A rake, some wire
two metal shovels.

Your house has seen
marriages begin, a grandchild die
photographs are the wallpaper.

In your knee high socks
navy polyester dress
pounding on pots and pans
guarding your crops
against curious rabbits, squirrels,
grandchild.

Mezzo giorno we sit together
the ground cool under the shade
munching on today's pick
laughing at the neighbour's stare.

coupled

Adriana Suriano

The virgin white lace tablecloth
awaits in my mother's night stand
crocheted by nonna in Italia
who barely remembers my name
who stopped calling three years ago
to ask if I was coupled.
"Si nonna. Hai ragione," were
the last words we spoke. I am
the shameful one who sleeps
without a wedding band
wakes up with my maiden name
signs my own rent checks.
Sends her photos
scattered private journals
poetry and its rewards on the wall.
Presses the keys
hard on my keyboard.
Receives photos of cousin Rosa
her handsome fiancé studying law
matching brown leather shoes and belt.
Adriatic Sea flowing behind
the smiling old womyn
who barely remembers my name.

Nana's Peaches

a memoir

Carol Mottola Knox

My Italian grandmother was the only person who could laugh at me and get away with it; no mean feat, for I was a child with dramatic flair bordering on the operatic. It was not uncommon for me to weep and whine with gusto at the slightest provocation. But when my Nana, who adored me and who beamed each time I crossed her kitchen threshold, would laugh at me, it was a safe signal for me to laugh back at her. And how I would! My heart tickled at the very sight and sound of her, transforming frustration into giggles.

For if the joke was on me, so was it on her. Picture it: on one side of the turquoise arborite table, across white crisses and crosses of the red oilskin cover, was herself, the lady who had crossed the ocean cradling her new daughter in her arms, comforting and crooning in the only language she knew: Italian.

Five grown sons and another daughter later, Italian was still her metier. The Calabrese town she had long left behind was reflected now in the small Italian community nestled in this railway town of Transcona, just outside the city of Winnipeg. Her identity, her comfort zone, the very atmosphere she breathed had remained inviolate. Although the periphery of her life touched Canada itself, all things intimate maintained their Mediterranean hues, flavours and sounds.

Across the spotless oilskin I preened, "drinking coffee" (only with you, Nana, only with you), performing my cosmopolitan act. Coffee at Nana's consisted of a cup of warm milk, a drop of coffee for colour, and roughly eight teaspoons of sugar. My grandmother knew how to make a lady feel grand! Poised as I tried to appear, I was, in fact, her inadvertent nemesis. I, firstborn of her own, beloved of her beloved, special one of her special one — speaking to her in, and only in…the dreaded English! Her eight year old granddaughter, the infidel. That was me.

The one who spoke no Italian. Come from the city to spend some quality summer time. And in less than the forty-five minutes it took to arrive by bus at what for me was the Continent, an infinite reserve of palliative laughter stood at the ready. Our painful predicament? On one hand, we were verbally challenged to the 'nth' degree; on the other, we had so much to say. Each time we met, we remembered. Our eyes quickly revealed a latent sorrow: just below the surface of two loving hearts lay a vast and indomitable void. An empty canyon that was somehow saturated with mystery; a power which drew us to itself again and again. Our desire and determination to follow were lured by a love that was greater than any obstacle. Not for nothing were we Italian women! We would fight with tenacity for communion.

"Commé stai, bellezza?" (cheek pinches)

"I'm fine, Nana, how are you?" (stinging cheeks)

"Ah, stai bené, gracia" (kisses to make the sting go away)

After establishing the well-being of mama, papa, baby brother, and scoala — (they were obviously bené, else I wouldn't be there), the river of our conversation began drying up. Our scintillating dialogue was losing its sparkle. Rather than indulge this dilemma, my nana rallied, and made straight for her prime arsenal: coffee and the biscotte she draped with icing just for me. She exhorted me to "manga, carissima, manga!" Rhetorical words, I might add, for I loved this ritual and notoriously ate every bit of food she ever gave me. In truth, she was adroitly fending off the lurking chasm. Sophisticate though I thought I was, it was she who had true class.

It was not that my Nana had done as some others and refused to learn English. Rather, as each subsequent offspring went through school, she acquired an adequate vocabulary, storing words and phrases as she went along. No, her mental filing cabinet was not where the problem lay. Her tongue was the culprit: it was set in its ways and simply would not cooperate. For just as Nana ordered her words out in English, mutiny occurred. Immediately upon stepping smartly to the beat of fife and drum, that traitor tongue would roll and curl towards its soul-mate: the roof of her mouth. Like prisoners-of-war released, rejoicing words linked elbows, danced the tarantella, and flung their partners about. Vowels frozen by the frigid English Channel thawed and floated on balmy Mediterranean waves. By the time her thoughts arrived at my ear, they were singing an old familiar song from home.

But not familiar to me.

My father, whom Nana adored, had nonetheless made some irrevocable decisions since marrying her daughter, decisions which were painful for both. Costly though they were to my grandmother's life, she had chosen not to challenge them nor reveal her sorrow. Her son-in-law was a man of great respect; for her daughter's sake she would champion him. She never wavered from this stance.

Small-town life would never do for my father. Thus my mother, a sixteen-year-old bride, went directly from the cocoon of her mother's kitchen to a new life-style in the city, exposed to all manner of people and backgrounds. How difficult this must have been for my grandmother: she lost the companionship of her eldest child before ever gaining the luxury of enjoying it. The rest of her family had come along too quickly; her daughter was leaving too soon. There had been no time to sit drinking coffee and laughing together as we were. In the blur of cooking, scrubbing and cleaning as a team, of changing diapers and nursing illnesses side by side; her right hand had somehow become a young woman. A woman-child with whom she had toiled; never dallied.

On the heels of this loss came her first granddaughter. A great moment, but bitter-sweet. My arrival was accompanied by a second Paternal Pronouncement; another stinging blow. My father ordained that in his city home we would speak only English — English was to be the mother-tongue of his offspring. This was not a value judgement but a judgement call, based on his understanding of what would serve us best in life as Canadians. Since my father justified himself to no one, the Italian community was left to form its own opinions. A vocation to which they were certainly called.

A radical decision, but a positive step in my father's mind. Designed to promote belonging in a Canadian world, it inadvertently drew lines in unnatural places: I (and my future siblings) would from that day be alienated from our Italian heritage in the most fundamental way — we would grow up in a world where that language was nothing more than strange noises, often much louder than we were accustomed to, coming from a people we could not understand.

Again and again, I was to stand beside my mother or father at some Italian gathering while they spoke lustily in this strange tongue and tone, hands flailing, their faces transforming even as they spoke. They seemed to smile more in Italian, really relax; it was as though they were different, happier people. And I was not 'in on it.'

My mother soon recognized my blatant signals of sighs and shuffling feet, and did her best to include me. I didn't want to be included, I just wanted to go home — where normal people lived. But we didn't get to the 'let's-go-home' part either swiftly or painlessly. Not without acting out the familiar farcical script, beginning with: "You remember so and so, she's the aunt of the cousin of Mario (or Carmella or Saverio)."

No, no, I did not! It made me furious! I am ashamed to admit it, but each year found me ruder than the one past at being expected to identify "those people." They all looked the same to me through the jaded eye mysteriously sprouting on the tip of my snooty nose. Frizzed hair, gold jewelery, a smattering of gold teeth, and the ubiquitous stale, black clothing. But the rub was that this band of strangers had a relationship with my parents which, although out of my loop, was tauntingly visible in its immutable splendour. A mystery; the thorn in my flesh. How it chaffed and tore.

I would stand on the sidelines and roll my eyes, blatantly projecting the message that they, not I, were the interlopers. I was the daughter here, after all. Their stars did not sparkle in my universe. I could never know them because of their strange language and customs, so I adopted a body language which spoke for me: I don't wish to know you, anyway!

Bear in mind there were so many of them, and only one of me. I think this is where I developed empathy for minority races — I knew what it was to be the 'only one.' A horde of people who were virtually deaf to my clumsy attempts at speech, a nightmare for a chatterbox like me, left an incessant need to be understood, and a secret belief that I would never be. This feeling of apartness, along with its partner, guilt, landed in my gut early on and never left. I was the Italian pariah who never failed to evoke that look on the face of a "real" Italian at the blatant evidence that I was deficient. An incompetent in the language of my ancestors, a handicap to the Community at large.

But not my Nana. The only disappointment on her face was there because of her own limits. As though she were letting me down. Doubtless there were treasures of wisdom she was unable to bequeath; certainly there were times of trouble in my life where she yearned to plant her love via words instead of taut osmosis. Yes, Nana, I could feel you trying. And if the words did not get here, the love surely did.

That was why this woman could laugh at me and get away with it. She had a magnanimous heart which invited reciprocation. There was no blame on either side, only recognition that we both got the joke. Our mutual hilarity landed us in a life-long bond of intimacy; ours alone to cherish.

In spite of the language barrier, Nana would often send me on errands to the store (I dreaded it when it was the Italian store), or to some neighbour or other to fetch or offer anything from beans to eggs to baking. Most often my aunt or an uncle was available to translate the instructions for me.

One particular day, just as I was beginning my summer holiday "abroad," there happened to be no one else around. Nana took her chances and sent me on an errand "downtown," a euphemism for the three business-lined blocks on the main street of Transcona. Not far; a pleasant walk. She requested that I go to "Roberts'a Druga-stora" and pick up her peaches. She was anxious because she had "losta the billa," and she admonished me several times to state clearly that they were for her. Since this assignment was accompanied by the inevitable nickel, gleaned from the bottomless sugarbowl for a popsicle, I went willingly. Besides, it was summer, and I was free to roam!

Has the sky ever been so blue since then, or the sunshine so caressing? Joy, joy, joy to skip along the wooden sidewalk, joy to see jaunty flowers everywhere nodding and waving me along. My friends. Riots of triumphant fuschia roses raced with alacrity along latticed Italian trellises and arbors; orderly rows of sun-yellow marigolds obediently lined the whitewashed fences of perfectionist Ukrainian residents, standing sentry under sparkling picture windows. Turn right, cross the gravel street, along two blocks which revealed inner secrets of every corner house: ubiquitous beanstalks and bandaged tomato plants holding sway over obese squash, with perky pink petunias bobbing in place, defining backyard gardens. How intimate this

Curaggia

glimpse; how thrilling! Onto the Big One — Regent Avenue. (New York, move over!) Dance left two more blocks. Turn in to Roberts' Drugstore. Remember exactly what Nana said. Losta the billa, losta the billa.

"Hi, Mr. Roberts, I've come to pick up the peaches for Mrs. Cantafio. She said to tell you she lost the bill, but you would know which ones." Popsicle already in my mouth, grimy hand outstretched, I looked up to see confusion pass across old Mr. Roberts' face.

"Peaches...hmmm, that's a new one! I'm sorry, miss, but you'll have to tell your grandmother that we don't carry peaches. Unless...yes, that must be it! She must have meant you to go to the Fruit Home. Sure, that makes sense."

Accustomed to these errors by now, I acquiesced and happily extended my mission another block to the town's only specialty shop: both fruit and soda fountain. Streaked with melted purple rivulets, baked by the blasting sun, I was not a welcome sight to busy clerks who wasted their time hunting for peaches that were not, it seemed, there, nor ever ordered, by any Mrs. Cantafio.

Since I wanted very much to please my grandmother, it was with some anxiety that I returned home empty-handed. Nana was most emphatic — the peaches were at Roberts'a Druga-stora waiting for me to pick them up. Mr. Roberts had said Wednesday, and today was Thursday. All I need do was pay for them. Did I show him the money? Maybe he thought I wanted them for free? Mamma Mia! What would he think?

The second round-trip was walked, not danced — but it was the third that rendered the sun unbearable, the houses with their ugly flowers hateful, and turned me into a muttering beast. How could I face Mr. Roberts yet again? He was as adamant (there are no...peaches...here!!!) as my grandmother (si...si...the peaches are-a there-a!!! Go backa, go backa!!!) I quoted radio's Gildersleeve as I stomped back and forth. "What a revolting predicament this is!"

I was grimy, sweaty, purple, and my burning feet were blistered. For the last time, I limped back to Yale Avenue East. How to get her to understand me? How to get her to understand the ways of the English-speaking world? Drugstores did not sell peaches, for gosh sake! Everyone knew that! I was humiliated. I was weary. And I was fed up. Why was she being so stubborn? Why did I have to be born Italian anyway?

When I crumpled through the doorway for the last time, bearing still no fruit, it was clear that she and I were battling mixed emotions. Laugh or cry? What to do? We had reached an impasse, a brick wall which neither of us had the skills to scale. I saw a degree of frustration on her face which in a lesser woman could have led to murder. Mine. Instead, my grandmother did what she always did when language totally failed us. First she shook her fist as at a naughty child. Then she threw her head back and laughed until the tears fell. We had landed in a comedy of errors yet one more time. "Peacheres, peacheres!" she squealed, "Oh, Madonna Mia, how I can say better...the peach...er...ees...!" Mrs. Cantafio was doubled over with mirth.

And then I got it. The light went on. She hadn't been asking for peaches at all! She had sent me to pick up the pictures that were ready at the drugstore, only she had lost the receipt.

What a victory celebration we had when I arrived home after a marathon run from Roberts' with that envelope of pictures in my hand, name of Cantafio indelibly printed on the front. Double portions of caffé and biscotte all around! What a triumph we shared. We had won! She had persisted in what she was trying to say, and in the end, I had understood. No Nobel or Pulitzer could ever feel as good as the prize that was ours on that lovely summer day in 1947. Understanding and being understood. Nana's peaches. A trophy indeed.

As if From a Great

The choco'
scratchy
felt th
I w
r

I remember you most in the kitchen
standing at the sink, a warm
washcloth in your hand, the soapy
water sending steam up, fogging
your glasses. Or standing by the stove
stirring the enormous pot of sauce
with the same wooden spoon
year after year, the six stuffed artichokes
in the blue and white speckled pan
covered with aluminum foil
waiting to be eaten. How you moved
from refrigerator to cupboard to sink
endlessly, the rhythm hypnotic, demanding.
I would stare up at you, knowing
your attention was elsewhere
knowing that was how you fed me
and I remember you buttoning
my new jacket for me, with the red anchors
on each white button
my hair cut in a pixie,
my teeth coming in.
I had shorts on and blue sneakers
you handed me a small brown sack
with some Hershey bars.
I think you spit into a tissue
and wiped my face before I left.
It was the first time I would walk
to the Andolina's house down the block
and across the street by myself.
I was scared and you knew it and ran
your hand through my hair once
before I started. I got all the way
to the bee bush and then stopped.
I could go no further, I stood crying.
Time passed, an hour, then two.

.e melted, the jacket felt
.d I peed a little,
.varmth down my leg.
.ed to run back home
i didn't, rooted there
.i my young body.
And I remember so much.
You driving us to the beach down Highway 8
when there were still cows in Mission Valley
their black and white bodies beautiful
against the green of the hills.
Once, we got a flat tire
in the black Rambler with the red tail fins
at first we thought it was just some
rough road and a helicopter above
but then we pulled over
and you looked suddenly tired
and open like a rose before the petals fall.
I remember the time
we drove to Sears to buy material
for my Home Economics class
there was a sale, it was crowded
and steamy and the women pushed and elbowed
and you elbowed them back.
On the way home it was raining
and a car drove by us, fast, the water
sprayed up through the window
and you had to stop because you
were drenched and couldn't see to drive
and we laughed so hard you had to stop again
and later at home with the pattern cut
and the fabric pinned
I accidentally sewed the sleeve
to the front of the blouse
and you had to rip out the seam
and do it over for me.
I wanted to tell you then
what I already knew
about the sewing I would never do
the cooking, and the men I would not love,
and the women I would. I wanted to tell you
that blouse with the queer sleeve
sewn against the cut of the pattern

Curaggia

was me, *don't do it over*
but you sewed it to perfection
anyway and I took the finished
blouse back to class
and I can remember the feel
of the fabric against my skin, the lie there
and I looked at you as if from a great distance
the sad spread of air between us
suddenly lost, suddenly known.
I remember you most
in the morning, the ritual
the warm milk, the hard bread
the sound of your hands
no longer touching me
clearing the table, washing the dishes
putting the food away.

Sunday Lunch

Stefania Vani

Ritornai da Mia Madre

Giovanna Di Lena

Ritornai da mia madre
e mia madre mai più mi riconobbe
il mio cuore palpitava lontano.
Ritornai da mia madre
ma ella non mi rispose
e fu allora che capii
che dovevo seguire l'aquilone
e fu allora che i miei occhi
assunsero un nuovo colore.

I Returned from My Mother

I returned from my mother
and my mother would never again recognize me
my heart was distantly palpitating.
I returned from my mother
but she did not answer me
and it was then that I understood
that I needed to follow the north wind
and it was then that my eyes
assumed a new colour.

I Dream of My Grandmother And Great-Grandmother

Maria Mazziotti Gillan

I imagine them walking down rocky paths
toward me, strong, Italian women returning
at dusk from fields where they worked all day
on farms built like steps up the sides
of steep mountains, graceful women carrying water
in terra cotta jugs on their heads.

What I know of these women, whom I never met,
I know from my mother, a few pictures
of my grandmother, standing at the doorway
of the fieldstone house in Sant Mauro,
the stories my mother told of them.

But I know them most of all from watching
my mother, her strong arms lifting sheets
out of the cold water in the wringer washer,
from the way she stepped back,
wiping her hands on her homemade floursack apron,
and admired her jars of canned peaches
that glowed like amber in the dim cellar light.

I see those women in my mother
as she worked, grinning and happy,
her garden spilling its bounty into her arms.
She gave away baskets of peppers,
lettuce, eggplant, bowls of pasta,
meatballs, zeppoli, loaves of homemade bread.
"It was a miracle," she said.
"The more I gave away, the more I had to give."

Now I see her in my daughter,
that same unending energy,
that quick mind,
that hand, open and extended to the world.
When I watch my daughter clean the kitchen counter,
watch her turn, laughing,
I remember my mother as she lay dying,
how she said of my daughter, "that Jennifer,
she's all the treasure you'll ever need."

I turn now, as my daughter turns,
and see my mother walking toward us
down crooked mountain paths,
behind her, all those women
dressed in black.

Summoning Death

Francesca Gesualdi

As though hailing a taxi cab
she stands by her vegetable garden and summons Death
to hasten her to her joyful assignation.

With august force and milkwhite lips
she sings,
I must return this flawed and battered vessel
to the merciful fool
who saddled me with it.
Its maintenance has grown much too obscene,
Hurry, Oh Death, with your proud wings
before the duty of the day rebinds me.

Mother of mine,
she prays, please don't banish me now
though I let you make your last journey
without this daughter's kiss upon your brow.

I'll be there soon.

She watches Death present itself outside her fenceline,
mulling something over in a neighbor's yard.
Arms outstretched, she calls
but Death flees upon seeing her ready smile.

She perseveres in a circle of morning light
her own scarecrow,
'til her garden asks for water.

Cara Mamma, I Write You This Letter That I Cannot Send

Gabriella Micallef

This is an excerpt from a work in progress that explores the themes of family, mother-daughter relationships and the issue of forgiveness.

Cara Mamma,

I write you a letter that I cannot send. Prompted by a dream. A dream I continue to try and interpret. To understand.

We are in your living room — myself, my daughter and my brother — though I cannot picture the room. You are there watching. We are packing boxes. I remember thinking I was glad I had brought the van so I could move the rocking chair. Remember the rocking chair. You had bought it for me a long time ago-one for me, one for my older sister, a piece of our hope chest. We were teenagers at the time. When I moved away, a long time ago, I did not bring the chair. I did not send it with other boxes that were filled with my belongings and left weeks before. It was just too big to fit into the car and wouldn't come apart. It was also part of a different hope chest of expectations. I had other hopes, other expectations. Since then, something had changed for me. Now I could finally take the chair.

I turned and saw you crying. "How can we be together for Christmas now?" you ask. I turn back, ignoring the question. I have not been "home" at Christmas for many years now. The question was not meant for me. There was very little talk as we packed. The moment passed. I became absorbed in packing the van. An adventure — or something — loomed ahead. I could feel it. I commented on heading for Texas. My daughter stopped to look at me. I shrugged. Didn't know where that one came from. Then, I heard your voice again. "She's here," you said. Everything slowed down. I turned my body and stood up to see you there with my aunt. Granny stood at the end of the hall holding on to each of you. I was surprised. Knowing of her death 10 years earlier, this was a long trip for her. I turned and walked toward her, arriving quickly. I reached for her extended hand and sunk to the floor in front of her. I held her hand as I cried. My body shook with a sobbing I have always been terrified of-a sobbing that feels endless.

It is too vivid, this dream. Too intimate. I cannot dismiss it. My sobbing: an act of confession? A premonition of something to come? She came such a long way. Held my hand as I felt my body collapsing. Her hand full of love, not letting go. "What did you mean for me to know"?

I write you this letter that I cannot send. There have been too many years of protecting/barricading my emotions.

There are many things that have happened in my life the last few months. New thoughts about lingering painful issues, confrontations, and a new life.There have been many times I have remembered that dream, and thought I finally understood.

I have felt much anger over the years. Anger that allowed me to stay away from a sadness that lingers underneath it all. A sadness that threatens to drown me in my own tears. I cannot weep for all that I have lost.

How can I cry when your sadness threatens to overtake the two of us.

Cara mamma, cho un grande desiderio che un giorno nel tuo sguardo vedro la felicita.

There have been many years of anger. Feeling let down. Let go of. Estranged from you all. FIGHTING, FIGHTING, FIGHTING. Wanting you to understand the decisions I have made. Especially you.

The issue of forgiveness is a recurring theme for me. Feeling as if I needed to forgive to be rid of the anger. "It's not that we don't love you, it's just that we are not strong enough to go down that road with you," my uncle said to me. My emotions had fought their way to the surface. My sunglasses remain on my face, an attempt to hide.

My heart could not understand and accept what my head knew and long understood.

I write you this letter that I cannot send. For my honesty will force your hand and then I will be left with the outcome.

My friend R.H. tells me, "It is birth and death that have the potential to shift us." And indeed it was when your granddaughter was born that I began a shift.

So many feelings: joy, pain, uncertainty, excitement and apprehension. As she struggled through her first few days, you were there, loving her, praying for her. I felt as if she redeemed me-your love so strong it could not help but penetrate through all my anger, all the years of it.

Then I began to see. Then I understood. It has been myself that I have had difficulty forgiving.

Forgiving myself for the sadness I see in your eyes.

Your life success shown through your children. But success is subjective and laden with ridged notions of gender, cultural and class expectations. What I consider my success, it seems, is your failure.

Curaggia

How do I take away your shame? What did you feel with your mother? What will I pass on to my own daughters? Lamentations?

Cara mamma, comme possiamo ristabilire il rapporto che abbiamo perso?

I write you this letter that I long to send.

Bottled Roses

Darlene Madott

"As if
The scene you play were mine"
— (Camillo, The Winter's Tale, IV, iv.)

Do I remember him? It was here I folded your letter, and crushed it. For days it has lain subtly unfurling in the corner where I threw it, a swatted paper moth. You don't ask about the London audiences these days, what the critics are saying to my Lady Macbeth, not about anything important to me now but about *him*. Do I remember?

Of the two women I am remembering, one knew the very secret of secrets, which is the art of keeping secret; the other knew how to *use* secrets, which meant at some time or other she let them loose. I don't know when I came to understand how confused their secrets were with mine. But I sense there is a pattern to it that the four of us complete — my grandmother, my mother, myself and now you.

My grandmother was a formidable, Depression-made terror of a woman. I say it with respect; for whatever cause my mother and I both had to resent the old stinker, Nicolina Leone was more interesting than the whole pack of aunts and uncles put together. My grandmother and I shared an instinct for the theatre. That was what we saw in each other and it made a bond between us. Not that Nicolina ever went on the stage in any actual sense. But in a deeper reality, I don't know that she was ever off it.

The last time I went to visit, she was still stubbornly entrenched in her own home (who could live with her?) Still turning the earth of a garden she swore each summer would kill her, still covering her moustache and offering her cheek if you went to kiss her (that dark growth disturbing her vanity; she'd wanted to have it removed at seventy, when she first heard about electrolysis). When I asked how it felt to be ninety-three, she said to me in broken English with her indomitable sense of humour, "I'ma ole. Thisa house, she stink. *Ma*, I never be so sick I canna wash miseff."

My great-grandfather begat Nicolina and seventeen others upon his first wife Francesca, and when she finally croaked (a horse having thrown her and the unborn twins twisted in her stomach), the old bugger married a widow named Nina. Nina had three sons of her own. Nicolina was sixteen when her father remarried and she fell in love with her stepmother's son Paolo.

Although she was her father's favourite, or perhaps *because* she was, Nicolina was never allowed to marry her choice, and both she and her stepmother wept the day Nicolina was compelled to join lives with my Grandpa Rosario. For as long as I can remember, my grandmother spoke with pride of having refused to dance at her own wedding. When my grandfather came to her window at *Carnevale* with a lantern of candies and a troupe of hired musicians, he was trying to woo her heart now that he'd won her hand. She bolted her windows and corked her virgin ears. They were married anyway, after Lent. And yet she recalled these things to me with a kind of grim satisfaction, as if she believed she'd still won.

I remember the day she told me her story. We were sitting on the verandah peeling beans because I hate to just sit, just as my grandmother hated to just sit, and it was fall, crisp and lovely. I was in love for the first time, which may have had something to do with it, for I was stirred by the sight of her harvesting her memories. She told me how my Grandpa had offered her a *bicchierino* of wine to celebrate their betrothal, and how her father had intercepted the glass as she reached for it. In the old country I suppose hands never touched. What must she have thought when all the wedding guests had left? My Granny blushed like a young bride at my implication. *"Che poi fare?* My Papa, he tella me marry. I marry."* And she dramatized her legendary innocence, how that night after the songs and banqueting were done, she got up to leave with her parents. Her stepmother Nina said, "No, Nicolina. You have to stay here now. Go to your husband." And this was when tears filled her eyes, as they always did with each retelling, right on cue, and when my own mother, hearing me repeat the story to my sisters, interrupted.

She's full of shit and don't you believe a thing she says about your Grandpa. My father was an angel. And he loved her. Paolo was just an excuse, a might-have-been. It's easy to talk when there's no-one around to say any different. I know what my mother was like. She just loved to make a scene. When we were kids she'd rage over nothing for days and my father would try to coax her out of it. 'Nicolina, Nicolina, aw c'mon.' She'd shrug him off, but you could tell she loved every minute of it. Then she'd threaten him right there with the loaf of bread she was slicing. They'd end up laughing. She didn't care who was around then. She's a bugger, your grandmother. Don't ever let her fool you."

A fascinating bugger though. Still, you can afford to be fascinated if it isn't your story she's rewriting. How many lives did she spoil, convinced that next to God, she of all his creatures was always right? Nicolina wasn't the least bit sentimental for all the tears she squeezed. If every now and then she plucked the dulcet string of feminine romance, you could be sure she had something else in mind.

When it came to her own children's marriages, she opposed all seven of them. Two of my aunts eloped with their unfortunate choices — one because she really loved him, the other because she'd rather die than marry anyone her mother loved. Granny's favourite, Nino, refused to breathe when he was three and so escaped the fate my Aunt Ninetta undoubtedly inherited by coming after. (Ninetta was the family's basket-case.)

Granny's sacrificial lambs. All except my mother. Being the youngest, she must have had her eyes full. Although my grandmother cursed my mother's marriage and its issue extravagantly, that marriage, of all her daughters' marriages, was the only one that wasn't cursed. As long as I knew my parents, their tenderness for each other never tired, never diminished, never grew old.

Perhaps you'll understand then why I was nervous the day I introduced my grandmother to my fiancé. Because Paul, out of all the introductions to precede him, was the first Granny had ever smiled upon. And he took to her instantly.

On her eighty-fifth birthday, with all the aunts and uncles, all their children and their children's children assembled to pay homage, Nicolina looked down from her place of honour, scanned the crowd of related faces and thundered, "*Dov' e Paolo?*" Paul was painting his mother's house. I had to get on the phone and summon him because Granny refused to open one gift until he arrived. She had worn her best black dress and her wig for the occasion. My grandmother would never have dressed up for her own. After she bore her children she had little time or use for their private feelings. She was too busy looking after herself. Here was a woman who had clung stubbornly to life through two bouts of puerperal fever. To die in childbirth was just not her style. She had a sense of gesture. To have so many was sweeping but definitely not the way to go. The house was always full of *paesans* from Italy, and Granny wanted her praises sung in every letter, every photograph of her verandah and herself, posed grandly with her little tin-types clinging about her skirts, which went back home. During the Depression she even made over old clothes so that no-one would suspect her family needed. They were thought rich while they starved. The guests ate meat while her own family filled up on bread. Undernourished, the whole lot of them. My grandmother was five-foot-eight. Not one of my aunts exceeded five-two. Yes, Granny was a clever chess-player, interested not so much in the pieces as in her own control over their moves.

So I didn't like that "where's Paul," nor did I like what came with it, my blessed-among-women status and the "*sangue mio*" with which she claimed me as her own.

By the next year and only one week before the actual wedding I had called it all off. My reasons had something to do with his jealousy, which at first delighted and then exhausted me, being so impossible and unpredictable it required all my energy. I say his jealousy, meaning that intolerable, love-only-me part of love that won't recognize anything your mind can spin

Curaggia

out singly, which says "I want no more than to see you happy," and means "I have to be your only happiness."

He thought to tempt me away from the world of theatres, insisting what I wanted to do most in life was superficial, not real, was making a spectacle of myself for an audience's amusement. Acting was not meaningful work. It was diversion, play. I knew of course that these were only words concealing the real reason for his resentment. I got tired of arguing; I told him *he* was the diversion.

An hour after I'd hung up the phone he was pounding on my door. I cried and cried on the other side but I wouldn't open. The wedding gown hung in the hallway. Nothing was disturbed. No-one knew yet. But I wouldn't open. My stubbornness was stronger than my want, for at the time I still loved him.

How do you explain these things? He was so beautiful. Like a Roman statue. A cold, challenging beauty. I was nineteen when I met him. What did I know? I had never been in love before, never even lived yet. I only knew that I adored the fine arch of his nostrils, his strong jaw, the way his eyebrows met frowningly across his forehead, the feel of him holding me from behind with my back nestled into his chest and his lips on my neck.

And then, he was so exotic, a lot older than my other friends, twenty-five when I met him. He worked as an engineer at an aerospace company, talked abstractly about the project that then engaged him, part of a telescope France was building with Canada to fill the top of some dormant volcano in Hawaii. I thought it romantic that he should be a star-gazer, never realizing how full of coffee cups and broken pencils his world of circuit-boards must really have been.

At first it was comfortable to have him always there, knowing his eyes were seeking me somewhere in the darkness of the wings. I felt singled out, protected. He had a kind of sad charm with his briefcase and his ties and his trying not to get in the way when his mere orderliness amidst the props and dusty curtains was in the way. We were so unlike. But I loved him, made love to him at first through my lines. It was only afterward I understood how much this playfulness grieved him. He put up with it because he loved me.

"Why do you love me?" I asked him once. "What is it you love in me?"

I had taken longer than usual to change, and when I came through the door beside the stage, expecting to find him somewhere in the empty auditorium, I saw him on the stage, sitting at an upright piano with his back to it, legs outstretched, elbows leaning against the keys where old butts were stubbed between the cracks. He was smoking a cigarette, and in the darkness the slow burn of that single glowing point was very dream-like, haunting. I was so moved by the sight of him waiting for me, I suddenly wanted to be forgiven. Why did he love me? He looked startled when I asked, as if to say, you mean you doubt me? But he never really answered. It often happened that his answers only silenced me, they didn't satisfy.

"If I could tell you, Jean, I wouldn't be in love with you."

This made me flinch. I didn't like the compulsiveness his words suggested. What if someday he should find himself wondering? Paul troubled me the way a woman in the front row had once worried me by fixing her opera glasses on my face. I was flattered by the attention and frightened by it too. However guilty it made me to acknowledge it, I did doubt him. I feared it wasn't me Paul loved, but some fixed idea of me, his own, which must alter if I were to remain my own, believing in my own changes. What then? He'd never forgive me. He'd believe I had deliberately deceived him. Whatever my doubts, I didn't want that to happen. I still wanted him to love me.

There was a dream I had about this time that I believed held some significance. In my dream I was locked in a dark theatre. Something insidious was expecting me and I knew where it was but not what it was. I went to a costume cupboard and threw it open, unhanging every costume until I found it. It was an actor's mask, tied by ribbons to a nail and gaping with a drooped, evil grimace that seemed to mock me. I tore at it violently with a hanger, sticking my fingers through its lidless eyes and ripping them apart. Even when it lay in shreds I kept tearing at it, relentlessly, furiously, surprising a wildness in myself that was as sinister as the mask. Only when it was completely destroyed did I realize my fear hadn't left me. *I* had left me. I was moving like a grey shadow into the thing, becoming what I'd destroyed.

I told this dream to Paul after we'd had a bad argument. Weakened by tears and afraid of myself, afraid of the stubbornness in me that wouldn't let go even if it meant sacrificing my own happiness, afraid of losing me in the masking of me, I asked Paul to make me a promise.

"Promise me you'll never let me leave you." I was serious. I didn't trust myself to make the right decision. It was a moment of supreme fearfulness, childishness really, because I didn't want the responsibility. He behaved accordingly, his voice soothing and parental. "It's all right. Everything will be all right."

It breaks my heart now to think just how seriously he took me. Paul gave me what I asked, tyrannically.

"But if she cannot love you, sir?"

"I *cannot* be so answer'd…"

But then, the Duke of Illyria didn't have Paul's mother. For I come to his mother.

His mother who had stood at the sink with her back turned to us, resolutely peeling beans and crying when he told her he was going to marry me; who sucked her teeth; who enjoyed misery because it broke the boredom of her days, because she liked to have her hand held and be coaxed back into smiles; who accused me of never looking her in the eye when it was her tongue whittling away at a back tooth I couldn't bear to watch; who accused

Curaggia

her son of having forgotten her, her reproaches sounding not quite right, sounding too much the whine of a neglected lover. His fiercely jealous Mamma, the only person I've ever truly despised.

It used to torment me that Paul didn't seem to recognize the game she was playing, that for every rose he bought me there had to be another on her kitchen table, that for every occasion she developed a sudden illness. In pulling him from her bedside I found myself playing an ugly tug of war where I lost with every gain because he was sullen when he came, because he passed his guilt from her to me like a plate of rancid meat.

Paul's mother was my rival. He belonged more to her than he ever could to me. He belonged to that silent apartment back in Italy where she locked him up as a little boy while she went to work at the factory. There was something dark and disturbing about him, something he must have carried with him from those distant rooms where he would play for hours at a time with the coloured buttons in her sewing-box. Half his thoughts were in another language, forever foreign to me. Even the landscapes of his dreams, always secret and impenetrable, were doubly alien to me, who could never know the sound of a cypress from that of a pine.

Perhaps it was wrong of me to blame his mother. Perhaps Paul was never really deceived by her aches and pains. I can almost understand. For she was alone, more alone than ever my grandmother had been when she undertook the same journey a half-century before. Nicolina Leone had more social sense, more inventiveness. She knew how to make her own fun and enjoyed her own company. Perhaps, too, I had never really understood the perplexities Paul faced, a boy of twelve with an immigrant memory, what bitterness he concealed when his mother embarrassed him, what guilt he felt, being embarrassed at all. I was a generation beyond having to undergo these humiliations.

Whatever the failure, there was something my father said to me when I went to him attempting to sort out my feelings, something I couldn't ignore or forget. "Acorns don't fall too far from the oak. He may think he doesn't like her now, but give him time. He'll want his wife to act just like her. You'll be peeling his oranges the way she always did, making pasta every night, or you'll never hear the end of it. Salmon return home to spawn. Look at the mother."

Appalled, I never could look at those self-pitying eyes, nor think of the ignorance that dwelt in her walnut of a mind without fearing the primacy of blood. Could he, even in some hidden corner of his being, be like her? And I'd picture myself twenty years from then buying purple sweaters and Woolco purses, the same dark fringe above my lips, standing in a field of dandelions with hands pressed against my back to keep my stomach from toppling me. I was terrified of ever coming to resemble *that*, and yet I was filled with what

I hated. And I hated her because she diminished life. *"La vita é dura"* was all she ever had to say about this hugely engaging existence.

Paul couldn't have known what he did the day I was feeling depressed and happened to tell him I was. He made a curious slip. It was like a revelation. He grew impatient and irritable, and when he spoke his voice was oddly spiteful. "You remind me of my mother." Aghast, I could think of no answer.

It wasn't too long after that we were playing out our scene on opposite sides of the door.

Had it not been for one terrible coincidence, that would probably have been that. I would have suffered for a time, but not been really damaged by it, the kind of mooning I overheard my father speak of one morning in the kitchen with my mother when I was thought to be sleeping late, like my sisters, but was in fact frozen in the hallway, convinced it was I they were discussing. "You can't keep flogging a dead horse," he said. And then I heard, "No wonder...can't sleep...walking the floors all night," which was what I had done the night before. When I laid my wounded righteousness on the table in front of him, my father looked up from his coffee and his only answer to me was, "You, Jean, could hear a butterfly fart." Later my mother assured me it was she he'd been talking about, but I suspect she just said this to mollify me. I do know we were then, and had been, conspirators.

The conspiracy I'm referring to is the one that made Granny our common enemy, and it was as much the outcome of coincidence as anything I've known.

My poor mother had to inform everyone that the wedding was off. I wanted it irrevocable as soon as possible but couldn't do it myself. I was afraid I'd crumble under the weight of a question. So after rehearsing her a few times I set my mother up at the telephone with a glass of scotch, and by the time she finished going down the list she had polished off half a bottle and a box of Kleenex. The ordeal took her about four hours. I sat with her the whole time. She had made me write out on a piece of paper what to say and it went something like this:

"Corine? It's Fran here. How are you?...Not so good. I've got something I have to tell you. Jean isn't getting married this Saturday....No, it's all for the best....*Well, I'd rather not talk about it.* (I had underlined this for her.) If you'll excuse me now I have a lot of calls to make....No, there's nothing you can do.... Yes, I know they looked beautiful together, but looks aren't...Corine, I have to go now..." And every time she hung up the receiver it took her ten minutes to recover. She'd tell me all over again everything she said and they said. And some said they had had a feeling all along, and others

Curaggia

said what a shame it was, and so on and on, and it was awful, and people are awful, though some were wonderful.

It took the next few days to unmake all the arrangements and I spent them in terrible mental anguish. Cancelling it all wasn't the worst of it. There were the calls from Paul, the priest, Paul's friends, for Paul was busy begging everyone to intercede, and everyone felt they had a right to explanations.

I was terrified of everybody, didn't want to meet anyone I knew, ever again in my life. I couldn't bear the thought of the pain I was causing him. I couldn't marry him. I couldn't live. I couldn't die. Finally, when I couldn't take it any more, I pulled a new dress from my trousseau, did my hair, put on some makeup to cover the puffiness, made an appointment at the Gold Shoppe to have my ears pierced and asked Mom to come downtown with me. We'd go to dinner, have a few drinks, book a trip somewhere, anywhere, it didn't matter, and maybe sleep that night for a change.

It was Friday, the twenty-first of June. I lived a month in that one day. When we got down to Bloor Street my mother and I were beginning to feel a little better. We were out and moving, though everything around us had a surreal stillness, as flat as those stagy train-window backdrops that move on rollers and return while the actors jiggle their bodies and get nowhere, undestined against their painted landscapes. It felt like high summer holding off a rain, for the sidewalks had that sewer-and-sweat smell, overbaked, dust-struck like late July. The sun beat relentlessly through the rain-filled air, sucking in the pale tops of trees and overexposing everything. Downtown the shoppers moved deliberately, so many flickering frames in a silent movie; overworn images flecked and brittle with dryness. I watched as in a dark theatre, feeling very distant. And yet the day closed in on me. It comes back to haunt me whenever the air is white and steamy, whenever I wait for rain.

Before we entered the Gold Shoppe we paused, unaccountably, and looked at the window displays. With that brief hesitation I saw him, inside the shop. He was handing something over the counter. I dragged my mother to the nearest doorway and stood there in horror, panting as if I'd just run a mile.

"What's the matter?"

"I've just seem him."

"Who?"

"Him. *Him*, of course."

"Where?"

"In the Gold Shoppe."

My mother's expression changed. It sobered. She drew herself up as if preparing for a blow and looked at me. Her question drove the last spike into my indecisive heart.

"Why are you standing here, Jean?"

"I don't know, Mom. I don't know." I was pleading with her.

"You know. In your heart of hearts you always know."

We were looking each other straight in the eye.

"We can go if you like." She was challenging me.

"But my appointment. What about my ears?"

"You can phone them from the next corner. Say you'll make it some other time." And then she said what we both knew.

"You want to go in there, don't you? You want to."

"We can walk quickly. Straight past him. He'll never even see us. It's at the back of the store anyway."

"Don't play games, Jean. Don't play games with your life."

But I was headed in and her warning struck upon deaf ears.

For I had seen him. Can you know what that means? I could have turned away a thousand times if I had seen him in my imagination alone. But seeing him there, in reality, his handsome face distraught from so much suffering, intent now upon something in the counter, unaware that I was watching him, his elbows and forearms leaning on the glass so that his broad back appeared hunched and sadly beautiful, I wanted to hug him from behind. I was overcome by a strange excitement that kept turning over in the hollow between my ribs.

For there was the unknown. I *wanted* this experience.

The strange thing is, he didn't see us. Not until I'd had my ears pierced and came out of the back room into the shop again. Hearing my voice, Paul looked up startled, frozen in profile like a listening animal. I tried not to look at him. I had only glanced over to see if he was still there.

He came to me like a sleepwalker. My mother sat stiffly on a Victorian chair not far from us. I don't think she could stand.

"How are you, Jean?" He said it very quietly, as if after days of telephone calls I wouldn't answer, he'd finally resigned himself to the fact it was over.

"I'll be all right."

"You had your ears pierced?"

"Yeah, it hurt too."

I tried to laugh but an unexpected tightness caught at my throat. I looked away and my eyes fixed on a pair of opera glasses inside the glass counter. He followed my stare. For a moment we were both looking at the opera glasses.

We talked, about such simple things, as if there were not that overwhelming knowledge between us, that coincidence too huge to speak of. The next day was to have been our wedding day.

I asked him what he was doing here, and he told me he was returning something he'd bought for me. He was careful not to sound accusing. He

Curaggia

asked what I was going to do now, and I told him I wasn't sure, I hadn't planned on this.

I don't know when the months of bitterness heaved into my mouth—bitterness for expectations disappointed, dreams you won't ever believe in again after twenty-three. I think it happened when my mother lifted her face to kiss him and wish him good luck, when she left the shop. I wanted to say something then that would make him know why I'd done it, know that I'd suffered too, something that would avenge me for his being so good about it now, when it was impossibly too late, something he'd remember for the rest of his life. I said the cruellest thing I've ever uttered.

"Someday, Paul, maybe you'll be able to hate your mother honestly."

"My mother has nothing to do with this."

"Hasn't she?"

He was livid. His lips were like chalk. They thinned to a hard line and I knew, I finally saw in his eyes the reason I had loved and hated him, drawn by fear to the person who threatened me most, running now to avoid becoming what he saw as me, escaping that final tyranny.

I turned, but his voice followed me.

"And you tell *your* family to stop calling."

"Who's called you?" Realization hit. "Granny!"

"How? I never said…"

"It's Granny, isn't it? She would."

I was furious. I could read his broken promise to her all over his face. I left the store before he could deny it.

My mother was standing on the sidewalk, crying, oblivious to the parting wave of people that passed her. I put an arm around her shoulder. She felt so delicate, like a frightened little bird. My rage left me. Left me extraordinarily without bitterness or defence. Sad, that was all. Such immense sadness. What had I expected? To steal the show? I'd come off poorly. I'd convinced no-one. Not even myself. And here was my mother, crying for me. For me!

I walked her toward the subway.

"Please Mom, it's hard enough."

"I'm sorry. It's such a shame."

"Mom, I don't regret it."

"Are you sure, Jean, are you really sure?"

"Yes. Please stop crying now."

Sobbing into one soaked Kleenex, she choked out her words.

"I'm sorry. It's just that love's such a precious thing. I'd be nothing without your father. Nothing. I can't stand to think of you without what we've got."

I knew that for my mother, this was one of life's unstated truths. My father was the still point in her life, a man profoundly committed as husband and father to being what he was. He let us commit ourselves to what we were, even if it meant letting us make our own mistakes. I think my sisters and I learned to trust our parents' love in a way so deep the knowledge of it could be assumed. It had that quality of permanence that gives life its whole shape and meaning. So my mother, at that moment on the sidewalk, wanting the best for her children, wanted love. Love such as she knew it, such as she defined for me with her simple words. Before her belief, I was overcome with nostalgia for something I'd never had.

"It's so important to love someone, to have someone you can share things with. What else is there? What does it mean? Without love it's all just selfishness."

I *had* to change the subject. I told her about Granny. Her crying stopped instantly.

"She what?"

"She called him."

We had reached the entrance to the Bay Street subway station. Mom hiccuped, saw where we were through swollen eyes and somewhat irrelevantly, reminded me of my promise to take her to dinner.

"How can we go, after this?" I said.

"Well, I'm not going home. That's for damn sure."

The minute we got to the Fifth Avenue Tavern my mother descended the stairs to the washrooms and got on the phone. She dialled with a fierceness I'd never seen in her before. Because this was her flesh she was defending.

"Ma. It's me, Fran. You know, your daughter. The one you're always kicking in the teeth. You called Paul, didn't you, Ma? Don't give me that horseshit. I *know*....Never mind who told me. *I want to hear it from you*....Okay, Ma, question number two. Who did the dialling?" (My grandmother was illiterate. We knew she had to have an accomplice.) "Ninetta! Why, Ma? Why did you make her do it? You had to find out. Couldn't you have asked me? I'd have told you. Do you think Jean did it for nothing? Couldn't you have given my daughter the benefit of the doubt? I don't care if he called you first. She's your flesh and blood....He wanted to find out how she was, did he? As if he cared. Don't you know bullshit when you hear it? Even if he did, what do you know about my daughter's feelings? You don't even know mine....Oh yeah, we've been having a picnic the last few days. Maybe I sounded all right, but I wasn't all right, Ma. Tell me, just one more thing, why are strangers always better in your books? Tell me, why do you always believe them first, over your own grandchild for Christ's sake....I'll swear if I like. I'm fifty-two, a grown woman with four grown daughters and I don't have to account to you anymore. I'm not going to forget this one, Ma. I'll never forget it. I've had it."

Curaggia

I think my mother surprised even herself. Still holding the phone, as if trying to figure out how it got back up there on the hook, she blinked in disbelief.

"I shouldn't have done that. She sounded so upset."

"Good. You've got her worried for once."

"But she's an old woman."

"Old! She'll bury us all. And don't feel guilty. It'll do her good to sweat for a change."

"You think that's right?"

"Whether it is or isn't, you never let it sink in. Be smart for yourself, Mom. She's not worried about *you*."

"She's just an old woman."

"With a thick skull. C'mon, let's get a drink."

My mother had three Bloody Marys. I had three vodka martinis: straight up, and straight down. By the time I'd finished them nothing was at all straight, not the room, not the past, not the next moment.

With that one Kleenex drying out on the table between us, my mother and I grieved together. *Had I said this, had I done that, it might have worked out, he might have loved me better. Who can say? What if I were not Jean, and he were not Paul?* We lost our sense of the moment and what this entailed.

What amazes me now is how incredibly innocent we must have been to look with such trusting eyes on this question of love, how it should somehow be possible to agree that the hug against the dark is worth infinitely more than proving who-hurt-who first. It seems to me now so obvious, I don't know how we missed it — that two people can fall in love without ever being able to tolerate each other's truths. I must have sensed this then, but not been convinced. My wings were only singed, not consumed, and as long as I could still see his face, burnt like a negative upon my mental plate, I had no will *not* to fly into that flame.

Three words to sever the silence. That's all it would take. I could even pronounce them proudly. Like me, he would be desperate for comfort. Three words ignoring everything that had happened, all that needed to be said, would have to be said if we were fools enough....

I hadn't a doubt he would receive me. His siege had me convinced that if at any moment I lowered the drawbridge he would still be there. For this was love, this wretched devotion, this unwanted humiliation that happens to you, making you want despite yourself, despite what you want. What other force could have made me compromise all those beliefs for the sake of which I'd left him in the first place?

It was dark when we left. The subway was a press of bodies that shuffled at each stop without altering the terrible density. The air was thick, oppressive. Darkness, flashing lights, closeness. My mother and I are disgorged into the upper air to wait for the bus that will carry us home.

A decision has grown in my mind to unbearable proportions. My desperate need to go to the bathroom lends it urgency. By the time the bus comes I have to go so bad I am almost nauseated. My head rolls on the back of the seat — my eyes closed, mouth an aching open hole. Even my mother's touch is painful.

"We'll be home soon," I hear her say distantly. She pats my hand. I have become numb. The only two realities converge in my brain. Must call him. Must go. Insistent. Relentless.

The bus stops at Bathurst and Lawrence. I tell my mother I can't hold it any more. The Bay Company Department Store is open and somehow I make it to the women's section on the third floor where I know there's a washroom. My mother is right behind me.

What happens next must be a dream. I hear his voice. His hello hangs suspended in the telephone's clicking void. Thin echoes of unreal voices cross the wire connecting our silence. I am called upon to answer. Say it now for God's sake. Answer him. The words are out. I'm committed. There's a pause, and then, a torrent of unleashed anguish. He wants to see me. He wants tomorrow still to happen. It can happen without anybody, just us, alone. But a doubt insinuates. Jean, you won't do this to me again? Jean, say you won't leave me again. That persistent doubt. Someday, maybe nothing. Someday I may howl with the sudden discovery of final desertion. Say I'm not alone. I say it. I'd say anything to stop the pain I couldn't bear for one day, for one moment longer, not to save a lifetime of suffering. He's so relieved. I've given him back his happiness. It makes me feel almost light. I've done something merciful for a change.

"I've got to tell your father. Somehow. He's got to know." We walked the rest of the way home. I shivered the whole time. My mother was sick with dread. We walked slowly, as if trying to postpone it. It started to rain just as we got home. My father had waited up for us. I came into the warm room with mascara streaking my cheeks and blood running down my neck. Not used to earrings, I had partly ripped one earlobe with the phone. My father came up to me and said, "You've had your ears pierced?" And I left the room to wash myself, abandoning my mother to the task of telling him. When I came back into the room he looked ashen. I'd never seen him so miserable.

"What can I say? You don't know your own mind? My God, we all get it sooner or later. I can't stop you. But if you ever blame me or your mother for not stopping you..." He was crying, inside. I heard one whimper behind his tightened lips like a tap turned to a violent close.

"You're going into this with your eyes open. You can't say you didn't know. I wish you luck."

We were married three months later and parted a year after that. I spent some time in a home recovering from a nervous breakdown and when I got out I went to visit my grandmother.

I was twenty-four. I went because my mother asked me to go. "She's old, Jean, and she's sorry. What good can it do to hold a grudge?"

I was sipping tea. My grandmother got up and went over to the mantelpiece. She took a glass jar down from among the figurines and *bomboniéras* and lifetime's worth of dusty museum pieces. She wiped the glass clean with a corner of her black sweater. It was the kind of jar in which little round gift soaps are often wrapped. She brought it over to me and I saw it held a dried corsage of faded roses.

She asked me if I knew where they came from. I told her I knew all right. *But she wanted to hear me say it.* So I said it, loud and clear. "Paul gave them to you to wear at our wedding."

"I'ma ole," she said. "I no understan' thisa worl' no more. *Tu lo ami. Lui ti ama.* You marry. Be happy. Ats all. Eh, whatsa use? Whatsa use? *Non capisco.*"

She told me to take my mother "fer sample." Did I think she'd always been so happy?

"Afore she marry your Papa, they have a fight. No see fer year. She tella him she no wanna see no more. But she get sick. Her hair alla fall out." And Granny waved her arthritic claw about her head as if tormented by some fly.

"*Ora,* you see *com'é.* They happy....Everybody fight. I know he good boy. *Lo so.* He good to me. Whatsa madder wi' you? *Testa dura* like your mother. *Ma,* Paolo no come back like your Papa. Paolo no come back."

A pattern was beginning to emerge, so claustrophobic I nearly choked on my ladyfinger when it occurred to me. For one brief instant I had a vision of the women in our family all giving birth to the same story, a tale that each successive generation must play out without anything ever being learned or redeemed. And if that weren't terrible enough, to witness it as well. Each player must pause in the wings for one last hovering instant, like the solstice sun before turning, and in that instant of outer darkness, to lose belief. For the play isn't done yet; another is taking up your script. While they pronounce, you must lip, powerless to utter or intervene.

My grandmother couldn't resurrect Paolo. Angered at her own impotence, she tried to take it out on me. She watched me, waiting for her revelation to sink in, while I sat with my finger locked in the tiny handle of her delicate teacup. How could I for one moment deny so extraordinary a thing as the human heart? How could I think all this stubbornness, this hunger, resilience and dignity no more than a fixed pageant, without substance, without life?

I looked Granny calmly in the eye and smiled. She smouldered. I smiled. She glared at me with pinched lips and wore her fierce look of pouting, disappointed childishness. She'd met her match for stubbornness. There are times when the most practical thing to do is to sit down. Granny sank into her chair. Raising and dropping her hand on the doily she'd put across its worn upholstered arm, she looked for all the world like a wooden construction sign waving Rough Road Ahead. Together we listened to the clock. Her refrigerator trickled. I felt sorry for her. Because she had to listen to these endless silent sounds. Because of the boredom in this last waving gesture. Because her head trembled on the end of her liver-spotted neck and her throat wobbled like a chicken's wattles. Because everything about her was old and powerless — the room smelling of dust and bad breath and potted plants and those God-awful snake plants you only see in Greasy Spoon windows; her greyed doilies, the matted wig she hatboxed every night, her chipped teacups and her warped old ideas.

"Whatsa use. I'm a no good for thisa worl' no more. I'm a sick an' tire." No, she wasn't. She'd had her wings pinned back is all. My grandmother never tired of life. She loved it up until the moment it finally had to shake her loose like a pair of knotted nylons — life, that fascinating puzzle over which she sometimes lost patience and loved losing it, because finding it engaged her.

No, Nicolina lived a long time after that, although at the time I thought she'd croak then and there just to spite me. I gave her bad gas. For me it wasn't that simple.

We are always limited by what we do not know. Granny thought she had my mother and me right where she wanted us. Because she had made me protector of the very secret that could hurt her daughter most, or, more precisely, had invited me to use it. Once I'd discovered one unknown, how could I ever be certain there weren't others? Nicolina had expected to rattle a whole chain of these questions. But instead of anger, I felt only awe — that I had lived twenty-four years with a woman whose capacity for mystery I'd never even suspected. I had underestimated my mother, and I felt immensely proud of her.

Nicolina may have been right about our hard heads. She was definitely wrong about our hearts. I never used my mother's secret against her, the way my grandmother tried to use it against me. I asked all right, and my mother told me everything. I told her it wouldn't have made any difference had I known. Knowing is not realizing. My mother had enough stubbornness to wait until she got what she wanted, by giving my father rope to realize what he wanted. My mother got her cake and ate it too. She was political. She was patient. Even if I had been these things I doubt if it would have made any real difference. For was there ever a time when I was certain of what I wanted? I've asked for much, and been reminded afterward that I asked for it. But the other — the knowing, really, what you want?

So my sister disapproves of your marriage. I can't say I'm surprised. And you think it's because she's had her eyes full of me. And you think you can find a friend in me, that I'll understand because I was once wild and impulsive. If only you knew how easy it would be for me to become your friend you would distrust me. I have only to tell you what you want to hear. But you'd better know I'm not committing myself to you the way my sister committed herself to you.

And when you ask, can I bring him to you…will you have us in your home if we stop over in England on our way to France? I want with all my heart to say, "Yes, yes, bring him with you." Because I see two young lovers walking arm in arm, eating ice cream in some January park just to be different; I see the Toronto of my youth; I see the darkly fascinating man to whom I gave so many hours; I see you, in love, with that radiance love spreads across a woman's skin. How charming your hopefulness seems to me. And yes, I want to be in love all over again. Because love, in spite of all it has made me suffer, is still so beautiful.

I was jealous of your mother when you were born. I wanted that experience too. But I must have known I wasn't cut out to bear my sister's pain. I can take most things that happen to me. I don't know that I can stand watching. The way mothers are forced to watch. Blamed if they do. Blamed if they don't. I must be in the play, not the audience.

So I've rounded my life out in many roles, and I have enjoyed playing many people. Make no mistake of it, I have enjoyed. But what do you really know of my life? The one story my sister told you about me, told her way, trying perhaps to use it against you. We all use each other's stories. You think you see yourself in me. I'm flattered. I'm angry too. What right do you think you have to play upon this one story? There are others, you know. You haven't heard the whole of me. But I'll save my breath until you come.

Because I'm alone now as I look out into this London. Because it's five o'clock and raining. Because I want to taste youth again, feel I still have a part to play in life. Because you are my blood, *sangue mio*. Ah, I finally recognize my grandmother smiling to me from the wings. As the curtain comes down, tossing me up on applause and voices, I feel the pain again, an unexpected rapture catching in my throat, there in the circular magic of the lights, revealing me as I bow to the nameless faces, there, a revelation astonishes me. I know what it was I wanted all along. The way I knew standing outside the Gold Shoppe when I said I didn't and it took my mother to know I did. She had that extraordinary gift of knowing almost by instinct. The way you know now what it is you want and aren't sure you're happy with the knowledge, because it's dangerous to say for even one day at a time.

But your question. Weren't you really asking me if I'd have written the script another way? Not whether I remember the lines, but what it does to me to remember? Whether I now believe it harder to live with one loud, unretractable word than with all the walking shadows of might-have-beens? My dear, without knowing you, I'd say you have my grandmother's taste for bottled roses.

Just Two Dagos Getting Some Gelati

(Rose Palazzolo)

On Naming

Edvige Giunta

The Italian tongue resists, even refuses, the clash of consonants in my name: *Edvige*. The letter *d* yields amorously to the encounter with other consonants: *dr, rd, nd, sd*, but rebuffs that awkward meeting with *v* in my name. In Italian, the *dv* of Latin, turns into the smoother sound of a double *v*: *adversarius* becomes *avversario* — opponent, enemy; a*dventus* becomes *avvento* — coming, birth.

Here I was, a child born in a small, provincial town in Sicily in 1959, stuck with a name that sounds more German than Italian — and even less Sicilian. I grew up among playmates and schoolmates with names that evoked the weight of Sicilian traditions, or the much desired cultural normalcy of Italian names: Antonella, Donatella, Sonia, Ornella, Valeria, Daniela. I did not envy those with Sicilian names, having achieved at a very young age a foggy but accurate understanding of cultural hierarchies. I knew better than to crave names like Maria Rosa, Maria Concetta, Grazia, Nunzia, Assunta, Margherita, Agata, Rita, Lucia, Domenica, names that these days I find perfectly lovely. As a child I craved the leveling of regional idiosyncrasies encouraged by Italian culture and language. And, as displeased as I was with my name, I considered myself more fortunate than those with names like Crocifissa — which means crucified and is often conveniently abbreviated as Crocella, little cross, or as the rough sounding Cuciuzza — or Rosaria — rosary, often abbreviated as Sara, from which comes Sarina. People from the mainland could glamorize a name like Sara, but the thick Sicilian pronunciation of that name, with its Arabic intonations, simply horrified me. Of course, there were people lucky enough to have names like Rosy, which was really just plain "Rosa" — as Sicilian as it gets — but that "y" replacing the "a" made all the difference in the world.

None of my relatives could pronounce my name. So I became *Edivige*, and the foreignness of my name was temporarily tamed. My aunt Gemma called me Giuggiuzza, from "Edivigiuzza," both intimate nicknames reserved only for close family on the maternal side. Nobody uses those nicknames any longer, though when my older sister feels particularly loving, she will call me a variation of Giuggiuzza: "Giuggiù." These are appellations that in time have come both to embarrass and comfort me.

Only my father, who had chosen my name in spite of my mother's thinly disguised disapproval, could pronounce it correctly, enunciating the word, making each letter resound. "Edvige!" he calls me, and from the emphasis I can guess whether he is pleased or angry, agitated or calm. I can guess whether he wants a cup of coffee or a hug, or whether he is irritated because, once again, he can't find his keys, or even whether he is about to question me about a violation of paternal rules. When I hear him call me, I anticipate a harsh word or a soothing touch.

My father used my name sparingly. He still does. I always feel strange when my name is on his lips: I experience both the shock of recognition and refusal at the sound of his voice calling my name. I feel surprise, fear, pleasure: a conundrum of emotions I struggle to decode.

The story goes that, as a toddler, my brother, three and a half years younger than I, could not pronounce my name at all — and with good reason — so he started calling me *Edi*. The name stuck. I liked it. I embraced it. I made it mine. Little by little, everyone — family and friends — began to call me by that diminutive forged by my brother. But the old name remained. My official name, my authoritative name that I never fully identified with, as if within me I carried two girls, and each answered to a different call, each spoke a different language, each told a different story. Relatives and family friends who see me rarely or have not seen me since I was a child, still call me "Edivige." My father has continued to call me Edvige and uses the name Edi primarily when he mentions me in conversation with others: "Dov'è Edi?" he asks one of my siblings. "Where is Edi?" To my mother, though, he typically asks, in dialect, "Unn'è tò figghia Edivige," — "Where is your daughter Edivige?" — turning to everyone else's incorrect pronunciation of the name he has given me. On rare occasions, he even addresses me as Edi, but I always perceive an awkwardness, a resistance, as if he is trying to reconcile within himself the contradictions of my naming.

Once, when I was ten or eleven, I asked my father why he had given me such a strange name, a name not suitable for a child. He smiled and laughed at my disgruntlement. After lunch he gestured towards me to follow him downstairs. This was a familiar gesture. Daily, my father would select one of the children to accompany him to the apartment below, where my parents' bedroom and his study were. My father would prepare slowly for his afternoon nap, and we stood there, like altar boys assisting in the performance of a sacred ritual. While we often resisted that ritual, we also treasured this rare moment of intimacy with my father. Before his nap he was mellow, even tender. That was often the chosen time to ask for his permission to go to a party or on an overnight school trip, requests that at any other time were sure to elicit a harsh rebuttal, a denial, an angry outburst. At times, he would grant that much craved "sì" — yes — and later forget he had. He would rebuke us for asking him about something so important, something that required such careful weighing of the situation, at such a delicate time, when his brain was not working properly, when all his energies were focused on the upcoming

Curaggia

nap. But it was before his nap that I liked my father best, when I got a glimpse of his repressed capacity for tenderness, his fragility, his desperate — rarely if ever articulated — need to be loved.

My father leads the way downstairs. He opens the door to one of his two studies, the formal one. He searches through his books — he has a wonderful collection of history and philosophy books, which at one time he told me would become mine after his death, since I am, of all the children, the one with a passion for books, study, and research. He pulls out a book, flips gently through its yellowed, frail pages. The book seems ancient, like most of my father's books. The most important are jealously guarded behind the black, thick curtains of the old-fashioned book cabinet. My father's library looks like a medieval fortress, dark and imposing against the wall of his spotless study, the locked room that never sees the light of day, that makes me think of a temple: my father is the priest and I am the occasional initiate, both eager and unwilling. His face lights up and his finger points to something he wants me to read. There it is! My name is in a genealogical tree. My father explains that he named me after a German princess. I have a glamorous, important name, and should be happy with it. And, for a while, I am.

My name has always felt like a secret, a secret that belongs to others. I embark on etymological and historical quests that will hopefully unveil the significance of the word, a word that apparently signifies *me*: but this signifier strikes me with the arbitrariness of its sounds which seem so unrelated to the person I feel that I am. As an adolescent, I read in a book of names that my name means "rich warrior." Somewhere else I discover I have another homonym, a Polish saint: St. Hedwig of Poland, born in 1371. In my *Treasury of Women Saints* I read that, as the legitimate heir of King Louis of Poland, Hedwig became queen at age thirteen. "She had been betrothed to William, Duke of Austria, at nine years of age and she had come to love him." As if the fact of being promised in marriage at age nine was not bad enough, because of changes in political alliances, in the end she had to marry someone else, Jagiello, Prince of Lithuania. Of course, like every good aspiring saint, she consented to marry Jagiello. Wearing a black veil, she went into a church to pray to God so that he would help her resign herself to the loss of love in her life. Thankfully, I learn from my *Treasury*, her sacrifice led to the conversion to Christianity of Prince Jagiello and his people, and Hedwig led a happy life, blissfully dying while giving birth to her first daughter, in 1399. She was twenty-eight. Is Hedwig related to the princess whose name appears in my father's book?

In college I read Djuna Barnes' *Nightwood*, a book that seduces me with its anguish and darkness. I am taken aback by the fact that one of its characters shares my name: Hedwig. Hedwig Volkbein. She, too, dies during childbirth. As I unravel the semantic threads of onomastics, I discover that my historical and literary namesakes have led lives more tragic than glorious.

The ominous history of my name takes a semi-comic turn when I reach adolescence and other kids tease me because of another homonym of mine, the actress Edwige Fenech, notorious for her appearances in what I then perceived as soft porn movies. My name continues to be a source of discomfort and embarrassment. Coming to live in the United States further complicates things since almost everyone struggles to pronounce both my first and last names correctly. I learn to recognize my name through a clutter of stuttering sounds.

The truth is, I was not named after a princess, a saint, a literary character, or even an actress. I was named after *zia* Edvige, my father's sister, crippled since she was a child, who has led a life of utter isolation. Her seclusion rivals that of the nuns of the order of the Poor Clares.

My mother tells me that just before I was born, the already tense relationship between her and my paternal grandmother became even more strained because of my mother's firm opposition to name me after my grandmother: Concetta. Concetta was both my paternal grandmother's and my mother's name. But my mother did not want to burden me with this Sicilian name, which to her evoked the past, tradition, but also the obscurity and infelicity of my grandmother's life. She wanted a light, soft, modern name for me, a name like Valeria (though Valeria, too, has ancient Roman roots). And Valeria they did name me. But a couple of days after my birth, my father, without consulting my mother, paid the then significant fee of 500 liras required by the Registry to change my name from Valeria to Edvige in order to pacify his irate mother. My mother was not pleased, but swallowed it all. And my grandmother was not, of course, satisfied by that tribute to her daughter. According to her, in respect of tradition and in respect of *her*, I should have been named nothing but Concetta.

Sicilian is nothing like English, a language where names are typically changed only to be abbreviated, to save time: Dan, Sam, Tom, Fran, Don, Jess, Liz. The monosyllable does not suit the Sicilian taste for excess and complication. The name Concetta, celebrated on December 8th, the Day of the Immaculate Conception, has a rich range of variations and diminutives: Cettina (my mother's name), Cettinedda, Cettì, Concettina or Cuncettina, Tina, Cetta, Cuncetta, Cuncè, and even the more modern Conci. But my grandmother's name did not generate any of these versions: her diminutive was Ciuzza. I assume it is a syncopated version of Cuncettuzza. To us, she was always Nonna Ciuzza, a name we never dared use in her presence or my father's. As children, we had come to believe that Ciuzza was a bad word, an insult suggesting unspeakable deeds, while in fact it must have been the amorous nickname conferred upon my grandmother by my great-grandmother, although I struggle to envision my grandmother, a dark and hard figure, always dressed in shabby black clothes when I knew her, as an infant dressed in pastel-colored baby camisoles, with a cooing mother rocking her in warm arms. In my memory and imagination she is always old.

Childbirth is a dangerous time. I have learnt this from the history of my ancestors and namesakes. When my aunt Edvige was born, my grandmother got sick: it was an illness that to this day remains unnamed. I suspect it was post-partum depression. I know she was so sick she could not take care of the baby and, I presume, of her three little boys, Rocco, Vincenzo — my father — and Remigio. So they hired a wet nurse to care for the new baby. I am told that my grandmother came from a relatively wealthy family and in those times this kind of arrangement was not unusual. But this one proved tragic. The nurse's baby had whooping cough, which my aunt quickly caught. The cough was so extreme that it often left her breathless. Then, she had a seizure. Perhaps she had encephalitis, a common development of whooping cough. This seizure did not kill her, but caused major damage to the right side of her body: her arm became limp and twisted in spasms, like the ones that shook her body in frequent convulsions. Her right leg became a useless limb she dragged behind her body. Her feet became forever trapped in awkward orthopedic boots. How old was she? She could have been a few months, one or two years old. For a long time, I thought that, after the whooping cough, she had polio, but recently I found out that was just a fantasy of mine, though one I shared with other children in the family. We knew about polio: I still have the round scars from the polio vaccine on my right arm, and so do my sister and cousins. We attached a word, a disease that was familiar to us, to my aunt's story, a story that still remains, for me, shrouded in mystery.

I imagine my grandmother sick and depressed at a time in which the words "post-partum depression" meant nothing. She finds herself with a baby, her first and only daughter, crippled because she could not care for her, because she denied her own milk to her child. The sense of guilt must have been overwhelming. And I wonder whether people in the family aggravated, if not induced, this sense of guilt.

"M'ammazzasti u picciriddu!" You killed my little boy.

These are my uncle's words to his wife *zia* Cettina, another Concetta in the family. It's 1963 and she is travelling back to Sicily from Switzerland, where they had, like so many Southern Italians, emigrated in search of work. On the train, their seven-month old baby has a seizure and dies. It happens in just a few minutes. Nothing she could do or say. She wants to get off the train, but they tell her she can't. The train will not stop for a dead baby. The conductor tells her to keep quiet and hold the baby as if he is still alive. If they — and I don't quite know who "they" are — realize the baby is dead, they will take him away from her. And that's what she does. From Salerno to Catania: down along the stretch of the boot, through the desolate Calabrian countryside, through the interminable ferry crossing, with the train cars slowly going on and off of the smelly boat. The air is stifling. During the crossing, passengers go upstairs to seek relief in the fresh and salty air. They look eagerly towards the Sicilian coast, where the Madonnina of Messina waits to welcome them home. They eat a greasy *arancino*, and savour the end of the long journey and the imminent homecoming: the embraces, the celebration, the joys of reunion and return. My aunt does not seek fresh air. Perhaps her sister-in-law, who travels with her, joins the other passengers for a while, while my aunt remains in the darkness of the second-class compartment, holding the tiny body of the baby she was nursing only hours earlier. Her husband and her three-year old girl are back in Switzerland. What was this trip for? To see the family? Was her mother sick? For immigrants, traveling is dictated by necessity, not pleasure.

Her baby will remain in her arms till they reach the station of Catania, where my parents and grandparents are waiting. Other family members are there too. Her sister-in-law had a chance to call them, perhaps from Reggio Calabria, perhaps from Messina, before or after the crossing of the Strait. It's morning. Or perhaps it's evening. Outside the station the silhouette of the fountain representing Persephone's abduction stands glorious and menacing, a reminder that Death always launches surprise attacks on the most vigilant of mothers.

What did she say? What did she think? My uncle's horrible accusation leaves her breathless: "M'ammazzasti u picciriddu!" My maternal grandmother, my uncle's mother, tells me this story, and shudders in indignation when she remembers my uncle's words. Female solidarity transcends blood loyalty. My grandmother knows what it feels like to lose a baby. And to be blamed for it.

It's night and my uncle Saro, my maternal grandparents' first born, is sick. My grandfather will take him to the doctor. There is no car, no cab, no light outside. It's 1932 in Gela, Sicily. My grandmother is pregnant with her second child. My grandfather tells her to stay home and wait, but after he leaves with their son, she cannot resist. Anguished, she runs after him in the dark and empty streets of Gela. She feels the baby moving inside her, a movement that does not feel normal, a movement that feels cataclysmic. She stops, without breath. When she gets to the doctor, her boy is fine, but the doctor scolds her upon hearing of her crazed run and that strange movement she has felt in her womb. His words are sharp and ruthless: "You ruined your baby!" He tells her, "What have you done?"

My grandmother takes a deep breath: the memory of that night overcomes her. The baby, her first daughter, will be born months later with some kind

Curaggia

of bone disease: I imagine the brittle bones of her tiny body that refuses to grow. I imagine my grandmother's despair. The baby will die at eighteen months. My grandmother is twenty-two years old. She still believes, today as sixty-five years ago, that she is solely responsible for her daughter's disease and, ultimately, her death. A year later a child is born and is named after that baby: Cettina. This new baby is my mother.

I wonder about these women and their daughters. My mother, her dead baby sister, my aunt, my father's mother, all with the same name: Concetta — Conception — the name of Mary, Jesus's mother, the name that should have been mine. I wonder about family history, the history of our names. What does all of this mean?

My two grandmothers are linked through tragic stories of childbirth, of crippled daughters, of self-blame, of guilt. But how different their stories! My maternal grandmother accepted what she saw as her guilt and lived with it. She tells me that a few weeks before her baby died, the Virgin Mary came to her in a dream, dressed in black, and told her she had come to take her daughter away. "*No, no, please,*" she cries in the dream. Then, she understands. From one grieving mother to another. They both know about loss. They endure. They survive. Religion — and my grandmother is profoundly, mystically, devoted — helps her in her acceptance. She has so much love inside of her to give to her other children, grandchildren, and great-grandchildren.

But Nonna Ciuzza is a different story. For one thing, her daughter survived. But this survival, rather than appeasing her, enraged Nonna Ciuzza. She felt so much rage against the world. But, most of all, I think she felt rage against herself, and processed that feeling tragically. It became the blood running through her veins, the lymph sustaining her, and it kept her alive for over ninety years, stole any capacity for empathy or love she might have had, if indeed she did, prior to the day when her daughter became ill.

For a long time, she and my grandfather tried to find a cure for their child, but to no avail. They went to see doctors in Rome and Genoa, at a time when travelling was neither convenient nor common. They kept trying until she was in her late teens. My aunt's cousins tell me a strange story of pills prescribed by a Roman doctor, which, according to the doctor would either have cured her or made her worse. The pills triggered incredible mood swings: my aunt, they tell me, was out of control. She begged the doctor, in tears, to restore her to her previous condition. And he did. That was, I believe, the last attempt. Then came the slow, irreversible withdrawal from the world, the lifelong seclusion in her mother's house.

My grandmother fiercely embraced my aunt's condition as her own. She would not part from it, not even for a minute. And she would not part from her daughter. Ever.

It's 1990 and she is on her deathbed, battling death. She has to stay alive. She cannot leave her daughter alone. She hisses orders to her daughter, who weeps quietly by her side. *"Don't sign anything. Don't sign anything. Don't throw anything away. Don't change anything in the house. Don't ever leave this house."*

I dream of my grandmother's will. In my dream, she leaves a hug for Gagliano, the owner of the ice cream store where we used to get ice cream when we were children; ten thousand liras for the owner of the fish store near my parents' house who always gives my mother fresh, exquisite fish; and a hand lotion for her mother-in-law. This last detail is not only preposterous, but also anachronistic, since my great-grandmother died long before my grandmother did. But the whole thing is quite absurd because my grandmother didn't leave anything to anybody. Everything was for her daughter. Nobody else. Not a jewel, not a picture, not a cracked china cup, not one of the many embroideries she made. Nothing. Everything went to *zia* Edvige. She made sure of that.

This is a dream about nurturance, generosity, gift-giving. It's a dream about softening rough surfaces, about rewarding the man who sweetened children's mouths with the chocolate and vanilla ice creams my grandmother never bought us. This dream is about making peace with my mother. It's a testament that comes late, a testament I myself need to write in my dreams.

In this dream, my grandmother is eighteen when she dies. Was she eighteen when she married? My maternal grandmother was seventeen when she married my handsome grandfather who had come back from Argentina to marry the child bride he had never met. Both my grandmothers were children giving birth to children, but in those days it wasn't called teenage pregnancy. It was the norm. Not as bad as Hedwig of Poland, betrothed at age nine. But still…

This is where I come from. These are the women of my family. The dead and the living. Their blood, my blood. Eyes, mouth, nose, ears, skin, hands. All from them. My name, too.

Curaggia

sicilia terra-cuore*

Nzula Angelina Ciatu

as the train pulls north above
the yellow desert plains of the mezzogiorno
what part of my soul
do i leave behind

hips
breasts
lips
buried the red sands of Minoa
ripped my chest
body
parts
touches
your peasant hands
endlessly work the earth
sun blazes
i roll along the dunes of Montallegro Marina
do you hear my screams
tear with the winds
tremble
breath pulsates each salty ocean wave
catch glimpses my shadow
haunts the narrow village streets
black hair flies
curls strip across yellow cheeks

as i leave the lands of my origins
what part of my skin scrapes away
landscape colours
my eyes refuse to see again

i lie
cradled in your womb
sicilia terra-cuore

still born
i walk the earth
until my return

* *Sicilia terra-cuore translates to Sicily my heartland.*

Grade One and the Four Basic Food Groups

Anna Nobile

I. Breakfast

others draw sepia toast with strawberry red jam or sienna cereals with royal purple raisins floating in bowls of lemon yellow milk (white crayons never show) david draws something beige and lumpy steaming out of an aquamarine pot he says it's oatmeal but when i ask him what is oatmeal he only shrugs and says his mother makes him eat it for breakfast and he doesn't like it the only good part is the brown sugar

mrs day picks my picture as an example so i tell the class how i dip S cookies into café latte for my breakfast mrs day shakes her head you're too young to drink coffee she tells me eating cookies for breakfast is bad no wonder you are fat the kids laugh she holds up david's picture see she says this is what a hearty breakfast looks like porridge in milk a glass of orange juice and a banana stuff that sticks to your ribs says mrs day with her maize hair and sky blue eyes and melon skin i imagine pine green woods silent as a white crayon remember that goldilocks and the three brown bears ate beige porridge too

II. Lunch

i run home from school don't want to miss anything mom didn't have time to leave me soup or stew in a thermos before she went to work so i open up a can of spaghetti-o's heat it up at the highest temperature even though she told me not to because it would stick to the pot i don't care the show's starting the flintstones get a new maid lolla brigida she listens to opera and cooks them spaghetti and meatballs they don't get any vegetables or dairy products either

III. Dinner

we ate *muset e bruade* one of my father's favourites but mrs day wants to know what is — what did you say? i can't tell her what it is i don't know what they are called in english i use the crayons instead she looks at the gray fat tubes and the lavender pile of mush and I hope that she recognizes the sausages and vegetables i have eaten and drawn so she can tell me what they are this makes no sense dear she says are you sure the sausages were gray? maybe you better draw something else something we both know is real she puts a gold star on david's picture of black pot roast and boiled yellow-orange carrots i look at my picture and feel hungry

Una Lettera Alla Mia Cugina Americana

(A Letter to My American Cousin)

A Letter in Response to
Crossing Ocean Parkway: Readings by an Italian American Daughter
by Marianna De Marco Torgovnick

Michelle Alfano

Cara Marianna, *Mia Cugina Americana…*
Crossing Ocean Parkway was significant for me as a writer of Italian origin, as a woman, and as a perennial outsider who, at times, has not found a haven in Italian culture or the North American mainstream. Your book is subtitled *Readings of an Italian American Daughter* and aptly so, because we are often defined by our roles, our kinship. This too touched me in the many secret places of the heart and mind.

"On Being White, Female and Born in Bensonhurst" had the most power for me, because it rekindled memories of my working class roots in Hamilton, Ontario and because it explored the volatile issues of race and ethnicity which also lay dormant in my old neighborhood. Issues that exploded with such velocity in Bensonhurst with the shooting death of Yusef Hawkins in 1989. Marianna, you experienced, as have many others in our large extended family, a profound sense of shame and anger towards *la communità* but also a fierce need to protect it from outside scrutiny. It is the need to protect our men — fathers, brothers, sons — from the caricatures which distort an accurate depiction of their lives and, implicitly, our lives as their daughters, sisters, mothers. Images of the primitive brute — the sexually potent but destructive Other — often contaminate perceptions of the community from without.

My father has been dead for twenty years. My closest male kin is my younger brother and what I feel towards him, aside from a loving tenderness, is the sense of safety and security that he inspires in me. A tremendous sense of loyalty and commitment emanates from him towards our mother and his two sisters. Politics, religious opinion and temperamental differences aside - he still makes me feel protected and loved. And when the image of our men is criticized or ridiculed I always think … that's not the whole picture … Yes, this exists and it is ugly and hateful to the extreme but you are not talking about *my* blood. And so I had many contradictory feelings reading your essays, particularly those that I read as an indictment of the way Italian men and boys conduct themselves in the world.

And yet, I remember the *small murders* of my teenage years in a large extended Italian family in Hamilton. In the small web of our family ... A male relative beat his wife and children and was defended by his sisters with the statement that it was his wife who provoked him to do such things. Another male relative attempted to molest some of the younger children, a fact which they never discussed until they had reached adulthood, knowing that their story would only inspire disbelief. A *paesano* tried to shoot his wife. That was explained away with the thought that she had probably cheated on him, without evidence to support this theory. A daughter who was beaten repeatedly was begged to remain in her father's home until her wedding some months away, so that the ugliness of her situation would not dishonour the family. Children were bribed to stay home or in town with the gift of cars and other expensive gifts, rather than leave for university outside Hamilton.

A beautiful and refined boy interested in fashion and design was labeled a "fag" for the freedom and delicacy of his dress. He left town. An unusual and shy girl who wore second-hand clothes and her own homemade fashions (out of, I think, not only a daring sense of fashion but lack of money) was treated like a parasite and a fool. She too left eventually. Girls who dated or befriended the few and often isolated Black teens were labeled as whores and treated as such with bathroom epithets and ostracization. A wealthy Indian girl raised in England defiantly exclaimed during a class that she refused to be called a Paki, to the wonder and shock of us all. The loneliness of the foreign students from China that no one could or would befriend. Each small, insignificant "murder" of the few who were different — who would not or could not be the same as the rest.

To escape this legacy of real or imagined violence and moral corruption which was so bloodily exemplified by Hawkins' death, I too assume and have assumed in the past, the mask of another. I turn my face from my roots. Michela became Michelle sometime before entering high school. I don't strive to retain the first language I learned from my mother's lips, much to her displeasure. I did not marry an Italian, do not move in circles made up primarily of Italians. I do not go back to pay homage to the village where my parents were born in Sicily. I have never seen Sicily.

And yet I love the myth of Sicily — the idea of it. Perhaps because I have never been there my vision of it is potent, vivid, drenched in the red blood of my family, in the blue of Sicilian skies, in the rock-coloured dreams of crumbling Grecian temples, in the ebony of Sicilian eyes borne of some Arabic ancestor. Cafe au lait skin burnt brown by a Mediterranean sun. My grandmother's lullaby like a mullah's call to prayer. The *piazza* of the small village bereft of women who dutifully remain home, so that their husbands and fathers will not be shamed. My father riding with pride an ornamental horse dressed in the colours of the flag in a religious parade. So beautiful, so pure, it pains me to look at his photograph. The houses which appear to be carved out of stone. My father calling out to my mother as she passed the field where he tilled the earth with his brothers — perhaps she gently exaggerated the swing of her hips for her future husband. Long black braids tossed back suggestively. My grandfather gunned down over a small dispute by a young boy who was duped into believing he would not be charged. The bandit Guiliano's mother licking the earth where her son's blood pooled after his betrayal and murder.

I slip into these memories, these dreams and myths like a pool of warm water and think of my family's life there. Somehow more alive, more real than this endless struggle for the acquisition of more and more which has become Italian Canadian life.

At times I felt that I would discard this too dark, too pale shell (neither white nor brown) which peels away not so gently with a touch. Trapped in this skin and with this face formed by history, culture and race and not of my own making.

I am struck by your words and have fumbled to express the same thought many times: "Occasionally I get reminded of my roots, of their simultaneous choking and nutritive power."

"Strega" the men muttered when you brazenly ordered a *cremolata* in the old neighborhood, having ventured into the for-men-only cafe. "I have broken the rules and will pay the price again and again," you intoned when you entered sacred territory, forbidden areas which would be defiled by a female's presence. Imagine the names they would have called you if you had gone further than merely venturing into the "wrong" cafe. Imagine that you were Yusef, a brown-skinned man walking with friends in the wrong neighborhood, mistaken for another boy who dared to date a girl from the neighborhood. The tribe of our people, my tribe, our tribe, is unforgiving, fierce, territorial and mesmerizing in the intensity of their hate.

Cugina, I too resisted inculcation in the domestic arts. I refused to cook unless compelled, refused to learn how to sew (even a button!) and took but one typing course in order only to type essays but never memos from a boss. I chafed against tasks assigned only to me and not my brother — making beds, his and mine; washing dishes and clothes. There were gifts: a bicycle for him yet none for me. Freedom and mobility were dangerous for young girls, even in small cities under the watchful eyes of many relatives. A parcel of land from my grandmother Michelina for my brother but not for me.

"You see ..." my mother murmured rather too complacently, "She's forgotten about you." But this was said matter of factly. The rage or disappointment were left to me.

Marianna, you wanted to go to graduate school. Your mother wanted you to become a secretary. I wanted to be a lawyer but was advised by my mother that being a bank clerk was more appropriate for a girl. One uncle prophesied "She'll never become a lawyer" and the prophecy came true but not for the reasons he ventured. Lack of confidence and fear slowly became lethargy and a lack of focus. He and many others tried to destroy my will in a thousand ways. "Destroy" is not too strong a word. Sometimes it was innocent, sometimes it was not. But always it was with the intent of molding a certain image of young womanhood which had more relevance to Sicilian village life in the 1930's than life here in Canada in the 1970's.

You say getting out of Bensonhurst never meant a big house or nice clothes or a large income for you. It meant freedom "to experiment, to grow, to change. It also meant knowledge in some grand, abstract way." *Cugina ... sorella,* escape from my working class roots and the chains of ethnicity is what I sought as well. To me it meant space — the languor of emotional and physical space where a locked door would not be perceived as hostility towards the family and where reading was not seen as an idle luxury. Where an interest in the other sex was not seen as an opportunity by which to ruin or shame the family. A place where difference did not pose a threat.

Why, I asked my friend, does independence for Italian women always equate with sexual promiscuity or emotional distance from the family? We say ... I want to be on my own, independent. *You want your own place so you can do what you like with whomever you like.* I want to meet other people, experience other cultures, other lives. *You hate your own kind, you despise your own people.* I want to sustain myself financially, emotionally. *Why won't you let us help you? Why do you hate us so much?* The questions lingered, stayed. They linger still ...

Marianna, you believed in an "idealized, almost imaginary version of what it meant to be Jewish." Crossing Ocean Parkway was the physical demarcation of crossing over from working-class Italian Bensonhurst to a middle-class, upwardly mobile Jewish neighborhood in Brooklyn — a world of learning, books, culture. For me, it meant escaping to the bigger, more glamorous city of Toronto forty miles away. It was a decision I made at sixteen. Not insignificantly it was the year my father died of cancer. It, too, was a decision to grow, to be free. Would it be cruel to say my father's death represented a sort of liberation for me? It would. Extremely cruel, but also true.

You should live with your widowed mother until she dies. It's your responsibility. Why can't you go to university here? Why can't you be with your mother? She needs you here. You've always been lazy/selfish/difficult … fill in the blank.

As a teenager at home, I receded into an emotional infancy, either consciously or unconsciously. It only accelerated when my father died. I made myself useless, lazy and non-productive by my family's rigorous standards. I was the least hard working, least responsible member of the family although I was the eldest. I was the emotional one, the difficult one, the childish one. But I must have succeeded in my plan because gradually responsibility in the family business shifted to my younger brother and sister. It was physically hard work and gut-wrenchingly important as the only means of our livelihood when my father died. But I selfishly decided I didn't want that responsibility for all of my life. And I knew if I stayed at home it would destroy any independence or courage I had. You see … I loved myself better than I loved them. That was my first crime.

My tribe … my blood. The intensity of my conflicting emotions: love, fear, anger, shame, pride threatened to engulf me when I was younger. I am more at peace with myself, at peace with my culture which has, as you described, both threatened to choke the life from me and provided me with great moments of pride and beauty.

My father's portrait sits above the plastic-covered couch in the never-used living room. His half smile hides a strong and sometimes cruel nature. *Don't slander the dead and above all don't slander the family* it says. I am warned by his and a hundred other voices within and without. Yet the truth, my truth, spills out of me like water from an overfilled glass, with nowhere else to travel but up and out.

Munda the Italian Witch

Rome, New York

K. Freeperson

She was old as
dried hot peppers
strung in the hallway
we tried not to breathe
or laugh as we watched her through high grass
on eleven-year-old bellies
fearing her witch's powers
dark, secret, musty like old widow's black
dresses stored in moth balls
in mahogany chests.
Fear and respect like old brick streets
for a woman who brought peppercorns in gold
to pin to diapers of newborn Italian babies
tiny protection from the evil eye, or malocchia
Munda's glasses thick like
the bottoms of beer mugs
scanned the herb garden in her dark backyard
strident voice rattling off and on
Italian and a touch of English
using eyes and wrists, finger
for emphasis
while our bellies on the cool grass full of pasta
from some "Welfare Dish"
Gramma made, were pillows on the earth
we watched the Italian witch on First Street
through grape vines
grown from grafted pieces brought over on the
boat from Naples, Sicily and parts South rule
her family manless.

Italiana Lady

Laura D'Alessandro

Religion (and all of its contradictions) was a definite early influence for my photographic constructions. I was never sold on the Roman Catholic concept of suffer now, while putting off pleasure for another day (usually after it is too late, anyway). There was no comfort for me in reading that the "Little Match Girl" joined her mommy in heaven — even as a child, I could find no happy ending for a young barefoot girl, who died of exposure and starvation on Christmas Eve. I was continually grappling with parallel worlds of the aesthetic and the grotesque, not realizing that I could have both, could incorporate both into my work. My first in-person viewing of Hieronymus Bosch's painting *The Garden of Earthly Delights* (ca. 1500) would be a major catalyst in my life and work to decree that life (and process) could be poetry. It had always seemed to me that heaven would be a dull place, but in *The Garden of Earthly Delights*, there was an illusion — between the fantastic fruits, hybrid creatures, and vivid sensuality — that hell *or* heaven could define unimaginable experience. It was bizarre, it was ugly, but it was orgasmic and beautiful, as well.

I have consistently dealt with women, relationships, and power struggles within my work in recent years. This seems almost like a natural extension of my life, considering that I grew up in an environment — with an Italian father — where I rebelled against the attitudes of virginity, passivity, and subordination, the predominant themes for a "good Catholic girl" to adhere to. Although my mother is supportive of my work, and my choice to attend graduate school, my father (who is a truck driver, and also grew up working in the coal mines of Italy and Belgium) always questions why I could not obtain a much better (more practical) job like that of a secretary or hairdresser.

I have grown up realizing the strength of the Italian-American woman, observing the way that these women in my life have had the task of being the backbone of the family unit — keeping everyone together — while at the same time, trying to fight against antiquated cultural mores that have only served to keep the women down. I created this photographic construction, *Italiana Lady*, as a reaction against these mores and an affirmation of the perpetual strength of the "Italian-American" woman.

Excerpt from

Return to Sicily

Anna Maria Carlevaris

It seemed inevitable that my hosts should be my cousin Salvina and her mother Lucia. Although Salvina and I had nothing in common — she disliked reading, had a talent for making money, adored Elvis and was passionate for soccer — no one questioned my internment in her fortress. It was a fait accompli from the moment of my arrival in my mother's home town, when my bags were secreted away to the guest room located at the very top of Salvina's tall, narrow house. From my window I could see the rising and falling rooftops of the town's southern extension, the 'bald spot' created by the half-built never to be finished kindergarten and, beyond this, a receding panorama of rugged hills. In the midday July sun nothing seemed to move except the occasional madly flying Vespa on the road leading out of town, a tiny blur and disproportionately large 'buzz' against an immobile expanse of yellow hills and azure sky.

Salvina's was indeed a fortress, for at night, after she closed her gift shop (on the first floor) she would check her safe (where she stored gold jewellery wrapped in black velvet), turn on the high tech alarm system, and the house became sealed. No one could enter or exit while the alarm was turned on. Salvina could sleep soundly several floors above her shop and her mother, on another floor, could listen to late night movies at a volume that would shatter Canadian eardrums, feeling fully protected against all imaginable intruders. We women slept alone, each in our own beds, each on different floors, fully insulated from a potentially dangerous world.

The fortress analogy is appropriate to the house's architecture whose irregular design is rooted in the town's medieval past. Monterosso Almo was built on top of a mountain centuries ago when vantage point was a defensive necessity. Over time, as the town grew, houses were forced to expand upward or to spread in random fashion along the steep sides of the mountain. This is why the house, although it has only eight rooms, is five stories high. The spectacular view from my room was no compensation for the fact that it was located five floors away from the bathroom. This alone would not be enough to discourage me although it did tire me. The real cause for lament was the fact that I had to walk through the gift shop in order to reach the bathroom. Each morning, as I made my way in nightrobe and slippers, I would lamely attempt to deflect the stares from Salvina's customers. More ignoble still, my passage back, when my hair would be wrapped in one of my Aunt's giant beach towels, a towering terry wig. My self-esteem was sufficiently unbalanced by this environment to make the morning walk-through feel like a dream of being naked in a crowd.

The gift shop was attached to a tiny garden that belonged to Aunt Lucia who tended it as well as the many stray cats that inhabited the oasis. There seemed to be no order to its growth. Walking along the narrow footpath, a tangle of thorns and bristles brushed dangerously close while white lilies and large, pink roses floated overhead between the hanging laundry. Now and then, cats' ears or paws appeared amidst the greenery, slipping away as you approached. Not that one wanted to them to come near. Scrawny, wire-haired, with feral, pale eyes, they stalked the undergrowth for insects and mice. But Aunt Lucia called them 'her' cats although she had never touched them, or allowed them into her house, or fed them anything other than table scraps. Often it was pasta in tomato sauce or stale bread soaked in water, which partly explained their sorry state. Occasionally one would be jolted by a sudden ferocious growl from Mad Julia, the neighbour's guard dog. Julia slept in the cool recesses of a nearby garage, locked in by a formidable iron gate. I had caught a glimpse of her only once or twice. Large and muscular, her reputation preceded her and I was careful to cut a wide path around her door. Sometimes, for reasons unknown to me, Julia would escape into the garden, taking the life of a pitiful kitten, a scene I was fortunate never to have witnessed. One morning, again for reasons unknown, she ran free into the garden and into the shop and bit a client on the buttock. I missed this too even though the muffled exclamations had floated up to my fifth floor window, distant cries I had mistaken for one of my cousin's more challenging sales.

Officially, the shop was open six days a week, from nine to one in the morning and four to nine in the evening. But invariably a customer would ring the doorbell at any time of day or evening because of an 'emergency'. If Salvina didn't respond, they would call to her from the street, pleading their case until she capitulated. Customers entered through a curtain of beaded strings, bowing their heads with the customary "buon gi-or-no" as a few strings lingered momentarily on a shoulder. The shop was small and overflowing with sparkling crystal, gilt frames with images of 'beautiful americans', perfume bottles, Swatch watches, lipstick displays raspberry red to iced mocha, costume jewellery and 'men's gifts'. Discretely out of view stood a rack of personal care products that customers would request in a whisper and Salvina would wrap in plain brown paper. All other purchases were gift wrapped with polka-dot paper (her trade mark) and coloured ribbon. Gold was elaborately packaged: thick chains, hoop earrings and tiny diamond studded crucifixes became meticulous presentations of curling ribbons, coloured tissue and shiny little stars that Salvina applied with the tip of her index finger. For dramatic effect, she would pause to stand back and admire her creative invention, sighing with satisfaction.

Salvina spent hours cajoling and coaxing her customers who were obliged by social convention to have a gift in hand for every occasion. She was persuasive, engaging, seductive. With gold-orange hair, freckles and milky skin, she seemed ill-suited to a Mediterranean climate. Short, chunky and hugely bosomed, she was a curious mix of genetic types. She had inherited her father's red hair but with him deceased by so many years, it seemed oddly of place. I wondered if there was Norman blood in her. It was not impossible. During her afternoon rest periods, laying on her white bed like an Odalisque, surrounded by stuffed toys and silk cushions and dragging on a Marlborough, she would tell me that she would willingly trade her financial success to be a "love-slave." But I didn't believe her. For all the complex manoeuvring of her make-up sessions, for all her lewd jokes and raucous laughter, feigned swooning as she chatted about her current "young friend," I think she took great pleasure in being a woman of independent means. Whether due to fate or circumstances, Salvina was different from other women her age. Although we lived in separate worlds, our bond was unspoken but clear — we were 'women without men.'

untitled

Nzula Angelina Ciatu

my stomach
is round, pudgy, flabby
like that of my strong-willed
owl-eyed mother
even if
i did not birth five children

round, pudgy, flabby
the determined large bellies
i imagine
my grandmothers fit proudly

my stomach
has a five by three inch distortion
trajecting vertically down to the edge
of my woolly pubic hair
a caressing reminder of my near-death
bout with peritonitis
and the vision of the Madonna
who assured i would survive

my midriff
pudgy, flabby, curving
is my very best feature
i insist to my thin-boned, seventh-generation,
Irish-Acadian Canadian lover
who responds a puzzled consternation

unlike
the fleshy, beautifully huge women in Reuben's
nineteenth century canvasses
i am not
lounging nude for someone else's pleasure
i have grown
into a full-bellied

sure-footed
stand tall and proud
Southern Italian donna*

if i am good, kind, sincere
Fortuna will smile upon me
i will grow further, further
expand into a strikingly fat old Sicilian woman
i will not shrink
into my vastness
as white North American society enculturates
i will
encompass space
large
wide
willfully
like a dutiful Iblean** daughter

*   woman
** *Ibla* is an indigenous Sicilian goddess

This poem is dedicated to Lucia Chiavola Birnbaum who taught me about Ibla,
and the truth about many other Sicilian deities.

The Sign of the Cross

Daniela Gioseffi

— for Gertrude Stein

Because of the cat's eye marble of your passion,
you old sage of roses, I slap my hand
on your big rump, old word whore!
You discovered the secrets of your body
only to keep them silent to the grave.

You contemporary of my late Italian grandmother
whose cadaver appears before me in my dreams,
her clitoris gleaming like a ruby jewel —
grandma who gave birth to twenty children
alone in her bed, her own midwife. Grandma
who never knew the numbing power of orgasmic
potency, pool of cosmic energy
for the tormented body.

For you, Dear Grandma, and for you, Ole Gertrude,
for all the women who were buried in their
living bodies, hiding sexual hysteria from doctors
who performed surreptitious clitorectomies,
so men might go on supreme through
thrusting centuries,
for you,
rain of the womb, spindle of Aprhrodite,
bud of Venus, tree of Daphne, moon of Diana,
I chant the song of the three, "Tender Buttons,"
the sign of the trinity:
        "THE NIPPLE, THE NIPPLE, THE CLITORIS,"
and the Holy Ghost
is "The Mother of Us All!"

The Oven

Rosette Capotorto

what are your chances for
mainstreaming
when you grow up
in a Bronx pizza parlor
   and no one
      knows your name only that you're
      eye-talian and your father makes
the pizza and you
serve the pizza and do
   your homework after school
  at the table behind the oven
and no one ever notices your mother
  but she's back there
    rolling meatballs
    tending your little brother and one in the belly
    that will be your little sister
      slows her down a bit
and you will change diapers
      in addition to doing your homework
        in back of the oven
and frying ten pounds of eggplant
for the eggplant parmigiana
and so will your sister
    who is two and a half years younger
   and you both do dishes at the oversized
    commercial sink
and after awhile you and your sister
will divide the work and it will turn out
that your sister is better at diapers and
baby hairdos and you are better at frying
   eggplant
and then your little brother will be old
enough to make the dough
test his strength against
the stain-less arm of the mixer

having been forewarned of its dangers
the little sister
   the last one born
will make tiny pizzas
      and there will be a photograph
   to remember this by
a little girl rolling pizza dough
which the family
will eat
in six
tiny
slices

Plucking

Mary Russo Demetrick

Long black hairs
grow from one
facial mole
in the right
corner of my mouth

My mother
would scrub it
hard
think it was food
or chocolate

Now hairs spring
not from my chin
or lips
just from the mole
and I go after them
with tweezers
or scissors
Sicily springs
from my mouth
hairs of the old
women now mine

Perhaps I'll gather
hair into a thin
small bun at my nape
throw a shawl
over my shoulders
knit endless
socks, scarves
like the old ones

Heritage sprouts
in more ways
than hairs
on a mole

no earrings for tina

Maria Lisella

i was about seven years old when i realized none of
the other girls in school wore pierced earrings.

my mother insisted.
said it was *buona fortuna* for girl children to start
off life with a piece of gold in their ears.

she didn't understand that this was america only the
*zingare** wore gold in their ears when they told
fortunes.

American girls never put holes in their ears.

it was saturday, my father took me to the movies;
when they were sad, i would cry a lot.

that day, we saw queen christina when greta garbo
laughed out loud for the first time in the movies.
she threw back her head and i saw that she wasn't
wearing gold earrings in her ears and she wasn't
even american.

on the way home, when no one was looking, i
unhooked my earrings and threw them out the
window of the El.
no one asked me about them again.

---

*   *Zingare*: a derogatory term describing Gypsies, members of a traditionally itinerant
    people who originated in northern India and now live chiefly in south and south-
    west Asia, Europe and North America.

Hyphenated Identities

Francesca Schembri

This is the biography of D.E., an Italian woman who arrived in Canada in the 1950s. To be more effective, the story is written in an English which an average, uneducated immigrant may use. The term 'mangiacake' is used without prejudice.

My husband, I wish you were here; but I'm glad that you are not. I have to tell you about yesterday. It wasn't an easy day for me and I'm glad it's over! Our son got married yesterday. He got married in a non-denominational chapel, you know? The girl is not a Catholic and she was married once. The ceremony was lovely and I felt as if you were there, beside me, holding my hand. At times, I could even hear your voice saying, "You look nice and elegant in this blue gown. Blue is not your favourite colour though, how come you are wearing it?" They told me to wear blue, not black. They said that black is not a proper colour to wear as the mother of the groom. Ho, yah! I'm the mother of the groom, even though he has an Anglo name. I felt strange, sitting in there by myself among those people with whom I have nothing in common. They are not from our group.

All these people talking English with sophistication! The servants, the chandeliers! It looked as if I was in a movie, starring as the mother of a promising lawyer who was marrying the daughter of a prominent personality. The only real thing in this, was that I had given birth to the groom. They tried to be nice, you know, as if they were talking to a child, with that certain condescension in their voices... I felt very uncomfortable and I wanted to leave even before the reception began. I was called by a different name, and I felt that I was negating you.

The wedding ceremony brought back memories of our own wedding day. How different it was! Shortly after the war, we couldn't even afford a wedding dress for me! I had to wear my cousin's dress and you had to wear your father's navy blue suit. It fitted you, as if it was custom made for you. Remember? Of course, I wanted to keep the wedding dress, but it was not possible. My cousin had previously made plans to transform it into a baptismal gown for the child. You promised me that one day, in America, you would have a dressmaker make one for me, "the nicest dress ever designed" you said.

We were in love, and we had made plans to go to America and make things work better for us. My auntie Antonietta offered to sponsor us. She sent us the fare which was paid by the Parish of St. Carmelo. We refunded the money within the year. Remember, how proud we were of being able to do so? It was possible because of the hospitality of my auntie Antonietta and the help of my cousins. They did not charge us for board until we found work. But, we had only just begun our lives together when the accident occurred.

Your tragic death left me struggling even more than before, without a husband and with two small children to raise, in a place far away from home. I did not have the expereince in taking care of things that were handled by you. There was, also, the financial struggle of making ends meet. I was an immigrant widower and this made things even worse than when we first arrived in Canada. In those days, we had to struggle to buy a toy for our son — remember that evening of December 1957?

We took our son downtown Toronto to look at all the Christmas decorations. The windows of the Eaton store were full of toys and we got caught up with the moment, and spent what little money we had on a toy for our son. But, it was worth it! Vincenzo was so excited that on our way back, he showed it to every passenger on the streetcar. He didn't stop talking for a minute. The driver became irritated and asked him to be quiet, and told us to stop talking our language and learn English. Then, he complained about us "filthy Italians" coming to Toronto and snatching jobs away from Canadians. We didn't respond because we were afraid of being deported if we created troubles. Instead, we got out of the streetcar. But we had to walk home that night in the cold because we didn't have any more bus tokens. We had spent all of our money on the toy. As a result, the next morning, our son was sick and you promised him that such a situation would never be repeated. "Son, this is your country and you are going to have a better life than us," you vowed.

I will never forget the difficulty in keeping that promise. In North America, people have to work hard to be successful, but we met that challenge since hard labour didn't scare us. At first, we could not find decent jobs. We had no skills, no education, and to make matters worse, we did not even speak the language! We took low paying jobs that nobody wanted. We did not want to be a burden to our sponsor or anyone else and so we endured the exploitation and humiliation. that came with the type of jobs we had. However, even though, your job was seasonal, we saved enough money for a down payment for our first house, so that all four of us did not have to share one bedroom. Then we sponsored my sister and family, and she sponsored her in-laws and they all lived with us to help pay for the mortgage, and then... the accident!

Many newspapers reported your death as another accident in the construction industry. For many people, it may have meant one less immigrant living in Toronto, but for us it was a tragedy. You did not belong to any union, and I did not have any benefits. Your boss gave us two hundred dollars for your burial and told your son Vincenzo that we should be grateful for the money. He claimed that he had no obligations, and that the accident had happened because you weren't "too smart." He had confused your inability to express yourself in English with intelligence. Then he added, that I should keep quiet and not try to pursue any legal action or talk to authorities.

Relatives and friends each donated a dollar or two to help with the expenses. This kept us going until the necessary mourning time was over, and I could return to work. The 'paesani' were very supportive. For a month, I did not have to buy any food because they donated it. The house was full of people every night and they all were very willing to help. Our people were great! They did not send a lot of flowers, but their presence helped. I felt protected as though, I had never left home.

There were other times, though. When auntie Antonietta died, four years ago, her children had a weird funeral for her. Only couples, the old generation, dressed in black. The ceremony was in English because they all know the language. They did not bother to take the body to our old parish for the funeral ceremony. Neither did they appear to be too interested in continuing our traditions. Instead, they seemed to care more about choosing the right thank you card, whether they should wear hats to the ceremony, and whether they should serve Italian or Canadian food after the funeral. Poor woman! After spending her entire life caring for her family and in-laws, baby-sitting her grandchildren, she was placed in Casa Verde to end her life there, among strangers. I wanted to take care of her, but her daughter made her decision. Her daughter who has a career, could not stay home to care for her. I was baby-sitting five children, I had to, if I wanted to survive. Back home, the government pays an allowance to a relative to take care of an elder, so that he or she can stay home. Here, they are sent to old folks homes, and away from the security of their families, to be placed in an environment as strange to them as if they were parcels. For her this was a degrading experience and also, a trauma. She could not cope with the new condition, and she was very unhappy.

The funeral parlor was in Richmond Hill where the daughter now lives with her family. The room where the body was laid was filled with flowers sent by relatives and friends. But, many did not come to the funeral. This reminds me of that advertisement — "Say It With Flowers!" Everybody seems to be busier than me these days — even our son did not show up for the funeral. He said that he had an important court case to attend. The young generation, nowadays, does not respect our traditions and has very little respect for us elders.

Aunt Antonietta was buried in a chapel. I'm thinking of purchasing one in one of those cemeteries, for you and me, and move you from the ground.

You should see how beautiful and expensive-looking they are! They are the replica of the ones in our cemetaries in our hometown. This Italian company phoned me last week offering me to pay them in monthly installments. Of course, it is expensive, but worth it. I can pay it with my pension. It means more sacrifices. The only problem is the distance. They are built outside the city of Toronto and this means that I can't visit you as I do now — every week. Our children will not have time to visit us often anyway. But, we have each other!

Distance today, seems relatively unimportant.The majority of Italians no longer live in the little Italies of yesterday (you wouldn't recognize Toronto anymore, because of the new and tall buildings). Now these neighborhoods are mainly occupied by different people. Imagine that on College street, there are now more Portugueses, South Americans and Asians than there are Italians. They have moved north. We no longer live close to one another as we used to… Many Italians have done well, and they all live in big new homes. We see each other much less now.

Things have really changed since you left. Shortly after your death, I began to work as a baby-sitter for a few relatives and neighbors. In the evenings, I did piece work at home for a garment factory. The pay was low, but it helped. On Sundays, I used to cook for our parish priests. With the money from this job, I was paying for our daughter's hope chest. But, I managed to pay for the mortgage anyway.

Even though Vincenzo was only 13 years old, he looked for work. Cousin Tony helped him to find a part-time job in the construction industry. He went to school during the winter. He wanted to become a lawyer, but his teacher recommended that he take trade courses, instead. He asked me to go talk to his teacher and make her change her mind. But what did I know about these things?! I don't understand all the fancy words they say. I did not get too far in school, and my English wasn't good enough. I did not have the time to study the language, because of work. Also, how could I have learned it? I always lived in an Italian neighborhood, shopped in Italian shops, and went to Italian churches. This means that I had little chance to practice English. I had to ask our priest to go and do the talking for me. Vincenzo completed high school and with with a lot of struggle, managed to go to University. I was very proud of him. But Vincenzo's problems did not end there. There was still the problem of the name.

According to many Anglo administrators, having a foreign name, at least in those days, was a liability and because of it, our son could not fulfill his dream of becoming a lawyer. His name, would not take him to the Bar. Without a Bar, he could not practice Law in this country. So, he was forced to reject his origins by changing his name and moving out of his neighborhood. Since 1976, your son has not been Vincenzo DiMartino but Vince St.

Martin! Please forgive him, at least he did not take a name such as Smith or Scott!

Due to this and the problem with your daughter, I wanted to sell the house and return back home. That was until I visited my homeland. I was in shock to discover that after thirty years, people changed there, too. My relatives were either old or dead in the grave. The new generation were strangers to me. They all speak Italian like the ones in the North, and they called me the 'Americana.' How ironic, I have been an Italian — but what am I saying? Many Italian people make a distinction between the real Italian people and the others: the ones from the North and the ones from the South. According to many of them, I have not even been a 'real' Italian, but an Italian from the 'South.' I had been a southern Italian immigrant in Canada and in my native country, I became Americana! That made me aware of my true ethnicity: Italo-Canadian! See?!

Now we have hyphenated identities. But, this is only part of the latest multicultural thinking. In reality, I do not feel either Italian or Canadian. It seems that multiculturalism has deprived me of my true identity. Prior to this, I was Italian. Once in a while, I was reminded of this by the prejudice of people or even by my own daughter. Whenever she was upset with me because I wanted my Italian traditions to be respected, she would say," I don't have to do things the ways you did it in the old country. You must understand that I'm not Italian, you are!" So, my daughter told me that I was Italian. The radio, newspapers and the government, and even the pizza advertisements also told me that I was Italian. Not Calabrese, Veneta, or Pugliese, but Italian! However, the Italian community tells me that I am Sicilian, particularly from Calmunta. I hear that it is all right to have all these identities because this is a multicultural society. Years ago, my children had to hide their identity in order to get ahead with their lives.

Maybe, this is part of the reason why I moved. Chiavalli was advertising large houses for sale. Do you know? The ones which have the circular stairs and the large entrances. We bought one in Woodbridge. I do not know if I'm happier here. How can I be happy when I miss my neighborhood, my people and my old house? I think that I did it because I felt pressure by those neighbors who were all moving to new and bigger houses. We Italians are doing good now, you know? I sold the house and moved, too. Maybe I moved because I felt that I ought to do it — for our children. I wanted to make them feel proud of us.

I do not think I will stay here too long. The house will be too big for one person. Don't you know? Your children do not wish to stay with me. It's not like before. They have their own apartments now, even the unmarried ones! What will I do in this big house all by myself? For twenty five long years, my nights have been too long and the bed too large for me only. Now, even my days are too long and I feel lonely. Sometimes, I feel like I want to talk to someone. To get out of the house, I take English lessons at the community center nearby. I'm getting older and there is a lot of work to be done to keep the house in good shape. I can't do it all! I may have to sell the house and move into a smaller senior citizen's residence apartment. It won't hurt, I have no memories here, nor have I made new friends.

Also, I must tell you, that I have given in to another custom. I will no longer dress in black. Apparently, this makes your children very happy. For once, I made Santina, your daughter proud of me. Santina and I are becoming closer now and this is mitigating the sense of guilt that I have been feeling for years... This reminds me of that day that I slapped Santina. You had died only one year. I can still remember, as if it happened yesterday,the day Santina came home from school mad as hell. She walked into her room and tore her black dress into pieces, yelling that she was fed up of our traditions. You see, the other kids mocked her for wearing black. They used to call her "blacky" and she would react through violence. Then, she got into trouble. This wasn't the only time!

She was seventeen when she met her "friend." He was a 'mangicake' and of course, she wanted to go out with him. She said, he was only twenty-two and that he wasn't thinking of marriage. I couldn't allow this to happen, because I wanted to protect her reputation. I did not want our relatives saying that because she did not have a father, her mother and brother did not take care of raising her properly. So, she rebelled against my rules.

One evening she didn't come home from work. She phoned the next day, to tell me that she had decided to move out of the house. She said that she wanted to experience life as a Canadian. She said, "I'm a Canadian and I want to live as such." In those days, many of the Italian children left their homes to experience Canadian culture — the other side. It was natural! After all, they have been educated in the Canadian system and they felt confused. After she moved out, I did not want to speak to her anymore. I felt that she had rejected you and me, our sacrifices, our love and values. I heard that she had an abortion and was not doing well. I wanted to forgive her, but she had offended you and I resented it. Also, if I were to take care of her, I would lose the support of our relatives. They were saying that Santina's behavior was not acceptable and that I did not know how to raise her. This made me feel very bad. I got so sick of melancholy. Because I still needed our relative's help, I turned my back on my only daughter.

I saw her again two years later. I was very sick in the hospital. Vince took her to visit me. I did not recognize her at first. She had dyed her hair blond, in the attempt to look more Anglo and she looked very pale, as if she had no blood left in her body. Her eyes were bulging out of her white face. Two dark olives in a hankerchief. Her pupils were so dilated that she looked like a mad person. It was obvious that she was on drugs. Not only did she require immediate medical care, but this time she needed my love, compassion and understanding. I had to be there, for her — our only daughter Santina, now called Sandy.

Sandy agreed to go to a rehabilitation program for several months. The place was run by an Italian priest and I talked to him about all of our troubles. He advised me what to do. At the beginning, it was very difficult to talk to a stranger about our family business. Luckily, with God's help, she managed to overcome her addiction. She then returned home and managed to finish high school. She took most courses at night and worked during the day. Shortly after, she moved out again. This time to live in a common law arrangement with a man she had met at a clinic. The relationship did not work out. She is now living on her own again and I respect her decision.

She is seeing an Italian guy now, did you know? He is divorced, but he's o.k. Maybe, one day they will have an Italian style wedding!

My husband, our children are not to blame, for being different. They are victims of a new reality. They suffered for being the first generation of immigrants born in Canada. These days, though, it seems that racism has found a new target in the new wave of immigrants. Unlike the old days, people are now coming from other places, such as the former Yugoslavia, Lebanon, South America, Somalia, and Sri Lanka, where there are wars and starvation. As we did, they also tried to escape an uncertain future, and like us, they too are victims of prejudice and racism. This time, though, they are victimized not only by the Anglo-Saxons, but also by us — the former immigrants. They are so many, but we all are called minority groups. We, the minority, as well, are the perpetrators of the pain caused to these people by our intolerance of cultural differences. We blame them for the increase in unemployment, taking jobs away from us, for the increase in crime rate, or because they are profiting on our welfare system, especially when we are in an economic recession.

Sometimes, I think about the past and wonder about the future. Since you left, the immigrants have changed faces, people have walked on the moon, answered referendums, made war and peace, and more war, countries have changed their names, others have split.

The past doesn't scare me anymore. I learned how to deal with the present, but I fear more changes. There have been enough already, and not all of them are positive. Often, I feel that my future is uncertain. Regardless of what it could be, you are there for me, and this is something that will never change.

Ciao Amore!

DIMI,
When are the Lesbians
Coming for Coffee?
(Laura)

Leaving Home: Refl[e...]
of a Catholic Lesbia[n]

Frances[...] [...] [...]uore

There is only one heaven, the heaven of the home.
There was only one paradise, the garden
that kept them little children even as adults.[1]

When Maria Giulia walked into my living room she was in her seventies, and had recently lost her eldest daughter to cancer. I was in my thirties and in my second year of theological studies at a local Catholic college. I had always respected Maria Giulia, a small woman who, like many other Italian women of her generation, spoke with firm conviction sharpened by an ever-present apologetic tone. On that particular afternoon she seemed especially burdened by her grief, and I, sensing her awkwardness at being in my home, felt unsure of my role. After all, we hadn't seen each other for years before our brief encounter in front of the flower shop she helped run with her son. And, more to the point, what spiritual guidance could I possibly offer this woman who was forty years my senior?

"How could God do this," she wanted to know, sitting at my side, tiny and demure. I wanted to gather her up into my arms.

Maria Giulia went on to describe how on one harrowing night when the grief prevented her from sleeping, she left her husband's side to seek comfort from a well-worn prayer book. Instead, she became disturbed, restless, unable to read on. Was it true what the prayer book was telling her? That her daughter who had suffered so much, who had left behind children and a husband was now in purgatory, suffering still. Suffering for an eternity. She looked up at me, incredulous, shaking her head. "You study theology," she said. "Tell me the truth." What did she think, I asked quietly. "No," she whispered. The book was wrong. God was merciful. Her daughter had gone to heaven. And yet...perhaps they were right. "They" of course, represented the voices of authority she had heard all her life. "They" were the black and white strokes on the page that located her daughter in the geography of eternity. I saw her vacillate, noted how she rose to her belief before doubt re-emerged, making her wonder, "perhaps, what if, perhaps they are right."

his dance between truth and doubt intimately. Other women have
ed a twisted dance with external authorities who deny, reject,
d, ridicule what they understand is real about their lives, their relation-
ps with others, and yes, even in their relationship with Mystery, with God.
Etty Hillesum, a twenty-seven year old Dutch Jewish woman who was killed
in Auschwitz wrote in her diary, *An Interrupted Life*, "And I listen in to
myself, allow myself to be lead, not by anything on the outside, but by what
wells up from within."[2] The great wisdom traditions of faith have both
advocated and feared spiritual disciplines of inner listening, prayer and
meditation precisely because anyone seriously engaged in such practices
knows the power that is released when, like Etty, you arrive at the knowledge
that "something inside [you] will never desert [you] again."[3]

Maria Giulia, a married woman with a husband at her side for longer than
she cared to remember, is most likely not lesbian, but she, too, struggled to
"come out" in the Italian Canadian community. In its broadest sense, to come
out is to affirm one's dignity when that dignity is assailed and undermined
by abusive forms of power. Balanced precariously between forces of self-
doubt and self-affirmation, she might be able to understand what an event it
is for a woman to claim a lesbian or bisexual identity. Coming out is nothing
less than leaving home, leaving the garden that keeps us as little children.

In 1983, barely into my twenties, still very much living at home, I
experienced a profound split in the relation between my body and the
mystical body of Christ sometimes referred to as the Church. The body whose
flesh is our first home, this body of mine quickened at the touch of another
woman. While other lesbians have described falling in love with a woman as
exhilarating, and euphoric, I experienced it as a wrenching of my flesh. I was
a daughter of the patriarchy, and it demanded heterosexuality; it would not
allow me to pursue my love without guilt and shame. I was backed into an
existential corner.

Perhaps because ties to the family and its prominence in my life were
becoming more and more tenuous, I reacted to this unnamed loss with a
strange blend of nostalgia and anger surrounding the rituals of family life:
engagements, wedding showers, family Sunday meals, any of the words and
gestures investing our sexual lives with meaning. Growing up Catholic, I,
too, would have been the recipient of such a well-ordered and divinely
sanctioned life. After all, I wanted five children and the rituals of family life.
I was Catholic and terribly romantic in the peculiar ways that only Catholicism can inspire.

In 1983, when I first fell in love, and my body awakened to the delights
and confusions of touch and tenderness, there was no one and nothing in the
Italian-Canadian community of family and Church that could have mirrored
back to me my own goodness as a sexual woman.

Curaggia

As is often the case my quarrel with the Church took me outside its ritualistic practices, but, inwardly, I refused to believe that the long wisdom tradition of Catholicism had no space for the likes of me and for the kind of love I was living. What do sexuality, Italian-ness and Catholicism all have in common, I wondered. They all ask questions of identity. What is Catholicism's prime contribution to the world today? Its notion of sacramentality. It's belief that the created world reflects and participates in God's love, the great birthing and redemption of the world. Why do we keep the bones of saints, and post dollar bills onto the statues of San Rocco? Because bodies matter. What Catholicism has to offer is the act of *redreaming* the garden. In that redreamed garden, bodies of the same sex can touch and be touched, offer tenderness and affection, become the image of God whose Being delights in diversity. In the garden healing can occur.

Notes

1. Mary di Michele. "Mimosa" *Stranger in You*. (Toronto: Oxford University Press, 1995), 10.
2. Etty Hillesum. *An Interrupted Life: The Diaries of Etty Hillesum 1941-43*. (New York: First Washington Square, 1985) 214.
3. Ibid. 160.

The Love Desserts

Ann M. Pardo

My Grandpa came to America with a cobbler stool and four tomato seeds in his coat pocket. A stranger in a starched white shirt and soft black curls stopped him on the docks and gave him ten dollars.

"Someday, you giva ten dollar to a paisan. Capisce?"

Grandpa did understand. Ten dollars, a hard day's work, a smile, a handful of flowers from the garden. My Grandpa from Sicily lived generously. He was born this way.

And he was born with a wicked sense of humour. Rose Angeles, my aunt, his only daughter, Rowie we called her, was pretty. Men asked her on dates. Grandpa would tell them all the same.

"Hello. I think I like a you. But. She's a my daughter. She's a very young. You touch her, you maybe die. You unnerstan?"

Every time he said it he would laugh and this would make the date laugh and Rowie would laugh.

Grandpa had what the family called Rules For Living. This was Rule Number One.

Made Rowie real popular.

Grandpa was doing pretty good just to let Rowie go on dates. His had been an arranged marriage which meant no privacy before the wedding and very little even after. He tried real hard to keep up with the changes in America. He and Gramma learned all they needed to know about love by staring out the back window, holding hands, staring into the layers of garden we called the back yard.

Grandpa and Gramma loved their three black-haired children and their lilac garden. Grandpa's solid cobbler stool and his hands made money to get that pizza oven and that black pizza oven made more money that became a real American restaurant.

Grandpa said, "The wooden stool, she hold the weight of pizza maker family."

When Grandpa cooked dinner, he said that the pizza is the story of the maker. This sounded like he was looking at life, but he was really giving us an important rule for living. So this cobbled, pizza-making-family bought a red brick, four room restaurant. The wooden sign out front blinked on and off, Red Rooster, Red Rooster, but the restaurant inside was decorated with a gigantic mural of the Texas Alamo, taking up two walls in the big dining room.

Grandpa laughed when he said that too much talk was like the steam blowing off the smelly boiling cauliflower. Another Rule for Living. Because of the Texas mural and the blinking Red Rooster sign, a family discussion happened without the smell of boiling cauliflower.

"The picture she's a good."

"We gonna keep her."

"Now she's a no red rooster, no chicken parmigiana. Now she's a de Alamo Restaurant. Good America family restaurant."

Growing up in a restaurant is the best growing up. You get restaurant meals all the time, you get to go to restaurant weddings, you get to hide in the coat room. You get to play with the most friendly of friendly retarded boys from the state school who do good dish washing. You drink Shirley Temples all the time. You are served extra cherries by the kind hearted bartenders. All this makes you popular at Girl Scouts.

Bein' popular is pretty important.

Friends at school think it's really neat that your Dad is a big shot. Or as Grandpa said, a bigga shit.

Dad and Grandpa wanted to make the Alamo a little more special than just a place with a Texas mural and nice State School boys washing dishes. So Dad came home one night and asked Mum about ideas for special and they had the longest conversation ever.

"We want to make it special."

"What about the waitresses wear Texas costumes?'

"Maybe that's it."

"What about having lotsa kids around so that everybody can eat with a kid."

"Maybe. Kinda strange."

"What about leaving the Christmas decorations up all year…What about extra special desserts? Lovely desserts?"

"Oh. Yeah. Yeah."

So Dad brought the idea to the uncles and they all liked the lovely desserts idea. The aunts loved the idea and Gramma laughed for an hour and seven minutes. The aunts laughed even more. Nine months later, two cousins were born because of this laughter.

Then Gramma spoke up.

"What's a lovely dessert?"

Everyone shrugged.

No one, not even Mum, who had the idea, could answer.

So I said, maybe a baker would know. At age six, things are simple.

Next day we met the brand new baker. Dad had made three phone calls and a baker happened. With Italians, finding a baker is a simple business.

We met the baker. Baker's name was Mike and the baker had a short wiffle haircut and thick black glasses. This baker wore a tee shirt, white, and an apron, white. Flat-bottomed shoes, white floury pants, and a heavy underwater wristwatch completed the outfit. This Mike was shaped exactly like my Girl Scout leader, Mrs. Aldentevecchio, kind of rounded in places and with big bubble hips. This Mike had arm muscles and smiles in the eyes. This Mike had a smooth face and wrinkly eyebrows. I didn't get it.

"Are you a man or a woman?"

My father held his forehead and shook off his embarrassment.

Mike was easy. Mike just told me.

"My name is Mike and I'm a woman with a man's voice and a couple of muscles."

Then she gave me a cookie from the white apron pocket and kissed both of my eyebrows. I'll never forget that cookie. It was soft and yellow with minty green stuff inside but when I finished it I tasted chocolate. And after it was all gone I felt sort of clean all over.

Then Mike turned away from me and my Dad and started throwing flour, handfuls of it, into the air all over me and my dad.

Mike was laughing wildly, shouting, "Madonna," and whispering something like, "espresso, permesso," and my Dad started to giggle. Dad called in the other fattened cooks and the red-headed waitresses and the smiling boys who came with their dishwater soapy hands.

"I'm gonna invent lovely desserts, so watch out," Mike said.

Sure enough, it was a man's voice.

Four and one half hours later, covered in flour, Dad and I smelled the deliciousness of a tray of one hundred and two different lovely desserts. Mike had explained that really these lovely desserts would be more special if we called them love desserts. Love Desserts.

The kitchen was floating in heavy vanillas and lilac smelling memories. The floor was soft with flour and crunchy with crystals from hand-crushed sugars. The desserts were smiling on trays layered with laces and paper doilies that Mike had cut with a sharp knife and a ravioli cutter. They were puffy little things, not cookies, not cakes, all coloured in gardeny ways. I remember thinking they were like little toys. They had little pastel painted pictures with them, that told what kind of love you'd get if you ate it. My favourite picture was of the two old people sitting holding hands in front of a window.

The trays were full of these lovely love desserts. There was a lovely love dessert for getting your Mum's love and another for getting your sister to love you. There were five different desserts for a boyfriend and fourteen for a girlfriend. There was even a dog lovely love dessert and a fish love dessert.

People back then loved the fishes.

Curaggia

There was a love dessert for quiet soldiers and a very lovely love dessert for archangels. There was a Manchurian love dessert and one for widow love. There was a fancy love dessert for dishwashers from the State School. There was a love dessert for an ex-wife.

Mike told me that in our town there was only one ex-wife and this dessert would turn her back into a wife if the right man ate it.

There was a love dessert with a picture of a woman who Mike told me was his own Francie.

One hundred and two lovely love desserts.

Mike made an announcement to my dad.

"I think, Vito, that you let me, Little Baker Mike, give away my love desserts, for free. One year, all free."

Dad tried to say no but Mike arm wrestled him. Dad lost to those baker's muscles and the desserts were free. Mike never took a salary, said there was plenty of money in her pockets and just made these desserts day and night. Mike never talked about money. Mike didn't need money for clothes, that was for sure. Mike washed that tee shirt and that apron every night and just put it back on.

During that year of free desserts, Dad took me to Mike's house. Mike lived with a real woman with a regular voice and soft pink outfits. She was a hairdresser with pointy high heel shoes and lots of red hair all piled up. Her name was Francie and she looked just like the picture that I had seen on the little dessert. Mike and Francie lived in a small three room house surrounded by pretty green grass and one red maple tree. Francie and Mike loved all of us restaurant kids.

Dad and Mum loved Francie and Mike.

In fact, all the aunts and uncles and cousins and the boxer dog and Gramma and Grandpa loved Francie and Mike.

I would have guessed that everyone would love Francie and Mike because they were so nice. We stopped noticing that Mike looked so much like a man.

It was a good year. The Alamo made a nice picture for the newspaper, Weymouth Sicilian News, and announced the creation, by Mike the Baker, of love desserts, free for one year. It was 1959 and the newspaper said that someone called the Dalai Lama was seeking asylum, and Grandpa got happy 'cuz Mr. Pirandello's *Six Characters in Search of An Author* premiered in New York. In 1959, Khrushchev could not get into Disneyland because no one could say he'd be safe enough in the Magic Kingdom. I felt sad for him and Grandpa and I wrote him a letter to make him feel better. Perry Como, who was the best singer ever, was offered 25 million dollars. I think that was a lot of money...

The restaurant filled up fast. Dad and the uncles hired more red-head waitresses and three more boys to wash the dishes. The piano man, Mr.

Benoit, added an organ so he could play popular Sinatra songs in two different dining rooms.

And all kinds of people came and ordered dinner and then ordered love desserts. People came from the next town and from Cape Cod and from the Midwest. Dad even wrote to some Manchurian who he met in the Korean war and the town raised money so the Manchurian could come to Weymouth. Dad wanted the Manchurian to know he was remembered, even though he was called the enemy. The Manchurian did come. The Manchurian kept his big fur hat on the whole visit but ate the food, except for the fava beans, and shook Grandpa and Mike's hand. It seemed like the desserts worked on people because the town began to look full of soft faced people and crime stopped. The Italians stopped bad mouthing the two Jewish people and the three Black families bought houses on the white side of town. Three white families actually traded houses so they could live beside the Black people and the newspaper wrote about the ex-wife who wasn't ex anymore. Weddings happened everyday, not just weekends and some people had to get married at midnight 'cuz the churches were so busy.

Naturally, people wanted to meet Mike.

So once every evening, Mike would walk out of the bakery and across all the dining rooms saying hi to people while Dad simply introduced her.

"Everybody, this is our Mike."

People would clap and smile and Mike would look kind of silly, smiling and just walking through the people.

If Francie was in the restaurant, eating dinner with the hairdresser club, Mike would stop by the table and would smile at Francie. Francie would talk softly with Mike for a moment or two. Mike would sometimes give Francie a very little sweet pat on the shoulder.

The newspaper wanted to do a feature story but Dad said it would have to be a short story because short was the family way. Grandpa explained about the wind of boiling cauliflowers being like too much talk. So the newspaper decided to do a short Alamo story every week. Mike's story was first.

"Mike doesn't take a salary."

The history of love desserts was the second instalment.

"Could have been lovely desserts; might've been costumes."

My favorite was when the newspaper interviewed the family boxer dog, Grumble.

"Grumble licks spoons while Mike bakes love desserts."

This stuff went on for a year. The restaurant was expanded and the windows were opened and lilac gardens bloomed. Gramma and Grandpa and old people like them could eat dinner, have a love dessert and then practice holding hands in front of a window, the way old people do.

One night, while the people were eating dinner at the Alamo and while people were deciding on which love dessert to try, a tall stranger came into

Curaggia

the restaurant. Dad knew many but not all of the customers. He figured this was another visitor from the midwest because of the way he was dressed in working pants. But this man was angry. Grandpa later said it was the ugly anger of rotten thinking. Grandpa told me to stop eating. He said I must never eat while there was anger in the dining room. I put down my fork.

Grandpa stood up from the table and went to the man. They just stared at each other for a minute or two. Then the man said, "Where's that goddamn stupid sister of mine?"

Grandpa asked him who he was talking about. Man barked, "She calls herself Mike. Idiot of a fool makes me sick. Where is she, my pig of a sister?"

Mike must have heard because she came out of the kitchen.

The stranger looked at her and growled.

Then he grabbed her by the throat and slammed her against the wall. He took a gun from his belt and pointed it at her forehead. He yelled, "Everyone move back."

Grandpa grabbed me and shoved me behind him.

The rest happened very fast or very slow. The man held Mike in a mean way. "Twenty years and you still make me sick. I ought to kill you right here. It was Ma thought you should know. Pa died two weeks ago. She's all broken up. Doesn't want to see you. Says you ruined our family."

Mike stood there looking at him. One tear rolled down her cheek but she looked him in the eye.

"It's just who I am. I never meant ... that's why I left."

"You're no sister of mine." He released her. He spat on her shoes. He clenched and unclenched his fists and then he pushed Grandpa out of his way. He pushed Grandpa so hard that I fell down.

He left and slammed the door so hard that the glass broke.

Grandpa put his arms around Mike, who stood there, in his arms, sobbing. Next day, Mike didn't come to work. Dad called Francie but there was no answer. So Dad and I went over to their house. This was almost one year after the time we met Mike and she threw all the flour around.

We walked across that pretty green lawn and passed the red tree. The front door was open and a rich creamy man's voice was singing something that sounded like opera. Must have been the record player but I never figured that part out because when we opened the door, the singing stopped.

On the table was a plate of pretty little pastel coloured candies, in the shapes of everyone in my family. A little marzipan Grandpa and a white chocolate sister and a pistachio Aunt Fanny. There was a note on the table.

"Time to make room. Love, Mike and Francie. P.S. We really love you all."

Dad started to hold his forehead.

"Oh. My God."

Dad came over and put his arm around me and steered me to the door and told me to stand there. He called the police.

The police were real polite.

The newspapers refused to keep the story short, even when Dad begged them, but there wasn't much of a story to tell.

Mike and Francie had lived together for about twenty years after Francie finished hairdressing school in the Everglades. Francie had no family. Mike came from a town in Wyoming. Her family was very wealthy from the beef business. One uncle was a priest somewhere in Italy. Neither had friends except for people they worked with and neither went out except for once a month to go to the movies with each other. Neither one went to church.

Nobody could find out anything else.

Neighbour of theirs said that a woman had visited them the morning they went away. She was a fancy woman, dressed in grey and beige and carrying a grey suitcase. Neighbour said that Mike and Francie sounded happy to see her and Francie said something about being glad it was that time again.

No one knew what that was about.

Neighbour didn't see the woman leave, didn't hear any noises.

Four months later on a dark road, Mike and Francie were found dead, in their car, both shot in the back. They had been living in their car.

There was a big humongous funeral for Mike and Francie, with an open casket and flowers, flowers, flowers. Sheperd's Funeral Home rented an extra parking lot from the supermarket so that everyone could park easy. Dad and the uncles closed the restaurant for three days.

I remember going up to the caskets. Both of them laying in there, side by side, in their boxes. The Sheperd's had made them look O.K., with a new tee shirt for Mike and a pretty green party dress for Francie. Mike even had her glasses on.

Gramma and Grandpa served anisette, right at the funeral home.

The angry brother was charged with murder. He said his sister and Francie didn't deserve to live, stinking up the world with their sins against God and man. I didn't understand.

Guess that's the story. They buried the caskets in a real pretty place by the brook in the prettiest cemetery in our town. All of us restaurant kids used to picnic by that brook so we saw their marker all the time. It had a picture of a tree with a vine growing up it and it just said, "Making room," like the note.

Sometimes I think I see Mike or Francie walking down the street but then I remember that they can't walk the street 'cuz they are sleeping by the brook. Sometimes I see a white apron or a red maple or a sack of flour and I remember.

The Alamo stayed busy and the waitresses got uniforms in grey and beige with bows in their hair and Dad hung a picture of Mike in one of the dining rooms. Mike's uncle the priest came to visit once and Dad let him eat for free.

A real pretty woman in a grey and beige outfit came once looking for Mike and Dad told her Mike had been shot.

The woman asked, "Francie, too?"

Dad nodded.

Grandpa happened to be sitting with Dad that day, sitting at the bar drinking Shirley Temples with us kids.

Grandpa asked the woman if she knew about Joe Green. Grandpa tested people this way. Joe Green and Guiseppe Verdi, two men, one name.

The woman shook his hand and said, "Do I ever."

Dad said Grandpa and the woman talked in Sicilian for awhile and then the woman left, but she gave Grandpa a small box. In it were a recipe for marzipan candies and a piece of red hair. Grandpa gave it to Dad.

Dad built a little shelf under the picture of the Alamo and nailed the box to the shelf. He put a picture of Mike and Francie on that shelf.

Dad and Grandpa decided to take a the train down to the docks like they did sometimes. Grandpa gave a quiet speech.

"Remember how the stranger give me a ten dollar, when I get offa the boat? He say to me to do this for paisan, some poor fool who alone? Remember, how I say to you, you too, you give the ten when you see them get offa the boat? Well. I have idea. Let's give ten dollar to a woman stranger this time."

Grandpa said this, shrugging.

Dad said, "Never gave a ten to a woman stranger."

"Might be a good thing, a good Mike the Baker kinda thing."

Grandpa smiled.

Bachelor

Laura Scaccia Beagle

Putting on my new black leather motorcycle boots to clean the house. So much for the pristine image of an Italian American mom shuffling about in her housedress and slippers, cleaning. When I was a kid, I wanted to grow up to be a bachelor.

I think I first learned that term from re-runs of "Love American Style" or "That Girl." I wanted to have a "bachelor pad" so my girlfriend could come over. She would be impressed with how cool it was and ask me about all the unique stuff I had lying about. I would tell her about the adventures I survived to get them all. She would be even more impressed, which would keep her coming back.

When I was a kid I wanted to grow up to be a bachelor.

untitled

Nzula Angelina Ciatu

shame & guilt
feelings i'm familiar with
anger takes getting used to

shame
when an italian literature professor
makes homophobic statements to the media
a group of dykes and fags
rally against him
shame
because i'm sicilian-italian
in white anglosaxon america
where one of us
represents all of us
i
carry
his errors
like sacks of grains
hunched-back heavy

shame
everytime i struggle
to speak italian
when sicilian rolls from me
naturally
smoothly
still i dare not speak
this forbidden tongue
shame
because even my sicilian is limited
a stabbing reminder
of all severed
by assimilation

shame & guilt
at every family gathering
my working-class secondlanguageenglish
suddenly shows off an education
shame
for having become estranged
from my roots
guilt
for what i can't turn back to
first generation
living the borderlands
piece together
identities
chewed up by oppression

finally
at the kitchen table
surrounded by italian dykes
hands swing
with gusto
high-pitched voices & accents speak
i savour
every word
sentence
phrase
gesture

at the kitchen table
reunited
with parts of myself
i'd always run from
guilt
for having hated my ethnicity
rage
for having been made to hate it
frustration
feeling i'm drawing attention
to myself
marginalized ethnic dyke
exaggerating

Curaggia

anger
because i know
this frustation is one part
of the whole fucking
racist system
hide cultures traditions
bury mother tongues
pass at all costs
as white-anglo-american

shame & guilt
feelings i'm familiar with
anger
i'm learning
helps spit out the bitterness

Dyke

Giovanna (Janet) Capone

At 23
I left my family behind
in New York.
I often picture me
at that time,
short dark hair
leather jacket
and a big black motorbike.
Screaming dyke.
I always liked
the colour black,
in fact,
I have aunts 4 feet 11 inches high
who wear it all the time.

I picture me
at 23
breaking the traditions I was raised by.
Che vergogna! Malafemmina!
Defying la famiglia
You gotta have alotta guts
to live another way.
No one bats an eye
when you're little
but at 23
Ooo Madonn-! They'd die
if they only knew,
those old Italian aunts
sifting clues
like lentil beans
They see me once a year
and stare

at my short dark hair
brown eyes
and olive skin.
I used to list my sins
in great detail
for the priest.
Say 15 Hail Marys
on my knees.
Acts of Contrition
are powerful ammunition
against a young gay child
trying to stay alive.

"Oh my God
I'm heartfully sorry
for having offended Thee."
At 23
the power of the family is strong
It's everything,
in fact,
and knowing that
you don't belong
brings misery.
How could I?
with my short dark hair,
olive skin,
leather jacket
and a big black motorbike?

I always liked the colour black,
in fact,
I have aunts 4 feet 11 inches high
who wear it all the time.

In another time
this paesana
used to make eggplant
with her mother,
drop breaded slices in a pan
and let them fry.

I got her soft brown eyes
and my father's darker skin.
Now, like him,
I drop my keys
on the kitchen table
when I'm home.
But I live alone
no paesana there
to greet me.

Even now, at 33,
I grate Romano cheese
fry eggplant in a pan.
When all else fails
I can always eat.
I can always
make a good red sauce

and remind myself
that despite the cost
I'm the boss
in my kitchen
and my life.

Curaggia

Dancing the Tarantella

Francesca Roccaforte

BASIL (Bay Area Sicilian Italian Lesbians) March at Lesbian and Gay Pride in San Francisco, California, June, 1992

Dancing the tarantella on the black sweltering street in the city of San Francisco
Pridefully strolling, the paesanas pound the ground
Like the beat of goat hooves ascending the craggy hills of our motherland, Italia
Olive skinned fac'ia bello, redheaded daughters, garlic breathed, spicy tomato-sauced, sesame-seeded,
lovely fem'mina
Sorelles of Napoli, Sicilia, Calabria and Toscana
Link arms and do the tarantella
Rejoicing in the melodic sounds of our homeland

This poem was inspired by a march of several members of BASIL, a group of lesbians who meet once monthly to celebrate our culture via food, exchange of family stories, and lesbian pride. This year Giovanna (Janet) Capone, the co-founder and Mama of BASIL, Lynn Razzini, Annette Cottonaro, Teresa Broccoli, Denise Leto, Mary Pelc, Vincenza Baldino, Rosemary Zapulla, Tina DeFeliciantonio, Lucille and myself marched through the streets of S.F. singing, dancing, throwing pasta at the throngs of onlookers and merrymakers.

The crowds just loved us as we held our BASIL banner, sweat dripping down our faces from the heat of the day. Denise and Tina started dancing the tarantella and a few of us started clapping and laughing as I was shooting video and still film of this precious moment. We all got into this high energy and it was just a blast!

Most of us were wearing black, the national color of Italians and I was wearing a tee shirt that said "Italian Girls Best in the World, Little Italy, NYC," with a tassel of red, white and green I brought from Little Italy. At first, I was wearing the tassel around my waste like a Middle Eastern dancer. Then I took it off and had it on a string and started waving at the crowds, giving them a mock blessing from the High Priestess of Southern Italian America! It was all great fun with Italian humor. It inspired me to write the above poem.

Touch

Francesca Roccaforte

Wet

Francesca Roccaforte

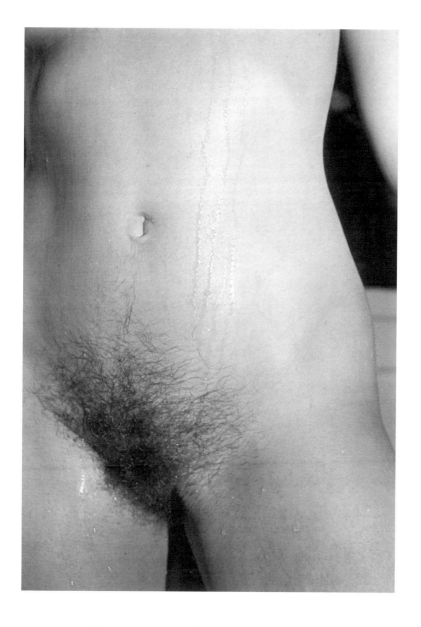

Self-portrait

Francesca Roccaforte

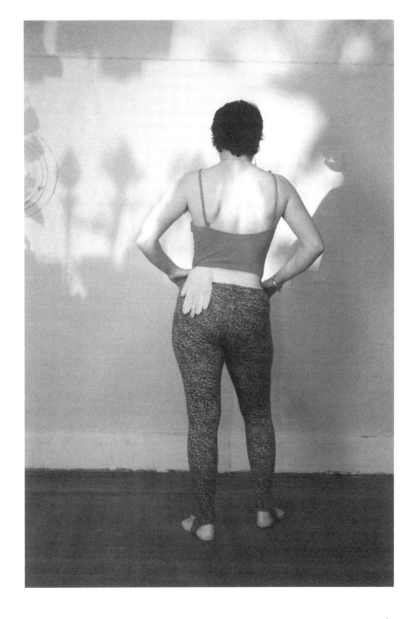

Last night I was visited by the ancestors

Giovanna (Janet) Capone

They sat heavy in my dreams
the dead ones
now undead
were talking, laughing
resting their hands on big bellies.
There was coffee
in demitasse cups
and crumb cake
on the table,
a cardboard box of cannoli
and almond biscotti
and lots of loud laughter
"Ha ha ha!
She thinks she's different from us
because she's queer?"

"Non farmi ridere!" one aunt said.
"Same problems, same pain.
Same old shit!"
Then the others burst out laughing
and they all laughed long and hard.
They seemed to share a consensus about me
and life in general,
which is that it's useless
to try too hard
to be happy.
"Hey, you get what you get and that's it.
Stop crying the blues."

Va fanculo, you ancestors!
You sit too heavy
in my dreams
as in my waking life
those times when
your immigrant resignation
is a quicksand
I sink into
a mud, so deep and familiar
I could make my home in it
— and suffocate.
Big hands rest on round bellies, thick fingers
and brown, fleshy arms,
your gray black hair done up perfect,
dark red colour
highlights your lips,
big gray dresses hang
past your knees.
You speak in loud, deep voices, wave your hands around
and keep a few small, slender men by your side
men like my father
who actually seem kinder
than you goddamn women
Madonn-!
with your volcanic laughter
you all sit in judgement
on me

Le sorelle di mia mama,
mia mama, i mie parenti, tutti
Molti avi
ieri sera
some dead
some still living
All of you flourishing wildly
in my soul
"Lesbian? Va Nabola! You think
you're different from us?
You think your life will be free
of pain?
Non farmi ridere!"

Curaggia

Syllables, Symbols, and Rhythm

Laura Scaccia Beagle

About Writing
"Syllables, Symbols, and Rhythm"

"Syllables, Symbols and Rhythm" was a prophetic permission statement, allowing me to experience and embrace my sexuality. It was prophetic in the sense that during the time I was writing it I was only speculating about what it would be like to be sexual with a woman. Feelings about "wholeness of identity" and the search for its expression, both in my sexuality and my lifestyle, were already there, dormant in a sense.

It was much easier for me to be Italian because I was taught to be proud of that part of my identity. Many of my artistic talents and charm my grandfather attributed to my Italian half. I have always identified my ethnicity as Italian. It was much more difficult to explore, take on, develop, embrace the identity of being queer. I honestly struggled with the labels, "lesbian" and "dyke." For me, the queer identity is uncovered rather than proscribed or apparent in the same way ethnicity is. I have struggled with a queer identity as shameful.

This story is a reconstruction of identity for me. It is an intentional smashing of the boxes that family and the institutional Catholic church have, consciously, or unconsciously, tried to impose upon me. While reflecting on many aspects of my identity, I became aware of how interwoven my Italian identity is with my woman-loving identity. I think it's impossible to view them separately.

In the beginning of the story, there is mention that Toni's (the main character) parents are dead. Their absence liberates Toni and she gives herself permission to explore her deepest desires, loving and making love with a woman. This shows the power the influence of her "familgia" has on her — respect and obey the rules and don't bring shame upon the family. This reflected my situation for many years. Though my parents are not dead, I was not out to them for fear of turmoil and rejection not to mention the extended family's potential uproar.

The story also addresses the issue of a Catholic upbringing and whether or not it delayed my sense of sexuality. There are clearly traditional Catholic images woven throughout the story. My intent, although at the time was quite unconscious, was to reclaim for myself the power of the images. The character rejects the "old ethnic chapel" and worships something much more alive and real to her, the beautiful woman who makes the bread at the bakery which nourishes her.

This mirrors my own spiritual journey of coming to accept myself and believe that my sexuality, especially my orientation, is a gift. I have many positive spiritual and "out" women who are models for me and with whom I celebrate a communal spirituality. I think Toni is searching and longing for this sense of community, family, "the familiar" when she fatefully meets the Madonna. When their eyes meet for the first time there is a sense of familiarity between them, much like the familiarity I feel when I know a stranger is a pasean, their features and gestures often indicate it to me. That same element draws Toni in, hoping to find some answers for herself in someone who resembles her. She seeks outward validation for her developing identity, rather than her own inward validation. The Madonna character replaces the validation she would be looking for in her family, she begins to develop a "family of choice."

In its original form, in the second-half of the story, when Toni begins to narrate her experience, she speaks in the past-tense. I thought about why I wrote it that way originally. It was a lot safer to speak about events after they occurred rather than as they happened. It gave me, in my fear, a safe distance from my own desire. Years later, I am feeling a bit stronger in my identity and thus able to be more present. I am grateful for the opportunity to pull this story out of the closet and examine it, may you all have the strength to examine intently your own coming out stories.

Part I

Looking through a stained glass window of an old chapel, "it was the eyes, the eyes." That was what was so familiar about her reflection. During all those years, the only constant was those two topaz colored pools on either side of her nose which sparkled when Toni smiled. She could always see through her eyes into her soul. Those who knew her said they could as well. Although her eyes stayed with her, her nickname "mouse-eyes" didn't. The first nickname for the first child of the family, a birthright of sorts. Yet still, she was a subtle combination of her parents, in her eyes and features, as well as her temperament.

Toni stared intently into her reflection, searching for definition and clarity to shine forth from her mouse eyes. She couldn't find either. Restless and discontent, she continued her snail-like walking. She passed the other window of the chapel and let out a pent up sigh.

Searching for clarity, a sense of belonging, had long been a recreational pastime of Toni's. Sometimes she would create stories out of half-truths just to ease her compulsion for identity. Loneliness had become a toe-hold for creativity. Imagination reared itself amidst oppression. Although creating takes an immense amount of energy, perfection always demanded more; more energy, more painstaking work, grinding day and night.

Toni found traces of herself in many obscure places. She recognized likenesses of herself in some people, strangers jabbing glances at each other in the street or hallway of a building, or the gods and goddesses she made of people who impressed her. She had lost and found her identity in an elderly woman or a young adolescent boy, back and forth, losing and regaining. Toni found herself in men and women alike. Some days she had more in common with men, whether rugged or graceful. Other days with women, strong, withered or soft. Toni lost and found her self in music giving her soul to it. She knew she could play percussion with incensed passion and become a graceful partner with the rhythm of dance. Most of all, she knew the sacred rhythms of eating, talking, drinking, singing, hugging and kissing that instinctively emerge from the decedents of Southern Italian peasants.

Yet she didn't feel she had a real identity of her own, not one she had a part in creating and that's all that truly mattered in the end. As a painter chooses paints, Toni wanted to choose from her available parts and experiences, emphasizing and de-emphasizing that which framed her, the colourful portrait of her identity.

Weighed down with the lack of knowledge Toni went in search of identity. The moment she saw her familiar eyes in the holiness of the chapel's stained glass she knew it was time to take on the divine quest of "self." She always looked outward for her self-definition. The only genuine things that belonged to her were her eyes, her "mouse-eyes." Now that the givers of that name were gone (her parents) those eyes belonged to her, even if nothing else about her seemed to.

Toni kept walking in this new found liberation. Allowing herself to experience, in order to pick and choose the medium for her self-identity portrait. It was the aesthetically pleasing aroma and the pangs in her stomach that lured her into the bakery's coffee house on the corner past the old chapel.

She lingered in the doorway and then meandered into the store front. This, she thought, would be her new shrine. This bakery ablaze with life will be holy ground. The bread was alive. The dough had risen, the coffee too, fitting for a chapel as it flowed out of the urn and its aroma wafted towards the ceiling like incense at high mass.

As Toni was taking in the sweet smells, the graceful Madonna of the shrine appeared. Her hair was pulled back, with wisps of flour clinging to her bangs. Immaculate and incarnate, her hands and forearms of virginal white carried the raw dough like the babe in swaddling clothes. Toni was captured in the revelation of the moment and could not answer the woman who questioned her at the counter. She didn't even realize there was someone other than the Madonna present. Toni stuttered, "Umm ... coffee ... black and bread ... whatever's the freshest."

The Madonna never turned fully around, as though disaffected and oblivious to the customer, to the bakery, to the mortal world. Toni was ensnared by curiosity and compelled to gaze upon her entire radiant face. She waited awkwardly, her mouse-eyes never abandoning her subject. Yet the Madonna seemed oblivious to Toni's gaze. Or maybe she was aware of it and was used to being adored.

Toni became mesmerized by the rhythm and grace with which the Madonna kneaded the dough. Toni took in the sights and made herself aware of every detail. Her eyes traced the slim muscles of the Madonna's forearms onto her flour-covered fingers. The way she was slightly bent over the back counter and the ease of her movements ushered a smile on Toni's face. The delicate tone of her shoulders and the sturdiness and strength of her lean angular back pleased Toni's mouse-eyes and made her aware of her own body.

Toni was startled, as her order of coffee and bread arrived. She fumbled through some cash in her hand and returned to watching her new deity. Slowly she moved to a counter seat, out of traffic and in better view of this holy creature.

What was it about the Madonna that infatuated Toni? Was it the transference of something divine and distant into the humanness of a woman standing a few feet from her? No, it was something more, something to do with creating an identity and something to do with the familiar.

So Toni waited, impatiently, wishing only for a glance at her Madonna's full face, and nothing more, she told herself. Toni had this awful habit of telling herself half-truths. Denial was her mode of existence.

The sun had begun its early evening goodbyes and now shone through the westerly window of the shop, revealing all the dust particles in the air from the constant use of flour. Just as Toni started to succumb to the rhythm of the sunlight dancing on the floating particles, her idol turned. The Madonna faced the half-empty shop and gazed out the front windows conveniently at Toni's back. Sunlight streamed through her hair and gave it a halo-like radiance. Toni wanted to stand up and obstruct the Madonna's view, force the deity to notice her. But, paralyzed by beauty, she remained seated at the counter. All she could hope for now was that the Madonna would catch her mouse-eyes as she retracted her stare from the window behind Toni. Mid-wish, it happened.

Toni forced herself not to look away, although she was sure she was blushing. Their eyes locked for a brief second and there was a benign recognition. The kind of familiarity that happens when you think you know someone or have met them before and begin to go on as if you know them but then uncertainty holds you captive and words and actions freeze motion-

Curaggia

less in mid-sentence. There were elements of that familiarity. As Toni drank in the Madonna's brief gaze she sensed a subtle wanting. The minute she began to recognize it, it was gone, and left her second-guessing herself, as usual.

The glance gave Toni admission to the Madonna's world, the minute she was acknowledged as a person, or at least as a customer, she was in. Toni knew how to take advantage, and with her admission ticket, a glance, she was determined to gain full entry into the this intriguing deity's life. This was her new obsession, a part of a larger one to create or discover or destroy her own identity.

Abruptly, Toni felt a heated urge to leave. It took deliberate effort to actually separate from the stool and start for the door. Consoling herself with two thoughts, she managed to rise from her seat. The first of those thoughts, was one of devotion. She vowed to return to the shop, her new shrine, her new found faith, and pay homage to the Madonna daily. This familiarity, this habit of locale would be a perfect vantage point from which to wait. And wait she would, for the opportune moment, the perfect segue into the Madonna's world.

The other consoling thought she had, somewhat more personal, was about the "fresh bread." The bread the Madonna had fashioned with her strong rhythmic hands and which Toni had consumed. Now a part of the Madonna, her divine creation, dwelt within Toni, filling up her hunger, taking away the pangs, filling her need. Slowly this image helped Toni wean herself from the glorious deity. She knew she would keep this thought tucked away and remember it at every time she ended one of her visitations to the holy shrine.

Toni was in a daze as the bus she meant to board passed her by. She looked for a taxi. Within minutes she hailed one, checked her pockets for cash and climbed in. Through rote memory she rattled off her destination. Her address had not changed in the last year, so for once she didn't have to second guess about that aspect of her life.

Three days passed after Toni's initial visit to the bakery. Each visit seemed to bring on more frustration. After all Toni had vowed to return there everyday and worship. The least the Madonna could do would be to show-up and allow herself to be adored. She inquired about the deity's whereabouts. The woman at the counter said the Madonna had taken another shift, the later one.

Toni was a bit disappointed. This shift change brought darkness. Later hours meant she could no longer watch the sun's rays through the Madonna's flour-basked hair. At least the Madonna still worked there and Toni knew where to find her, "for devotions, of course," she deluded herself. Toni decided to return later that evening. Hopefully the older woman at the counter wouldn't be working and wouldn't mention Toni's inquiry about the Madonna directly to the deity. The counter woman might become suspicious if Toni showed up there later and realizing she was a stranger to her co-worker, mention something.

Toni forced herself to think of something else and calmed herself with thoughts of attire. "Ah, yes of course, what will I wear tonight upon my return? Will she remember me from three days ago? Will I be just another faceless customer to her ... my beautiful Madonna?"

Toni went home to change clothes. She decided on something not too flashy, something that would create a mystique about the wearer. Although Toni had little of her own "true" identity, she always managed to create her own style of dress. Her particular style was a periscope both to the world outside of her and into her soul.

Toni got off the bus a block or so premature and inched her way to the bakery in anticipation and apprehension. She was surprised to find out that her cousin Joey worked at the bakery. Yet she was quick to realize he was part of her admission ticket, and would usher her into the Madonna's world. Toni couldn't contain her frenzied heart, pounding with excitement about worshipping her new idol. At the same time she was fearful that things would not be quite as perfect as the first time she knelt at the shrine.

Part II

I round the doorway of the bakery's coffee shop, pretending not to look directly, yet seeing all that my heart desires. Each second stretches as I wait impatiently to speak to the Madonna alone. Beauty captivates me and we linger a breath's touch away, curiosity waxing. We meet in the rear of the kitchen as she walks through the door. She moves briskly past me, and the wake of her body against the air caresses my being. No escape. Immediately, desire sets in. Will it be? Could this finally be the chance? Joey introduces us, our eyes meet as we acknowledge our mutual existence. I secretly want to know everything about her. Bubbling inside, uncontrollably, I eke out a "hello." All too quickly the introduction wanes and everything acquiesces to routine, not quite sure of how fate had brought us here, I am certain by evening's end we will be together.

My cousin leaves and the Madonna is to close the shrine-of-a-bakery. She is as familiar as I am at this point and does not mind that I am there after closing. She seems to welcome the company. I am someone to talk to as she checks off the tasks from the instruction sheet taped to the formica counter next to the register. The trash was the last task on the list. I offer to help carry it outside to the alley; she welcomes the offer with night-shift weary eyes. Our conversation is uninterrupted as we ascend to the alley from the basement steps. She mentions that her apartment is not far away and it is evident she wants to continue the conversation. I am so enthralled I fail to notice we are already around the corner from her building. She asks me in and I can barely rasp out a "yes."

The one bedroom apartment which "came furnished" she said, is extremely spartan for a Madonna of her stature. "High expectations lead to disappointment," I tell myself. She offers me what little orange juice was left in the refrigerator and joins me. The Joni Mitchell album is all cued up on the stereo and ready to go. She asks if I am a fan. I say I haven't heard much of her material and allude to Amy Ray's style of guitar playing instead of focusing on my lack of knowledge about Joni.

Then the Madonna announces her brief departure, a must, as she insists that her ability to be comfortable relies on whether or not she can rid herself of the "ugly" flour and grease stained uniform. As she changes behind the slightly opened door, shadows tantalizing, she never abandons speech. Her actual words pass by me, yet the timbre of her voice draws me closer, closer to her soul's voice. Like an unquenchable rhythm that rises from within, I know we will be together through this balmy night of early spring.

She stands at the partially opened door in a glow of soft lamp-light offering to make some toast, attesting to its medicinal qualities. In the short time we are together I take in each of her delightful mannerisms and sayings. I hone in on the absolute, the ones that give her distinction, unique personhood, falling in love with every syllable of body language.

After all the evidence of the toast has been exiled from the couch, we sit in a pensive silence, staring into nothingness. She breaks the trance by shifting her robe about her. She does this in an unconscious, matter-of-fact way which I can't help but notice. We talk of the universal trials of being "woman" in this society. Our conversation swells and through many transition topics, it seems to point directly to her need, which paralleled mine, belonging.

Much of the conversation, words, thoughts and movements become blurry, and we settle into a quiet non-verbal language; one of thought, touch and hesitated pleasure. Heart pounding I do not flinch as she touches my cheek and neck with her work-worn dove-like hands. I follow in turn.

We hold fast to each other's grasp and linger on the brink of no return, mutually choosing to plunge into what the other offers. There are no words, just syllables, symbols and rhythm. Almost telepathically the lamp light flickers off and we begin a dance of the unknown in each other's comfort and trust. Lightly back and forth we move, first me, then her. Tingling inside from the moist lips on my bare shoulder I try desperately not to spasm with a shiver. It is unavoidable, and entices her further. With glazed over eyes I give back to her all she gave me, with willing intentions and taut limbs, we dance.

Her knowing hands trace my dormant body and call it to life in the spring again. With her back arched she looks like an angel stretching towards heaven. My lips find a home among the dark, familiar hair nesting at the core of her being. She welcomes my lost lips home and sings an eternal song of joy upon their arrival. Turning and stretching, hungering and writhing I succumb to the noblest of her intentions, wishing we were clay and melting together into one.

As she lies silently on and around me I revel in her warm scent, so unique to her beauty so ingrained in my soul. We begin to dance once more, searching for our eternal sacred home, our sanctuary so private, few know the exact route to it, still fewer are let in.

She traces my outlines as one who had drawn the map. This intuition both surprises and excites me. We dance on and on, uninhibited, unlike with others.

My eyes are wet with joy. I lay tucked in the arms of this transfigured woman, feeling a familiar sense of home. I float off to sleep lulled by the syncopation of our breathing.

Curaggia

La Nipota Diversa

Deb LeRose

"Is not a trick," Nonna says sternly while she rubs her special San Antonio icon over the back of my injured neck. I was in a minor car accident several months ago and my neck still hurts a little. Because I live in the city, 400 miles away, Nonna waits for my rare visits to practice her healing on me.

I'm back in my home town for Nonno's birthday. The small house is filled with family for dinner. Nonna takes my hand and leads me down the hall, away from the loud voices, the hum of the TV. She brings me into the bedroom where, after 64 years of marriage, she and Nonno still sleep together in a double bed.

An invitation into the bedroom is reserved for special *sotto voce* talks or to get the good silverware from behind Nonna's blue polyester dresses in the closet. This time I was invited in to receive a miracle.

One of the bedroom's walls is a shrine to dead relatives. I recognize the faces in the photos from Nonna's stories. Nonna's two brothers who both died young. One of cancer, alone in California; the other, by his own hand—a result of his unrequited love in their village in southern Italy. But no one talks of these things. *Omerta*. I've made up their stories from decades of hearing innuendo and half-truths.

There are other photos on the wall. Nonna's parents: a handsome father who spent many years working in America until an explosion on the railroad tracks sent him back to Italy for good; his somber-looking wife, left pregnant after his annual visits home, raised six children. Next to them is Nonna's older sister who died here in Canada. The largest and oldest photo on the imitation wood-panel wall is of a five-year old Nonno and his mother who died in the 1918 Spanish influenza epidemic that swept through Europe. The photo was taken the same year she died. Nonno's father later married his dead wife's youngest sister. She was only seven years older than Nonno. More like a sister than a mother.

On a wall adjacent to the "family wall" hangs a giant beaded rosary; around the room are statues of Mary, including a plastic one once full of the slowly evaporating sacred water from Lourdes. Another wall displays a large framed Jesus in a garden whose name I should know, and year after year of small crosses woven from dried palm leaves.

My grandparent's bedroom reminds me of my childhood, when I would beg my parents to let me spend the weekend at "Nonna's house." Both Nonna and Nonno lived there, but Nonno worked shifts at the smelter and wasn't around much until he retired; by then, I had left home for university and never moved back to my home town.

Nonna devoted all her attention to me, making me feel like a princess. And she wanted me to marry a prince. She'd let me stay up until after the late TV news. At bedtime, Nonna taught me my Catholic prayers in Italian, so I could pray *ave maria piena di grazia* before going to sleep. I slept in the room next to theirs, in a small bed with a soft rolling mattress, on rough sheets hand-woven decades earlier by Nonna's mother. In the mornings, Nonna let me eat sugar-coated cereal, a treat denied by my mother. She taught me Italian card games; I was an adult before I learned that standard card decks included 8-9-10 cards.

Nonna, Nonno, my mother and her siblings immigrated after the second war. They joined Nonna's sister and settled in a small industrial town in western Canada. This is where I was born, barely a decade after they had settled here. Nonna didn't work outside her home, so she never spoke English very well. I don't think she spoke Italian very well, either. She had only studied up to grade five. When I visited, she would teach me Italian words and I would teach her English words. We each kept a list in our dictionaries.

On rainy days we listened to 45s — records — from Nonna's 1965 trip back to the "old country." We sang and danced around the dining room, which housed the small record player. I can still hear those melancholy lyrics about the *nostalgico emigrante* who left behind his *cara mama* and *Calabria amata* for the new land, this *terra desolata*. Those songs were Nonna's only link between present and past. S*tanno cambiando il mondo*, but Nonna would never change. I heard those songs as happy tunes, not sad stories from a world that no longer existed.

Nonno and Nonna never really knew how to dance; they bounced up and down with no apparent rhythm. The dancers were on my father's side of the family. My great-aunt, Z'a Teresa would dance the *tarantella* with my dad's father at all the family weddings while my paternal grandmother threw "confetti" — candy-coated almonds — at the feet of the dancers. As a child, I imagined them living forever to dance at my wedding. When I was twelve, my paternal nonna crocheted a tablecloth for me to put on the table under my wedding cake. When I was 20, she moved into a facility for the elderly. Before leaving her home of over 60 years, she gave my mother her silverware to give to me when I get married. Now I'm 38. I'll never marry. I'll never use the tablecloth. I'll never get the silverware. And no one will dance the *vera tarantella calabrese* for me and my lover.

"You have to believe. *Ricordi*," Nonna says, "ten years ago when Nonno almost died, he was in intensive care and the *dottore* didn't know what was wrong with him. When he was sleeping I rubbed this S. Antonio medallion on him and he got better. But, shh…'' she raises a finger to her lips, leans towards me and whispers, "Nonno doesn't know about it. Don't tell him or he'll get mad. Il dottore said it was a miracle.'' I nod. S. Antonio is Nonno's saint. Every year there is a new S. Antonio calendar hanging on the kitchen wall above the telephone. He is the saint who protects our family and especially our patriarch.

The one-inch square metal that Nonna rubs over my neck has a small round hole in the centre through which shows a tiny piece of cloth. Nonna says the cloth is from the robe of S. Antonio. She mail-ordered it from Padua. Coming from Italy alone makes it sacred. Nonna has added her own sacred touches: she's slipped the icon into a cut-to-fit plastic Air Canada luggage tag holder. Plastic. Like the plastic left on their lamp shades. It's a new-world product that preserves the few precious things they have.

Nonna continues to rub my neck. I no longer pray *ave maria*, instead I think about being a lesbian and how I will never tell her. I think about her experiences as an immigrant and how my lover is also an immigrant, one that I could not sponsor because no one considers it my right to have a same-sex partner.

Unlike my working-class grandparents, who couldn't afford vacations except to visit family, I travel often. I met my foreign lover while on vacation; not long afterwards she came to live with me in my country. Immigration became part of my personal story.

My *Cara*, my love, lived with me as a visitor for many years. At first, it wasn't a big concern. We knew if we kept quiet, Cara could easily slip across the border to renew her visa and return to our home without problems. But after three, four, five years of not working, running out of money, and living in constant fear of forced separation, we knew we had to come out and get support for our situation.

Coming out to my parents was disastrous. They behaved badly, and privately hoped that Cara would be deported; then I wouldn't be lesbian. After ten years, they still don't want her in their home. Nonna and Nonno love her because they know her as my dear friend who loves and takes care of me. And they are right. But she is also my lover.

Without the support of family, I looked for the support of community. I became an immigration activist. After years of struggling, I was able to get my partner into Canada on humanitarian and compassionate grounds. My family doesn't know this; they don't want to know my stories.

All Nonna has to give me are her stories. Stories that taught me not to trust people, stories that valued obedience, not truth. I've learned my lessons well, too well. I will honour the code of silence — *omerta* — I will never "come out" to her. She will always know me as her little princess who dances around the record player.

Nonna rubs S. Antonio across my neck one last time. When she's done, I'm cured. "I love you very, very much, my dolly," she says. "I love all my *nipote* the same, but you're the only one who understands me when I talk. You're different, *diversa*." If she only knew.

Curaggia

La, Are You a Lesbian?

Laura

"So, what would it mean if your son was gay?"
    "Well, I know, his father wouldn't handle it very well."
    "Why? What would he do? Strangle him? Kill him? Just because he was gay?"
    "No, well, it's just, he would be upset."
    "What if I were to tell you that my daughter is gay. What then?"

I came out as a lesbian when I was eighteen. Suddenly everything felt new, exciting, electric even! And just so incredibly right. A whole new world had opened up. There were marches to go to, meetings to attend, dances, parties, new friends, a real sense of community and of course, there were women to meet. It was absolutely hot and positively profound. But then there was how am I ever going to tell my family??? Thankfully, there was no time to think about it because there were marches to go to, meetings to attend, women to meet… But more importantly, there was, HOW THE HELL AM I EVER GOING TO TELL MY FAMILY?!!!!! Well, actually, it was more like how would I ever tell my mother. She was who mattered the most. We were always very close, visits several times a week and phone calls several times a day. So, I knew that lying to her about anything, for any extended period of time, was going to require extreme forethought, planning and pronoun changing agility. But lying was exactly what I was going to do, what I had to do. I had convinced myself that my mother's ill health would never enable her to cope with my sexuality. No, I had to protect her. She must never know!

    Eventually I introduced my lover to my mother, as my friend and roommate. I then had insisted that my 'friend' come over for every birthday celebration, every wedding and just every so often. This complete and utter deception went on for a few years. Or so I thought (hoped). On one particular visit, my mother quietly asked me to sit down, she had to talk to me. Well, what could it be? Her health? A family crisis? A bad day? I was completely unprepared for her question, "La, ma, are you a lesbian?" Stunned, wouldn't even begin to describe how I felt. How did my little Italian mother even know the word? More importantly, how did she ever figure it out.

    She told me that she had known for a long time, that a mother always knows. Slowly, after the initial silence wore off, she began asking me about

Dimi, When are the Lesbians Coming for Coffee?   149

all the women that I had ever brought into the house and whether they, too, were lesbians. These questions and answers were interspersed with longer and longer silences. Much to my shock, she had figured out who all the lesbians were and just who was with who. The tension finally eased when she asked me if my friend Bev was the 'man' in her relationship. I laughed, nervously, but I laughed. Was I really having this conversation? What did my mother know about the complex world of lesbian butch/femme relationships? Anyway. My mother ended the conversation in a way that I had never ever let myself even imagine. A simple statement. The reason behind this piece.

"La, no matter what, you're still my daughter and I still love you."

Recently, I asked my mom about that night and what her thoughts and feelings were back then and what they are now. I also asked her what or how she had come to know, what kind of exposure she had had to gay and lesbian lifestyles in the past and to try to shed some light on just what makes her so amazing.

Okay, Laurie, first of all, you used to go out before and I knew that you had a boyfriend. But then, after awhile, I had to start asking you why you weren't going out with anybody. You used to say, "Oh, I don't know, I'm still young." Okay, so this was the first question I had. Time passed and then you went to live with this girl and when your sister got married, this girl came with you. Then my imagination started to go wild.

So, one day you came home, I don't know the date, but you came home and stayed with me a little bit. And then before you left, you said, "Ma, I have to talk to you." So because the world is crazy and I suspected something anyway, the first question on my mind to ask you was, "What happened, you a lesbian?" And then you told me the truth. So, to tell you, to tell everybody who's listening, if this is the destiny of my child, that's okay, because I accept it and whatever else comes to her life.The only thing I don't want is, you know, anybody in my house kissa here and kissa there, that's the truth, right? I have never seen your sister kiss in front of me. So maybe I'm still a little old fashioned, but the real truth is, maybe I just want a little bit of respect in front of me, from both of you.

It was the end of 1968 when I found out about this 'other' life, we say. I saw a couple, two guys, you know, kiss each other and love each other. I knew they were, because we used to talk about it in Argentina. But you know people, Italian people, they, in that time, you know, nobody liked it. Maybe I didn't like it in the beginning, when I found out about all this. But later on, I started to understand. I came here and my life changed. So, because I had seen it with my own eyes, I already knew that it wasn't just me and my child.

Curaggia

So, I want to tell all of you who are mothers, no matter what, no matter what your kids do, please forgive and accept them because they are our kids. We have to love and respect them and they'll love and respect us.

One night, I was really really sad and depressed and for some reason, I saw God in a spiritual way and he helped me to be strong. And from that time on, no matter what, I have found inside of me, more love and more forgiveness. That's how I accepted, you know, my daughter being a lesbian.

Has our relationship changed? No, no changes. We still love each other, no? I accept any girl that you want to go out with, you know, you have to like her, you have to make a future with her. And I want her to respect you and to respect me and my family and that's all. Whatever you do in your life, has to be your future, your destiny. For me, I still love you. I don't know about the rest of the world, if they accept it, but I'm telling all you mothers out there, to accept and love your kids, no matter what.

My mother continues to amaze me. Her courage, compassion and wisdom are a constant source of inspiration for me. She has transcended all of the societal and cultural pressures that seek to make her think of and treat us as outsiders. She has never treated anyone in my life with anything less than respect and I love her tremendously.

What if Someone Found
Out We Wash Dandelions,
Cook them in Olive Oil
and Garlic, Eat Them
with Thick Crusty Bread?
(Mary Russo Demetrick)

The First Italian

Rose Palazzolo

Francesca

In the summer, waiting for Anthony, I sat on the stoop. He came home by 9 a.m. from his midnight shift at the radio station and I left for work at 9:15. I made sure the stoop never seemed large enough for both of us. I sat on the third step and spread my legs over the lower four, leaving little room for Anthony to get by. He'd show up with a sandwich wrapped in a bag swinging happily at his side. He left it in the bag until he crossed the street directly in front of our apartment. Then he'd stand in front of me, mouth full of his first bite, and place the tips of his tennis shoes against the bottom of my shoes. This was his hello, a small press at the soles of my feet. I'd look up, fake surprise. It was a game, a small one, I know. But we always tried to say a lot to each other without saying a word.

Mornings have always been rough for me. I get stuck in a half-fluttered, half-fear state at the beginning of a new day. It lasts until afternoon, when I finally just let the day happen without expectations of becoming a better person, a more contented person. I didn't always put these goals ahead of me so early in the day. The morning usually just meant a regular new day, a new sun, as they say. It was something about mine and Anthony's divergent schedules that threw me off, though. Anthony was always waiting for a new moon, me a new sun.

We lived on the near north side of Chicago just two blocks from the lake. Three months ago Anthony started working midnights at KCLU radio. The fifteen minutes we had together on the stoop usually set the mood for my day. I'd either look forward to another morning on the stoop watching Anthony's lips wrap around another sandwich or sit in the bewildered state of dating my mother's dream man: a central Italian with an education. But these confused states only occurred when Anthony didn't press his foot against mine, the times when he walked past me, eyes red and weary and his dimples flat lines on his cheeks.

The day Anthony brought back ham and cheese in a long baguette I told him my prosciutto story. To avoid a prolonged moment of uncertainty I thought up stories to tell Anthony, my first Italian. I'd sit up at night and go through my childhood and pick the anecdotes that would define me to him.

The Prosciutto Story From a Good Italian Girl

The prosciutto story went like this: My uncle used to cure his own prosciutto. The side of the salt-cured ham was yellow and crusty like a hardened shell of spit. Inside the casing was the salty red meat streaked with sweet white fat. The only reason I even tried it at first was because no one else would. I prided myself on being the daree.

As I told the story Anthony looked up every once in a while with just his eyebrows so that when he lowered them the sandwich and our shoes was all that crossed his vision. I looked down to see what he saw, just two pairs of shoes, his canvas tennis shoes, my pumps.

"This is ham, not prosciutto," he said.

I told him that I knew that, but I never liked ham. I liked prosciutto. I then told him how Uncle Tommy would stand close enough to me so that I could sense his movements but not so close that I could feel his breath on me or even sense the weight of his body. Again Anthony's eyebrows.

The meat looked hard and difficult to cut. But the knife slid under the shell of fat easily and Uncle Tommy pulled out a thin piece small enough that I could hold in two fingers. The first taste left me speechless. I sucked hard until most of the salt slid down my throat. All that was left was the feather of meat on my tongue, stringy and fragile. I'd stare at the hulking side of pig sitting on the counter and swallow hard. I swear I was probably drooling. Then Uncle Tommy would cut a second piece, thicker than the first, and I'd look up at his brown eyes, big behind his glasses, and I'd just smile. He barely spoke English and I was the only one in the family who liked prosciutto.

"I never liked it. It's too salty," Anthony said. "Going to work?" He looked bored. He juggled the sandwich from hand to hand, examined each side of the bread. Then he held out a palm to catch the drips of oil and vinegar as he bit into the thick bread. He just needed some time to process the story and decide what he thought. I left it open for him to find his own kind of prosciutto story to tell. He never did.

He pushed his toes hard into the soles of my pumps until I bent my knees up so he could get by and he swallowed the wad of sandwich that was just rolling around the innards of his mouth and caressing his cheek. I hardly ever expected Anthony to have much to say in the mornings. The randomness of my stories never bothered him, though.

Anthony said that it was the bizarreness of most of my stories that he liked. He'd look at me and just say, "You look so normal, like a good Italian girl, and then you tell me about the time you shaved all the hair off your Barbie and threw her down the stairs with your bother's G.I. Joe dolls. It's all so peculiar. Were you attracted to your Uncle Tommy? Is that it?" He was joking, but it was just this kind of response that I was trying to avoid. I didn't mind being a good Italian girl. I just never wanted to be a peculiar one.

Curaggia

Anthony

Being the first Italians for each other meant monumental family gatherings. Francesca met my family on my twenty-seventh birthday. I called to tell my mom that I was bringing Francesca and she said, "Latina or Italian?"

I told her Italian. Then added Sicilian and she was just silent. She called back and said that she knew I was expecting sauce on my birthday but since Francesca was Sicilian her family probably makes it different and she didn't want to "start off on a bad foot" so she'd make something else. Then she said, "Anthony, an Italian? Really?"

I was raised in a family of Italian women, three sisters and a mother. My father was the silent type and tended to cry at all weddings, funerals and Disney movies but never otherwise. My sisters and my mother ran the family. My father and I sat back and watched. We weren't benign by any means. They doted on us, the women, left of us two guilt-ridden men. We didn't even have to learn to speak. Everything was there before us: a newspaper, coffee, a plate of food, even a fucking back rub without a request.

On my birthday we ate a dinner of risotto surrounded by leaky shells of mussels and clams. My Uncle Nino brought over a cassata cake from Balluzzi's bakery. He told Francesca that he never thought I "could take an Italian girl. He liked the blonds," he told her. "He thought he was too good for anything but an Amerigance." Francesca just smiled. She does that when she feels humiliated, which I realized then was all too easily accomplished.

"In fact," Uncle Nino continued, "Anthony thinks Italians are stupid. Don't you Anthony?" He was about to tell the freezer story. He thought that it best demonstrated how I thought Italians were stupid. But it made no sense. The stupid ones in that story weren't just Italians. They were me and my mother. He always told the story, though. I took Francesca's hand under the table and cut off Uncle Nino at the beginning.

The Freezer Story, or the Boy Who Would be Rocky

The freezer story went like this: It was on one of those overcast muggy days in Chicago when the sky seems to hover just above your head pushing the heat down on your face. No blue in the sky, it was all gray. Francesca always wondered why I was so interested in what the weather was like when she told a story. I always know how the air feels on my skin. It's the truest way to temper a mood, or change one.

I was ten and had just started working at the store my Uncles Gino and Nino opened when they were just seventeen. It was on Taylor Street when the neighbourhood was still filled with people from the old country. Me and my mother used to close the store. One night my mother simply forgot that I was with her. I used to go in the back and punch at sides of beef in the freezer. It was right when Rocky came out and I was into punching beef, even if it was lying on shelves and not hanging from hooks. Part of closing, though, was locking the freezer door. By the time they found me my face was blue and tears had actually frozen on my cheeks. My hands were still numb, all red from punching the meat, and under the blood was this translucent blue skin. All I could do was moan and shove my hands in my mother's face.

"Can't you remember anything nice?" my mother said. "You kids never remember anything nice. How about when I took you to the park and that little boy, that blond kid down the street, the Irish kid, he was picking on you and I pulled him away from you by his little collar."

She always brought that up. I can't even remember that story. Francesca looked around at the faces at the table. My sisters were clearing the table. Francesca wanted to get up, but I held on to her hand.

"If you kids grew up with my mother you could never tell stories like that. In Italy you could never do that. You'd be out immediately," my mother said. She had a very high opinion of her old country. It is the best place to raise children, she said. Even though she never raised any children there.

Later that day Francesca and Paola sat at the picnic table in the backyard and finished off a bottle of my father's homemade wine. Paola later said that she liked Francesca but that she seemed a little too deliberate. "But then, all Sicilians are a little too deliberate," she said.

The Real Reason for the Prosciutto Story

I was trying harder and harder not to remember peculiar anecdotes of my life. I'd sit up at night and remember things like my Uncle Tommy's prosciutto, things that don't seem awkward, just personal. But, the only real reason I could think of for telling the prosciutto story was so I could hear myself repeat a family story, say Uncle Tommy's name. It was the whole point.

I hated the silent spaces that lingered in conversations with Anthony. I was never sure what they meant. I don't have the usual standby stories most people come up with in awkward silences. I made that private pact a short time after I met Anthony. If I started telling him about my first dog, Sophia, he'd smile apologetically and that was my clue. "We've already been there," he'd say, or "You're in reruns." But, inevitably, because of laziness or personal reasons there were details missing that I wanted to tell him. The stoop on that summer day, for example, was an inopportune time to mention that my Uncle Tommy shot himself in his garage just two months after my first taste of prosciutto.

I was reminded of all of this the day before as I walked down Lincoln Avenue and saw some prosciutto hanging in a store window. In front of the window at my feet was a bunch of rotten pears that had fallen out of their box. The brown, pulpy pears rested in rows surrounded by the green tissue that separated each one while they were still in the box. Left to rot on the sidewalk they obediently stayed in their previous order. My brother had to

Curaggia

clean up Uncle Tommy's brains off the garage walls and told me that the tissue wasn't gray as he imagined it would be, but brown and emerald.

But I kept my reason for telling the prosciutto story on that day hidden. Ambiguity made Anthony think for a minute, maybe picture it. Besides, it was all so peculiar. Later in the week he asked how tall Uncle Tommy was. What part of Sicily was he from? How did he meet Aunt Frances?

But that day on the stoop, when my story was over, Anthony turned his attention to the piece of cheese that was making its way out of the bread and onto the palm of his other hand.

"Going to work, Francesca?" he said again.

I kissed him and placed the leash in his hand. "Walk Jack," I said. He winced. He liked to call the dog Giacomo, his father's name. We'd begun to revel in our Italianness. So in the name of tradition we named our first dog, a male, after his father.

We met at Balluzzi's bakery of all places. I remember looking at us standing there next to each other. A queer distorted reflection sat in the glass counter. We were a picture. Anthony looked down at the reflection, too and smiled. I was never much of a flirt, so I just stood there like a good Italian girl and smiled. His fat dimples punched into his cheeks and he raised his heavy eyebrows at me. But it was his voice that really stuck with me. He had one of those deep radio voices that seem to vibrate and stand still in the air right in front of your face. Anthony remembers that it was a hot day in the middle of August. "The sky was so blue and the sun so full that everything could be taken for granted," he says.

Maria's Wedding: The Only Dago on the Block

I met Francesca's family for the first time last Christmas. We drove to Michigan in my new Jeep. Francesca was hoping for a long four-and-half-hour trip so she could explain her family to me. But I told her that I had to break in the jeep and had to drive 90 miles per hour the whole way, leaving little energy for conversation. We made it to Grosse Pointe in three hours, full of adrenalin. She had this self-satisfied grin on her face by the time we arrived. She didn't think I could handle her family and somewhere between Chicago and Detroit she must have decided that it would be fun to see me unnerved.

Her cousin Maria was to be married Christmas Eve. We arrived just before the reception. It was held in Francesca's Uncle's backyard. Their house was a mix of white aluminum, Spanish fluting and twenty-foot-high pillars which, Francesca told me, are adorned with flashing Christmas lights each year. Their neighbours, who lived in what Francesca's family thought were old creaky relics of brick from the turn of the century, wouldn't talk to her Uncle Frank or her mother and father, who lived a couple blocks away, for two years. "Just thought we were tacky dagoes," is what Francesca's mother said. "But once they gave in, I think they liked us."

We got drunk and watched Francesca's family talk about us. Her Aunt Frances convinced Sal to act as Francesca's older brother since Mario was too stoned to notice anyone new at the wedding. He asked me what my family did and then asked if I was "Sicilian or Northern."

I told him Central and didn't wait for an answer. Sal walked away and I saw him mumble something to his Uncle Tony. They both looked at me and tensed their chin up the way old Sicilians do when they think they have been insulted.

I wore a tuxedo that Francesca picked up at a second hand clothing store on the North side of Chicago. It hung on me like an old zoot suit and I looked too terribly stylish amidst Francesca's relatives. Most of them wore dresses draped in glittery beads and stones or black tuxedos pressed and cut to fit bulging biceps or stomachs. Francesca wore a more subdued style of the beaded dress, just enough to fit in.

The Boblo Island Story: Detroit in 1975

A couple months after we met at Balluzzi's Anthony introduced me to his family at his birthday party. The meeting wasn't as formidable as I thought it would be. I genuinely liked his family and cherished the fact that I was able to impress them with conversations about my grandmothers' black polyester outfits and the secret to my mother's sauce. We all discussed with vast knowledge what goes in red sauce and what definitely doesn't. We laughed at each family's crazy Aunt Frances's recipe. His Aunt Frances used too much oregano, mine too much garlic, at least eight cloves for just one pot.

"Bitter and strong," Anthony's mother said and waved her thin, vein-laced hand in front of her face. She looked at Anthony and they laughed. He was her only boy. Anthony then launched into a humiliating story about being locked in a freezer when he was ten. Not humiliating for himself, of course, but for his poor mother, who stared at her only boy all day with this incredible look of bemusement and awe.

I try not to do things like that, I told him that night. We laid in bed recovering from the huge meal we had just eaten. I remembered my Boblo Island story. Anthony's heavy legs rested over mine and I stared at the white ceiling trying to picture Detroit in 1975.

Boblo Island is a tiny island in the Detroit River. It's really a part of Canada but for the sake of an amusement park the U.S. and Canada decided to call the territory neutral. The boat ride to Boblo Island was a thirty minute ride of disco music and hot dogs. Amidst the blaring music and the sound of the boat's engine we ordered lunch. I was a picky eater. I didn't like red sauce until I was at least sixteen. My mother ordered me a plain hamburger and

Curaggia

fries. Aunt Frances ordered my cousin Sal two large orders of fries. I just had to look up at my mother and she ordered another plate of fries for me, too.

I have a picture of that day in my photo album. In fact the only other time I've told the story was when my friend Alice was flipping through it. In the photo I have on a white t-shirt with the flag of Italy on it. It says Italia under the flag. My Aunt Frances sits next to me wearing what I called her Adam Ant sunglasses.

Once we arrived at Boblo my mother played the water gun game that involves breaking a balloon that comes out of a clown's mouth. She gave me a twenty to ride all the rides I wanted with Sal. When we met her and my Aunt Frances back at the game five hours later, my mother had ten life-size stuffed animals with her. My Aunt Frances sat on the bench chain smoking with not one stuffed animal to show for her day. The one that I remember most, and will 'till I die, was the banana that was taller than my mother. It sat in the corner of my bedroom until I was sixteen.

But you'd have to know my mother for the story to truly resonate. The day that we went to Boblo was in the late seventies so she was decked out in full orange bell bottom gear with a top-heavy blond wig. She used to say, "Since we're the only dagoes on the block we might as well flaunt it." Anthony asked if it was hot.

"I mean," he said, "July in Detroit. It must have been hot and the orange thing must have been polyester." He laughed and said, "It's a better story because then you have to picture your poor mother standing at that game sweating bullets just to please her only daughter with a shit load of tacky life size stuffed animals." He wrapped his right leg around my left thigh and under my calf. I hated the fact that his legs were thinner than mine. His bony knee jabbed at the back of my thigh.

He has a way of wanting to humiliate a person in a story. It makes a better anecdote, he says. But, I tell him, the only dagoes on the block thing, that's funny. He agrees but then says, "So what? That's just not human enough."

"I just don't think humiliation is the essence of humanity," I said. "And isn't being the only dago on the block humiliation enough?"

"Yeah, it's peculiar" is all he said. He clumsily untangled our legs and turned on his stomach, placing a heavy arm across my chest. End of conversation.

Finding Giacomo: The Stranger Story

Since we've been together I wonder what on earth I could have talked about with the others. I know Anthony fancied big blonds with giddy laughs. I'm sure it was easy for him to slip in some humiliating anecdotes about his family without embarrassment. It's always easier for men that way. Whenever I tried I felt like I was being painfully self indulgent. So I listened to Freddy talk about his father and advertising and Michael and his mother's art collection.

I told what I thought may have been even more self indulgent stories about things I did in high school. But they just turned out to sound like rebel stories and everyone enjoys a good rebel story.

When Anthony moved to the midnight shift we got Giacomo, or Jack. Since I worked days it seemed like the perfect time to get a pet. For weeks we went to every animal shelter in the city to find the perfect dog. We saw Jack on a Sunday at a place on the west side. He sat at the back of his cage and cautiously jumped into play with the other puppies every once in a while. Anthony liked him immediately. It seemed wrong to separate any of the other dogs from each other but Jack had an independent quality about him. Anthony called it the "stranger look."

My grandfather once told me that a stranger was the only thing you ever needed to really see yourself. We sat in the cafeteria at Hudson's in Detroit. I was to see Santa Claus for the first time. He ordered me a hot dog which came in foil shaped like a boat with a bag of fries as its' anchor. He told me not to be afraid of Santa Claus. I thought about telling Anthony the story when he mentioned the look. While we played with the puppy in the cubicle I tried to figure a way of telling the story that would just make my grandfather seem wise, not crazy.

The stranger story went like this: I stood in line at Hudson's next to the other kids. My grandfather wore a brown suit and tennis shoes.

"He's just a stranger, Francesca," he told me. I looked up at the big man with the obvious fake beard. "Strangers are the only thing you'll ever need if you want to see who you really are. They are happy to show you, too." Then he punched his tiny forefinger into my bony little girl chest. My grandfather repeated this in every new situation. When my grandmother, his wife, died he brought me to the casket and made me stare down at her purplish, yellow skin.

"Look, Francesca, another stranger," he said.

I told this to Anthony as we left the shelter. Jack was in Anthony's arms. I didn't mention the Hudson's part until after I told him about my grandfather's hard, yellow hands and the fact that he played the accordion in a band when he was a kid. I thought the Hudson's part was too regional. Anthony had only been to Detroit once to visit my family. I told him that my grandmother never learned to speak English and never met a single person in the neighbourhood because there were no other Italians. She used to walk to the grocery store every day.

Detroit is a car town, I told Anthony. And Grosse Pointe, I added, is where all the auto executives live and there was my poor little grandmother walking to the corner store with her cloth bag. I told him that my grandfather called her a stranger right there at the casket and immediately I pictured the hot dog wrapped in boat shaped foil, but left that part out and told him instead that I kissed my grandmother's cheek and crossed myself. All day I could taste the oily makeup they put on her face.

Jack licked Anthony's face as he told me his dead grandmother's story. We sat in his car.

Anthony's Dead Grandmother Story

She left a list of the food items she wanted prepared at the wake. She wanted my dad's sausage sandwiches with the green peppers and onions and my Aunt Frances's mozzarella rolls and Uncle Dominic's pasta carbonara. The weather was one of those mixed-up days: rained in the morning and then became painfully bright and sunny in the afternoon. My mother prepared the basement for the party. When it got sunny everyone wanted to go outside. I played bocci in the backyard with my Uncle Gino until everyone left. We lived on Pulaski when it was all Italians and my grandmother was the neighbourhood grouch. She hated everyone on the block but seemed to know everything about them and they always came to her with their problems. The most she ever knew about me and my sisters, though, was what our favourite food was. I liked her anise cookies. She always made pancetta sandwiches for Paola and those hard little cookies with the pink glaze over them for Josephine.

When I finished my story I held out my chin, like I saw Francesca's cousin Sal and her Uncle Tony do. It was more an effort to stop me from crying. The story got me all emotional and the damned dog wouldn't stop licking my chin. It was more than insulting of the god damned puppy, it was like a nagging little child. The whole scene got so serious. I never felt so close to another person and so alone at the same moment There was nothing left to say.

Anthony's Rib

The part of the story that Anthony left out and that Paola told me later was that Anthony puked all day the day his grandmother was buried. At the party he got beaned with a bocci ball by his cousin Miguele. He had to go to the hospital and it turned out that he had a broken rib. To this day, right under the right side of his chest a rib sticks out like a bent tooth on a plastic comb. When I asked him about it he told me that the jutting rib had always been there. In the summer he walked around the apartment with no shirt. He rubbed his chest and the jutting rib easily and often. He seemed proud.

The first night that I saw it was a couple weeks after we met at Balluzzi's. We decided to meet each other at Danny's. I brought Elizabeth and Alice with me and Anthony brought his friends Peter and Nathan. Danny's was an old Victorian apartment that had been turned into a bar. It contained two floors of dark little rooms, each filled with small groups of people huddled together in private conversations.

Elizabeth liked the stained glass room. The light was a fluorescent neon which made lint and white colours glow. Elizabeth, Alice and I sat in the room with cold beers and I looked out the tiny opening of the room for Anthony's head. Once he arrived we had to deal with a couple hours of uncomfortable sobriety. His friends sized up Alice and Elizabeth to see if there were possibilities for them later that evening, although decisions like these seemed to be made before the night even began. It's funny how the stories about the evening are made up of what Anthony and me think of as filler. Elizabeth remembers the evening beginning when a couple of preppy looking men walked into the tiny room and laughed at her. Elizabeth had the most lint on her sweater. The tiny round balls lit up her black sweater. She took one of their cellular phones and began to play with it. She ended up calling their answering machines and relayed what she thought of them into their machines. She then described Alice and me to the machine and said that Nathan was hitting on her. Finally, she told the machine that Anthony was cute and ended it with, "Finally, Francesca bags a paisan."

I went to Anthony's apartment that night and saw the jutting rib for the first time. It was so curious. I rubbed it softly and thought about asking about it, but decided it would be bad timing. That morning he made pancakes impregnated with buttery apples. He smiled at me nervously across the table. He wore a white, ribbed t-shirt. I stared at the bumpy mass under his right pectoral muscle.

Francesca's Stitches

It was 4 a.m. when I first noticed the side of her leg. An uneven pink line traced the place where the stitches once were. The edges were puffy. She said that she sat on a piece of glass and the shard stuck in the flabby part of her upper leg. It was one of my days off. I couldn't sleep at night. So, I'd go to bed when Francesca did and then I'd lay there pretending to sleep until she turned her back and her breaths became slower and deeper. It was a hot muggy day and it had just started to rain when I decided to get up off the bed and watch television in the other room. But I stopped to look at her and right there on her leg was this scar. The streetlights made the room gray instead of black and a diffuse beam of light shone on Francesca's leg. I pushed down on the squishy scar with my finger. It gave easily and then formed back into its puffy shape.

That morning I asked her about it and she said that "this was one of my rebel stories that I only told the wasps. But since you asked."

She said that she was drunk and went to see the Billy Squire concert with her cousin Sal. When they got home her parents had neighbours over. So she wouldn't embarrass her mother in front of the guests she went to her room to talk with Sal. She didn't notice the broken mirror that Mario left on a chair and sat right on it. When she got up she felt some kind of wetness on her leg and felt for the shard of glass. She said that she pulled it out and wrapped her leg in a towel and went to bed. The next morning she went to the hospital and they put in twelve stitches.

Later when I asked Sal about the Billy Squire concert he told the same story. But what Francesca left out was that Sal was the one that wrapped her leg in the towel. Sal, of all people, her suave dago cousin Sal with the dark brown eyes and buff chest. They used to hang out together all the time, Francesca said. Really, when I think about it, Sal was Francesca's first Italian. They sat there, watched Billy Squire moan Stroke Me, Stroke Me.

Losing Giacomo

Anthony thought it was on purpose. The dog just liked to chase birds. I walked Giacomo down by the lake every day and he'd pull and walk hard ahead of me. We looked ridiculous fighting each other for pace, my steps uneven, his hard and fierce. He liked the water. I brought a ball to the lake and let him loose near Belmont Avenue where there was a small beach.

The day the ducks fascinated him was the day I lost Giacomo. I threw out a ball and he just kept going. I saw about a dozen mallards ahead of him. They flew low and headed for the lake. Jack, or Giacomo, kept running and when his paws touched the water he just kept going. His little head poked out of the water and he rushed towards them. I was so proud at first and I couldn't stop laughing. He'd been such a wimpy dog. He followed Anthony everywhere and would whimper when Anthony left the house. So to keep Jack from pouting all day I used to take him for long walks. But that was to be the last walk for Jack. He swam off that day and I ran the length of the lake once I stopped laughing. A man on a row boat tried to stop Jack. He thrashed his oars in the lake. But Jack just kept swimming and whining. The ducks were having a good time teasing him, paddling hard and fast in front of him, quacking the whole time. I called the police, then the firemen, and they said there was nothing they could do. They suggested I stand at the edge of the lake with a favourite snack of Jack's. All I could think of was that Jack's favourite snack was Anthony's socks. I couldn't bring myself to stand at the edge of Lake Michigan with a pair of socks yelling Giacomo.

What Francesca Leaves Out

I realize now that with Francesca it's not what she says but what she leaves out. That's who she really is. It wasn't the loss of Giacomo that finally ended it for me. I mean it could have been. The fact that the dog never trusted her, never came to her voice. But it was all the holes in her stories, her days. If you ask something that could possibly change a story you won't get to the real point with her. It's like when someone requests a song at the station. The reason why someone wants to hear a song has nothing to do with the song, or even what it says. Music is never about that. It's about some shared emotion, not experience. It's a seduction of the masses, that's all.

The day she lost Giacomo was the day she fucked Peter. I should have seen it. I was just the dago she needed so she could tell a story about later. Peter was the real thing. They both think life owes them something because there is no unity in simple existence. At least that's what Peter says. It's what Francesca's stories were all about. She was trying to convince me that we had this common experience with all her peculiar anecdotes. What it all came down to was an anecdote in the making. It was how the only dago on the block fucks a blond boy and loses her woppy lover.

Francesca's Roller Skating Story: The Pull of Chuck

Peter reminded me of the time I got pulled around a roller rink in my favourite dress. I was, remember, the only dago on the block. But I was unaware of all that until one day some kids down the street said my dad was in the mafia and that I couldn't play pickle with them anymore. They said that their father was afraid that I'd get hurt and that my dad would come over and break their knees. I had this vision of my dad laying the kids down on a block of wood and whacking their knees with a two by four. Sure, my father had friends, but that was it. But we were odd. We were surrounded by wealth and blue blood. Holden Caulfield was my hero. I had a crush on my cousin Sal. It was all normal in that way. My parents tried to set me up with Tony Badalamenti. The ultimate boy for me though was Chuck Roberts, the roller skating guard.

The roller skating story went like this: I went to the rink every Saturday with my friends. The Macomb rink was a dark, dusty place filled with kids wearing thick, pink combs in their back pockets and corduroy elephant leg pants. I wore my favourite dress, a floor length red and white checked dress. It was 1979. When the boy's choice dance came up I was stunned, pressed up against the wall of the rink. Chuck, one of the roller guards was dashing towards me on the wooden rink. He held his hand out to dance. Chuck had golden blond hair that tucked neatly under at the ends and swung softly at his right side, sometimes covering his eye. I thought he was the most beautiful person I had ever seen. He took my sweaty, 10 year-old palm and proceeded to whip me around the rink. We were flying. My right foot was still and rolled on the floor without my knowledge while my left foot swung chaotically out and back. I was trying to hold control and my calf started to ache as my leg wobbled and flung. It finally gave way and my planted right foot seemed to collapse. I was soon flat on my back, my palm still clinging to his. Chuck swung me around the rink twice, oblivious to the fact that I was sliding, my dress splayed out, wiping the floor, pain shooting up my right arm.

It was humiliation that flashes in front of me in all times of embarrassment or awkwardness. Anthony would love it. When Peter held out his palm for me that day we walked his dog Benny by the lake I felt the same tightness in my back that I felt when I whipped around the rink with Chuck. I knew then I couldn't avoid it.

Peter used to come with me and Jack on our walks sometimes. Peter had hair something like Chuck's, except he kept his short. When he held out his palm I took it. I couldn't look at him, though. I stared at Benny's short stub nose and the gray, still lake. Peter's smell, a mix of sweat and ivory soap, overwhelmed me and when I thought I was beyond surprise, I shocked myself by leaning closer, my arm fit into a crook in his bent arm. We walked hand in hand, arm in crooked arm and I breathed in the lake smell and Peter. We went back to mine and Anthony's apartment and locked Benny in the bathroom. Peter bought a bottle of wine on the corner and opened it in the bedroom. He held the bottle in both his hands and smiled.

"It's Italian," he said. "Fortissimo. Kind of like formidable or fortuitous."

He touched the hair at his temple and brushed it back with two fingers.

Driving to Taylor Street

So we had the obligatory talk about Peter as we drove to Taylor Street, Chicago's Little Italy. We both decided the talk would be best in neutral territory. But I couldn't stand the stale air in the car; even with the air conditioner on, my back stuck to the seat with sweat. The car still smelled like Giacomo and with the heat it seemed like the smell was weightier than the mass of our bodies sitting there.

Francesca was sweating too. Tiny beads of perspiration balled up and rested on the ends of her tiny hairs above her lip and on her eyebrows. She said that she couldn't explain why she turned to Peter. She said it was probably for comfort. I was in a sweaty half-alert state, unable to feel truly angry or deceived. I opened the window and moved closer to it letting the hot breeze whip at my face. Francesca shut her eyes and held her hands together on her lap. I watched them rub against each other for awhile. I circled Taylor Street five times looking for a parking spot. An Untouchables tour bus took up five spots in front of the gelato store.

I touched Francesca's hands with the tips of my fingers and pointed at the bus.

"They make you feel like zoo animals, don't they?"

She looked at the tourists. The Untouchables tour takes tourists to all the mobster hotspots in Chicago. They go to the spot of the St. Valentine's day massacre at Clark Street and North Avenue. Then to the Biograph theater where John Dillinger was shot. Finally, they stop off in Little Italy for some ice cream. The bus is an old school bus painted black. Francesca looked at them and stuck her tongue out.

I looked at her and laughed so hard the sweat pooled up on my forehead. I felt one bead trickle down the side of my face. It almost felt like a hug. I double parked next to the bus and leaned over to unlock Francesca's door. When she took my arm and just held it for a minute, I marvelled at the whole of the moment: the heat, the sweat, the discomfort, Taylor Street. It was too overwhelming.

"Just two dagoes getting some gelati, huh?" I said.

Francesca looked at me and solemnly, quietly said, "Sorry." Her clammy hand clung to my forearm.

I thought she was simply pathetic, but I admired the pitiful nature of just wanting some comfort on an afternoon and finding the coolest thing that could give it to you, a small cup of gelato. I appreciated the simple pleasure of it and thought that simple pleasures were all that one could hope to obtain even if you feel like you're sitting next to a perfect stranger.

Curaggia

Food, Religion, Death and the Family

Francesca Maniaci

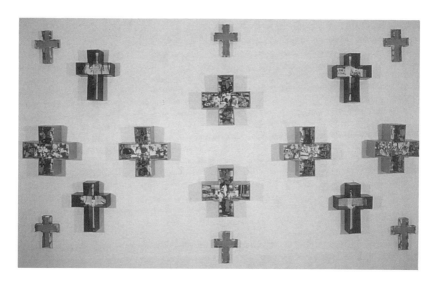

1. & 2. A la Famiglia-For the family 1991

Materials: Crosses made of foam core, acrylic paint and photocopies.
Size: situated on a wall space of 1.5m by 1.5 m. Crosses vary in size from 24cm by 24cm to 12cm by 12cm.

Idea: I have always had a facination with old family photographs. Each time I visit one of my family members home I find a few more photographs for my collection. I wanted to use these photographic images in a piece and this is what I came up with. This piece is a tribute to my family and family members.

3. Mamma-Mother 1996

Materials: box made of wood, collaged with colour photographs of food and assorted personal objects.
Size: 30cm by 40cm by 4cm

Idea: A three dimensional portrait of my mother in which I try to demonstrate the things that are important to her.

4. Pappa-Father 1996

Materials: box made of wood, collaged with colour photographs of food and assorted personal objects.
Size: 30cm by 40cm by 4cm

Idea: A three dimensional portait of my father in which I try to demonstrate the things that are important to him.

5. Family Cemetery 1996

Materials: crosses made of wood collaged with photocopies.
Size: each cross is 30cm by 10cm (12 crosses)

Idea: I made a cross for each deceased family member that I knew personally in their lifetime to demonstrate my respect for the family.

6. Nonna's Kitchen 1998

Materials: installation of furniture and various objects.
Size: installation in a space of 4m by 5m

Idea: Ever since I was a child my grandmother's kitchen has been the meeting place for all of my mother's family. This kitchen is very important to me because the house belonged to my family before it became my grandparents house and every member of my mother's family has at one time or another lived in the house.

Curaggia

Artist's statement

My work is an exploration of my identity that attempts to establish a relationship with the viewer by stimulating his memory with symbolic objects of my personal history. The work is multi-media, using a variety of techniques that invoke many layers of meaning and emotion.

Like many I was forced to grow up too quickly and now feel the need to search through my childhood and adolescence for something that I have lost. Part of this loss is the result of being born in Canada of Sicilian immigrants. Eventhough I was born and raised in Canada I still have experienced feelings of being and outsider; of my family being foreign. The primary subject matter of my work is my family and their domestic and religious rituels.

In my work I use photography and video as a seductive "means" for "truth." Photographic images have a remarkable ability to both preserve and distort our perceptions of the past. I consider the photographs and videos as documents of my life. With this "evidence" I am attempting to find my truth and at the same time questioning the relationship of my memory to that of my imagination.

Although my work is personal I hope to communicate my sensibility towards a collective family. As I attempt to communicate my experience of this internal loss or longing, I hope to awaken these memories or longings in others.

The Discourse of un' Propria Paparone

Joanna Clapps Herman

"You're such a papon'."

"What's this new curse you're putting on me?"

"Not a curse. It's a slur on your character."

"What're you calling me now?"

I'm in my Upper West Side kitchen talking to my Jewish husband. I'm protesting, insisting, injecting my ethnicity into the New York Jewish intellectual world I live in. The world I escaped to and by which I am now held hostage.

"Look, a *mammon'* was the worse thing you could call someone when I was a kid, anyone who was a *mammon'* was a putz, a jerk. But really it means mama's boy," I explain a bit pedantically, as I have learned to do in my life in New York. "O-n-e is a suffix for big, so when you add it to the end of a word it changes that word from an ordinary nominative to a noun that is somehow adjectival — the noun, made big, bigged up, remember James" (our son) "used to say, 'you're going to big them up,' when I borrowed his mittens. Not that my family ever pronounced a vowel at the end of any word. We didn't say *mammone*, we said *mammon'*."

"So if you're a *mammon'*, you're big for your mother — too involved with her."

"When Marcello Mastroianni died, the New York Times obit referred to him as a sex symbol who was actually a *mammon'*. I was stunned, thrilled, a word from my childhood in the New York Times!"

"You know how I always say 'I'm a *chacciaron'*,'" — *chaccia* means someone who talks a lot, but I'm a *chacciaron'*; a really big talker. "Annie's family calls it *chacciarese, e-s-e*, that's from her dialect." Annie's family is from a different town, they use e-s-e. It makes me sad that I have to explain these words instead of being able to just use them in a community who knows what I mean, the way my husband does with his friends, all those childhood sounds that convey what no other sounds can — *intimacy*. Occasionally, I say to my classes which are made up largely of minority adults, "*Stai zitto*." And because I love them I expect them to understand me. My students tolerate my explanation and translation because they are a people who recognize oral affection when they hear it.

Curaggia

When I was a kid, *mammon'* had been the worst insult you could fling at someone. That and *cafon'*, which really meant someone with no class, a lowlife. But for me and my cousins a *mammon'* was worse, anyone who wasn't tough, capable of doing whatever, climbing trees, swimming out to the island, staring down somebody in the school yard.

"But *you*," I say to my husband Bill, "you're a *papon'*." Bill loves this stuff, at least as much as he loves me. My Italianness. It goes with the circles under my eyes, my dark moments, all the garlic browned in olive oil for almost everything I cook.

But where we live on the Upperwest side of Manhattan it is assumed everyone middle-class is Jewish in reality or by association. And in effect I am Jewish by association. It's where I've found a home, where there is enough of the kind of talk I love, lots of it, too much of it, too intensely full of jokes and condemnation. It's where I found people who care more about reading or music or have some similar attachment that burns in them, that has little do with what was valued in Waterbury, Connecticut where I was raised. There people care about food, kids, gardens, fooling around, the loss of which burns in me still. But I had to leave because only my father who had been an ironworker, had been a serious reader. I am at home here on the Upper Westside of Manhattan. But I hate the fact that it's assumed I will be pleased to have my ethnicity replaced, "You're Jewish — everyone ethnic is Jewish," I've been told many times.

"I'm not Jewish, thank you very much and I'm very happy being Italian," I've found myself saying priggishly many times. Where I grew up it was a point of honor to declare your ethnicity defiantly. "What're *you*?" we asked the first time we met another kid. Everyone understood the question. We were Italian, Irish, a couple of German kids. Elaine Mann was the only Jewish girl in school. Maybe because I was *Italian* I still feel funny saying "Italian-American."

Just as I feel funny saying my family is "working class or blue collar." These are not words my family would use to describe themselves. They didn't define themselves by their work. That wouldn't occur to them. They worked hard. They were good at what they did. They mostly voted Republican. So those labels, although accurate, sound condescending, or as they say in Waterbury, Connecticut, brass capital of the world, "That sounds stupid." Italian-American is a name given to them by people who didn't live in our neighborhood. I feel as if I betray my family every time I use those words.

Another one: "That makes me anxious," instead of, "She makes me nervous," or alternately, "He gives me *agiata*." My husband's brother would say, "Don't get all noyved up." How about replacing, "She was so inappropriate," with "I'd like to give her a slap?" I can feel the sting in my hand when I say it. Is one more articulate than the other? The one with the sensation attached makes more of an impression on my synapses. But my language has changed. I only occasionally use phrases like, "Gimme the *mapine*," to mean, "Hand me the dishcloth." But these decontextualized phrases have taken on the ring of pretentiousness, because I use these words deliberately now, I'm doing something, not just talking in a world in which I belong. "Get the *scola macaron'*," I say to my son sometimes, because I don't want him growing up not knowing my language, where the phrase get the *scola macaron'* means literally, "Get the strain the macaroni."

So now I accuse my husband now, "You're such a *papon'*."

"You're saying I'm a papa's boy, right?"

"Aren't you?"

"Just because I'm mourning my father after forty years. I was a kid, I was only eight. I never got over it. My father..." he looks off dreamily into the kitchen cupboards. "If my father had lived he'd be 98."

"*Managga diavole!* Bill, if your father were alive, he'd be dead." I can't help it. I'm irritated this morning, sick of the endless talk about the dead father, who's haunted my married life to Bill. We've walked this hallowed walk at least once a week for our twenty years of marriage. I'm tired of this man I've never met. Bill looks at me, stunned. Then he flings back his head and roars. He's laughing so hard he's crying. "You, *you* kill me." He comes over and throws his large body onto me, grabs me and holds on while he laughs and laughs.

I never get over this. This is acceptable here, it's expected, you make small deflating remarks and if they hit their target you're a hero. I always feel sheepish for daring to go after "the father."

New York is my home. This is where I grew into my maturity, where Bill and I have lived our married life together. This is where we've raised our son James, a large Slavic looking boy, has his father's fine ear, which is why he wins prizes reciting poetry in the Tuscan version of Italian that my grandparents were unable to speak or understand. This Italian has little to do with the dialect I grew up with and can't speak except for a few scattered defining phrases. "My Russian boy," I call James, when I come upon his large blond presence with surprise again. "My big Slavic boy."

James doesn't seem to be in any way confused by these contradictions. His friends call him half-a-wop. He calls himself a dago-yid production. His girl friend is the Freaken-Puerta-Rican. Despite the language police, he and his friends use these terms as forms of affection. For them all this is grist for pleasure.

The girlfriend is pleasure for me — she looks like family, she has dark hair. She's strong and smart, still she looks at us, her boyfriend's parents, eyes wide asking us to like her. I do. This is stuff that I understand — a second skin to me.

James is a *papon'* too. "What did Dad say when you told him I won the Italian recitation prize? Was he happy?"

Curaggia

Why is there a dialect word for *mammon'* but not for *papon'*? Why is it bad to be a mama's boy or girl, but not mentioned if you are papa's boy or girl? Is it that these things are understood, part of the paradigm?

How about *un propria nu paparona*? Here I've modified in dialect this invented noun to describe the Italian girl obsessed with her Italian father — a real bad *papon'*, that's me.

These are the kinds of questions that I can ask here in New York and the people I'm talking to will pick the question up, look at it, turn it over and add something to what I've just said. Where I came from that kind of talk is considered silly. Anything that made you self-conscious is embarrassing. To be embarrassed is the worst.

"Can you imagine, he called my sister-in-law for *directions*? So embarrassing, a man asking a woman for *directions*!" My father had shaken his head in disgust and deep shame for his Jewish son-in-law when Bill had asked Aunt Tony for directions to the Cape, a place she drove to often. Where do you begin with something like that?

Especially if you are a *un propria nu paparona* — just like my husband and son — I'm one obsessed with her father. Whom I had always adored, who read Emily Bronte to my sister and me, at least once a year, sitting at the kitchen table in his undershirt and grey work pants, not blue, full of welding holes that my mother washed and ironed every day.

"Listen to this," he had said and I had, though I never learned how to talk comfortably to him. Because girls don't talk to their fathers, they listen. Anyway after a while I no longer spoke his language fluently.

He said things like, "You know what happened down the street with Cockroach Rhinie?" And this had made me want to ask two questions, "Is Cockroach Rhinie the guy who gets the stolen stuff from the colored kids?" And I wanted to ask, "Is Cockroach Rhinie typical of the environment in the social club setting?" Even thinking the second question was a betrayal of him. Thinking the other was a betrayal to the person I'd become. So sometimes it seemed best to stay in my kitchen among the *paponi* of my own and insult my husband in words I've invented, because he knows what I'm saying.

Bargaining*

Vita Orlando Sinopoli

Vincenzo, che vendi oggi, cosi buoni?'' Mama asked Vncenzo if he had something special to sell. When this door-to-door salesman walked into our bakery in Boston's North End, I saw him place his large black suitcase on Papa's desk and open it.

He smiled proudly as the ladies gathered around and scrutinized the merchandise. He knew they were familiar with European open cutwork embroidery on fine linen. Some had become skilled in this craft in their Italian homeland.

Mama picked out a linen tablecloth and asked, "Quanto, Vincenzo?" Price was important.

Mama disliked the price quoted. "We can buy it for less on Hanover Street," she and the others said.

"But this comes from Spain," Vincenzo said. " Magnifico lavoro!"

The women expected bargain prices from Vincenzo because he had less overhead expenses than the local merchants. He bickered with Mama and the ladies, reminding them of his willingness to collect as little as twenty-five cents a week. Of course, a weekly visit to their home gave him an opportunity for another sale. But that day, no one purchased anything.

Bargaining was a daily part of buying in our Italian community. People bargained with the produce vendor, fish peddler, hardware merchant, shoemaker, the baker and even the barber.

"Joe, I'll bring all the kids tomorrow," the barber was told. "You give me two haircuts for the price of one — okay?"

During the fall and summer months Vincenzo traveled through the streets of East Boston and the North End with his pushcart. Various sizes and colours of stockings and underwear hung from a makeshift wooden canopy attached to the sides of the pushcart. My friends and I giggled and pointed to the articles, eager to catch what might fall. But, Vincenzo kept close watch on his merchandise.

Josie and Anna called to him from kitchen windows of their apartments. "Vincenzo, aspetta." He waited for them to join the others on the street.

Josie asked "How much?" as she picked up a pair of stockings.

"Trentacinque solde," Vincenzo replied.

Curaggia

She frowned at his reply, thirty-five cents. "I'll pay you fifty cents for two pairs. That's all," she said firmly.

Vincenzo displayed anger but saw the opportunity to sell to those watching. "You make me lose money," he complained, taking fifty cents each from Josie and Anna. He completed three additional sales at the same price, before proceeding down Charter Street.

Jewish, Greek, Italian, and Irish merchants catered to the bargainers. During the depression years, they helped many families who preferred shopping in their North End community for day to day family needs.

Mama often said, "Come with me to Joe Shuman's." She liked to purchase her sewing fabrics and supplies there.

I enjoyed going to his store on Hanover Street. While Mama checked the prices of the various bolts of cotton and wool, I looked at all the other items. I yearned to have her purchase a pair of socks, a tam or beret I saw on display. But Mama's interest was only in the bolts of material and thread she needed. Mr. Shuman smiled patiently.

"I have some new yarn, Lucy," he said, knowing Mama loved to knit. He took a box of yarn from the shelf, removed the cover and placed it on the counter. But Mama only wanted her thread and material. In her calculated manner she managed to get a five or ten cent reduction in the materials she purchased.

Whenever Mama and I visited Clayman's apparel shop on Salem Street, she waited for Lillian to approach her. Lillian recognized familiar faces of customers and immediately asked about the family.

Boxes filled the shelves of the narrow compact store. A four-foot long counter separated the customers from the clerks. We saw folded bedspreads, infant and children's clothes, house dresses, and tablecloths displayed on hangers overhead and on the wall behind us. I stood next to Mama and watched Lillian's arms scan the boxes on the shelves for Mama's requested item. With her somber face, Lillian skillfully moved from one customer to another, serving two or three ladies consecutively. She allowed each an opportunity to think about the price quoted before returning.

Mama and the others knew how to be patient, but the young children became restless. I sighed when Mama asked to see two or three more of the same article. "Do you have this in blue?" Lillian diligently searched the shelves again.

While Mama examined the items, I listened to other customers. Some raised their voices in anger, others bargained quietly. Some threatened never to return because of dissatisfaction, while more women entered and filled the spaces at the counter. Back and forth Lillian walked, each time ready to stand by her employer's merchandise.

"Take it home, Lucy," Lillian instinctively said when she felt Mama really wanted to purchase that item. "Pay me a little each week." If Mama hesitated, Lillian added, "I'll hold it for you here, Lucy. Leave me fifty cents or a dollar."

Inventory and lay-a-ways rested on shelves in the small back room. The merchant's little record book for weekly payments was as handy as Vincenzo's.

Mama bought bed linens, tablecloths, and towels, in this fashion. She stored some in her cedar chest. Then, I wondered why. I learned later that Italian women prepared for their daughter's trousseau early in the child's life. When I married, I received those bargained goods as gifts from my parents. They lasted many years.

When Mama said, "Come with me. We're going to look for a new coat for you today," I knew I was in for a major bargaining experience. We always started in Wolfe's Clothing Store on Salem Street. When we entered the store Mama had a price in mind, and the merchant did also. That did not frighten Mama.

After the customary "How are you today, Lucy? What can I do for you?" Mama selected a few styles for me to try on.

The clerk, looking at us asked, "Do you like it?"

I knew not to show enthusiasm yet. With each coat I tried on, Mama asked for the price, but never revealed her pleasure or displeasure.

After four or five coats, I tried each on a second time. The clerk repeated the price, and added "But for you, Lucy, I can give you this one for..."

Of course, he quoted a lower price than the original. It became a theatrical performance. If Mama liked the coat, she started bargaining with seemingly unending offers and counter offers. If she became displeased, she took the coat off me. She took my hand, and we walked to the door after two hours of negotiating.

"Lucy, where are you going? That's a good price. Let's talk," the clerk cried out.

Mama and I continued out onto the sidewalk with the clerk following, cajoling Mama to return. How embarrassing, I thought!

The farther we walked from the store, the less my chances were of going home with a new coat. We only re-entered for more bargaining if Mama had her mind set on purchasing that coat. Otherwise, we moved onward to another store or returned home. Mama knew when to try again and eventually, she purchased a coat at a price that pleased her.

I became aware of these experiences again many years later, before retiring. Things had not progressed well for several months in our bargaining for a new contract for teachers and my secretarial co-workers. An evening mediation meeting extended into early morning hours. We found ourselves unable to reach an agreement. About 3 AM, I began to feel like I was in the coat store on Salem Street.

I said to another worker, "They *know* how far they want to go."

"And *we* know what we want," she replied.

I sat back in my chair quietly and thought of my mother, saying to myself — things might be different if Mama were here.

---

*   *Bargaining was a part of buying in the North End of Boston during the 30's and 40's. People bargained with the produce vendor, fish peddler, hardware merchant, shoe-maker and even the barber.*

A Day Like Any Other

Rita DeBellis

I'm still not quite sure if my parents really understand why the Fourth of July is celebrated. It wasn't till I moved South eight years ago that I became truly cognizant of the Fourth as metaphor for Americana — parades, flags, baseball, hot dogs, apple pie and Chevrolet. Back home in the Bronx, the Fourth was a decidedly male affair. It turned streets into battlefields where driving and walking were treacherous. Punks and nice boys alike would pool their resources to purchase, not the most colourful munitions, but the loudest, most dangerous, most illegal.

My mother, who after 40-plus years in the States is far more conversant in English than my father, has taken little notice of these nuances of the American way. For reasons of pure practicality, she has busied herself over the years with learning how to balance a checkbook, hearing the difference between "fifty" and "fifteen," learning to drive at 56, and discovering that "sale" meant a special "offerta," not the Italian word for salt. Imagine her confusion when she saw: Salt! children's shoes, Salt! home appliances, Salt! women's dresses.

My father speaks neither English, nor Italian, but the secret language of Jerome a strain of New York Italian-immigrant English culled from the construction sites where Jerome worked and the collective vocabulary of the neighborhood (a sort of informal *Sesame Street*, where my parents and their countrymen pondered new important words like "superintendent," "benefits," and "time-and-a- half"). What makes Jerome's language secret is the thick, once- hard-of-hearing, now-gone-certifiably-deaf slur through which his speech is strained. The slur, a WWII gift from the Italian army, happened when, during heavy fighting, Jerome stood too near to detonation. Hours later he found the river of dry blood that flowed down his neck from both ears. Ack, ack, ack. Ka-boom! Fifty years later he's still asking "What?"

Too vain for a hearing aid and too deaf for the MiracleEar, Jerome has over the years codified his version of English. His wife and children are his best students. I'm not as good with Jerome at the hardware store as my brother is, since the days when he just wanted 2x4s have long passed. Jerome's hardware needs have gotten much more demanding, sophisticated. Conveying these needs at Builders' Square of El Paso rather than at Carlo's ("Se habla Jerome!") Hardware Store, Bronx, New York, is no easy chore.

Jerome fell off some construction scaffolding and into a utility ditch 23 years ago in lower Manhattan. He landed on one foot, shattering his ankle. Most of his leg was set in a cast for most of the following year. He has not worked since.

After 25 years in New York and for reasons too long, complicated and uninteresting to relate, my parents beat a dry, dusty path to El Paso. My father now reads an English-language newspaper every morning. In New York he read *Il Progresso*, an Italian-language weekly published by the Pope family. (They endowed my high school with the "Generoso Pope Scholarship." I never knew anyone who received this honor, so my fantasy persists of it being a perpetual serving of a steaming bowl of pasta with marinara sauce). *Il Progresso* concerned itself with old-country political and soccer happenings and always had one page of group photos of fancy (not really) Bronx Italians that had convened for "dinner dances."

Jerome gets a lot out of the *El Paso Times*. He now follows football, and reads about important legislation, natural disasters, and wars. My mother never reads the paper, never has. She doesn't like the way the newspaper dirties her hands and the smell, she says, makes her sneeze. She does however, read supermarket circulars. These boneless-chicken-breast and Pepsi hawkers are generally printed on a better grade of newsprint than newspapers.

The burger-flipping clip-art dad, fireworks and screaming Fourth of July display type give Mom one up on Jerome. She *knows* the Fourth is coming and, more than anything, that it's a good time to stock up on ground beef for making meatballs. As for Jerome, he's had the day off for 23 years, and his associations of the Fourth with long weekends have long since faded. On his calendar, it's a day like any other. Very quiet.

Comare Rosa

Maria Fama

Comare Rosa died of too much happiness. Angelina DiStefano told her granddaughter this on the day Stephanie got engaged to be married. At thirty, Stephanie had never been married. She'd had a string of mysterious lovers who nobody ever saw and now was living with this Chuck. Chuck Del Giorno had some gray hair, but he was a man with a belly, a man of "presenza," presence. He had been married twice before, had five kids, yet Angelina liked him anyway, because he could eat and joke and drink without getting mean. Chuck loved his mother and was kind to his kids; he was generous and could marry a wayward, but lovable, hard-head like Stephanie.

Angelina Di Stefano had prayed for this marriage. Practically every candle that flickered in front of St. Jude, the saint of the impossible, in the church of St. Anna, Angelina had lit for Stephanie. Countless novenas to St. Anthony, patron of lovers, Angelina had said to find Stephanie a good husband. Angelina had even cast a few prayers St. Stephen's way just in case he could help. She didn't have too much faith in him, but he was Stephanie's patron saint, and the family's name was his, so that might count for something.

Angelina looked into her grandaughter's eyes. "My eyes," she thought. Black olive eyes Nino called them. He won't see this grandaughter wed. Angelina hoped she'd live to see a great-grandchild. Caution. Patience. She remembered Comare Rosa.

Angelina had to listen to Stephanie tell the marriage plans. When? December. Cold month for old people, but good. Nino and she had married in January. It was the marrying month in Sicily. Nothing better to do. Nothing to plant, pick, or make. May was the bad luck month: marry in May you'll rue the day they said. The Madonna's month, a busy time in the fields, and the Madonna probably wanted all the attention for herself anyway.

Did Chuck want this marriage? Yes. Chuck with his booming laugh and his kind hands. Angelina was glad it was him. She felt joy rising in her chest. Careful. Chuck would father Stephanie's child. Maybe a little boy with black olive eyes, or a tiny girl with a loud laugh. Good families start with a girl her mother used to say, but nobody got depressed if a son was first born. Joy. A baby! Oh, Comare Rosa. Tears came. Tears of joy moistened Angelina's eyes as she hugged Stephanie to her. So firm. It's good. She's huggable. "I am proud," Angelina said as she embraced this grandaughter. She felt warm

Curaggia

energy coursing through her body centering in her chest. Was this joy or a heart attack? Was this a terrible overabundance of happiness building inside her? Angelina felt a touch of fear. She pictured herself as a small child by her mother's side at Comare Rosa's funeral. "Too much happiness," she thought, "I mustn't tempt fate."

"Comare Rosa," Angelina said aloud. "Who?" Stephanie asked, disentangling herself from Angelina's arms. Angelina felt she must tell Stephanie the story now. Thirty was not too young to die, although Stephanie never looked her age. At seventy-eight one was more likely to die, but everybody said that Angelina didn't look her age either. "Comare Rosa never looked or got old," Angelina stated and told her grandaughter the story.

Rosa Vespania was the best friend of Santuzza Biaggi, Angelina's mother. Angelina remembered how Rosa and her mother were always together. They laughed, sang songs, worked hard and never got tired. To Angelina they seemed very tall and pretty.

Comare Rosa was a comare to Santuzza because they were friends, but also because for seven generations there had been many different kinds of honours between their families. There had been godmothers of confirmation, and godmothers of the baby's hat, witnesses at weddings and births, and pallbearers at funerals. Rosa had helped Santuzza at Angelina's birth, and Santuzza was with Rosa at the hard birth of Rosa's son, Gianni. Their husband had picked other families for the godparents of these children.

When Santuzza became pregnant again, she told her husband, Vito, that her little dead grandmother Lia told her that Rosa was to be the godmother of the baby. Vito agreed. When their son, Letterio, was born, they formally approached Rosa and her husband, Cola, to be godparents, the highest honor Sicilians can bestow on each other. Rosa and Cola were to be the "compari di San Giovanni" the godparents of the baptism, like St. John who gained the highest honor for baptizing Christ.

The little Angelina witnessed the unbridled happiness of Comare Rosa at the acceptance of the honour. She danced, she jumped. Her face was alive with colour. She embraced everyone in the room and showered the infant Letterio with kisses and blessings.

According to custom, Letterio was to be baptized at one year old. In the meantime, Comare Rosa's joy grew stronger and stronger. Her smiles were unceasing, her songs clear and sparkling. "A St. John godmother!" she'd often shout to Santuzza, "I'm standing as a godmother for the first time. It's more of an honour than being a mother!" She was carried away with emotion whenever Letterio toddled toward her. Angelina recalled how she loved to be in this flood of ecstasy, but her mother warned her friend to be careful with her joy. Comare Rosa merely laughed a wonderful laugh and hugged her friend. In Rosa's presence, the children gathered bouquets of kisses by the hour.

Throughout the week before the baptism day, Rosa was ebullient. Her happiness at hurricane force, she polished and decorated her house, ordered special liqueurs made, planned the cooking of delicacies, and on the day before the baptism, she died. Her heart stopped. Comare Rosa had died of happiness at twenty-eight. Comare Rosa, a martyr to joy, was buried, and the mid-wife was pressed into being Letterio's godmother.

Angelina shuddered as she remembered that funeral. The screams of her mother, the rantings of the men, the curses to heaven and the saints. St. John, wild, stupid, mountain man, inarticulate eater of locusts and honey, had played such a cruel joke on gallant Christian families. Choking on tears, everybody reminded themselves that such is destiny. Happiness is not for here on earth, if it's for anyone anywhere. Our joy is always mixed with tears, and too much happiness might hurry fate and stop a heart.

Dignity and tempered contentment had become the way for Angelina, though the men could always mix in anger, hatred, and revenge to dilute joy. Angelina Di Stefano told her grandaughter all this to warn Stephanie, but also to soothe herself, to rid herself of the crushing burden of too much happiness. This was Comare Rosa's gift to those she loved. At every event where happiness could overtake one, Angelina had called her name as an incantation against a most horrible fate. Comare Rosa.

Angelina said, "American Stephanie, remember that your grandmother will think of Comare Rosa on your wedding day. You do the same."

Dandelion

Mary Russo Demetrick

Embarrassed?
Sure!
I saw my relatives
in the thruway median
small paring
knives in hand
cutting
first tender
dandelion shoots

What if
someone
from my school
found out
we wash dandelions
cook them
in olive oil
and garlic
eat them
with thick crusty bread

Instead
my friends collected
yellow dandelion
flowers
wove them
into summer crowns

Now, vitamins
in these greens
just what I need
to return
to become well
to replenish
what was lost
like
intravenous feedings

Embarrassed?
        No!

Her Tongue the Culprit
(Carol Mottola Knox)

Blending In

Mary Russo Demetrick

Wild-eyed Italians
wild-haired Italians
loud speaking
loud laughing
women and men
fascinate me

I find them hiding
behind Anglo names
like Kennedy, Litz
and Scott
wanting to be discovered
dreading the exposure

I home-in on them
as if genetic
devices
clue me

Watch the eye color
the humour
skin tone
the length of the nose
that little
diction give-away

How they say "sang-wich"
"spaagh-hcttti"
"It-ly"

If they admit
they like large
Sunday dinners
at home

I meet them cowering
in the olive oil aisle
of our city's only
imported grocery store

Watch their excitement
as I tell them about
the best semolina bread
in town
as I describe the
bruschetta I make
by drizzling
extra virgin
over toasted rounds
fresh mozzarella
basil

Sometimes they ask
if my name is Italian
I have to explain the convoluted
        Americanized-version-of
        a-Russian-name-changed
        at-immigration
        for-spelling

At marriage I accepted
inched away from Italy
toward an almost
Greek-sounding Russian
surname
moved up in the alphabet
moved away from Italia
toward mainstream

Now I claim
like so many others
both names
the name of my adulthood
the name of my marriage
the name of my children
along with the name
of my childhood
my catholic-school name

Curaggia

my budding-artist name
my father's name
my mother's name

My business card
carries my full
ethnically rich
name
there is no doubt
when they hear Russo
unless they mistake it for
French

My mother
always said no one
ever thought
she was Italian
they took her for
French
her hazel eyes
her white skin
she enjoyed
the masquerade
wanted to be different

Spoke fluent Italian
at home
wrote letters for *comares*
but in the world
French exotic
acceptable

Ginney, wop, spaghetti vendors
Italians need not apply
grease balls
paisans
ka-beesh? the Anglo at work
asks the Irishman?
ka-beesh?
fractured
syllables of the mother-tongue

When I say someone's
name with true Italian
pronunciation
they smile
I linger over Mallozzi
Pallotta, Oscgunizzo

They discover me eating
dried Italian black olives
and provolone cheese
at lunch
at my computer
longing for *vino*
knowing it is against policy
longing for a nap
knowing that this country
thinks unwell of sleepers
longing to shout

I am Italian
don't you understand?
it's all right
I can handle it

Curaggia

Little Etna

Mary di Paola

Not Always as Easy as Breathing

Identity as Context

Susan Raffo

My uncle used to whisper to me, leaning in close with the smell of beer and the feeling of whiskers on the edge of scratching my face, he would whisper: "You got bad blood in you, real bad blood. You got to be careful, bad blood always shows. You got to watch yourself."

Then he would pause and look around, making sure no one else was listening:

"It's nigger blood you got."

I always knew what he was talking about. Knew that he was talking about my Italian father, seeing this Italian-ness as something that riddled its way through my body, treacherous and hidden. Something that, with his racism, he understood. It was about race to him. About something essential. "It's dangerous blood," he used to say. "It always shows. You can't hide from it."

My uncle whispered at me with an urgency, a sense of mission. His role was to teach me the things other people would forget. He knew I would not learn about my dangerous blood from my father. My father was dead. He died when I was young, before he could teach me about being Italian. I looked like parts of his family, had ways in the world that he gave before he left, but his culture, his being Italian as easy as he breathed? He took that with him when he died. Had my uncle kept quiet, the only way I would have defined myself was out of the jumbled German of my mother's mother and the hidden, the assimilated Indian, what he called "French," of my grandfather. Had my uncle remained silent, "Italian" would have been an unknown adjective that I used to describe what might have been. But instead, every warning, every whisper shot a fierceness, a wild thing into my blood.

* * *

"What's your name from?" he asked me when we were both in the sixth grade.

"It's Italian. My dad was Italian."

"Oh yeah?" Even though we were both in the sixth grade and supposedly pre-sexual, I knew what was coming next. It had happened before. "I know all about Italian girls." And he grabbed my arm and tried to pull me behind the white barn where the fast kids made out, each one taking turns to watch out for the teachers.

It made sense to me that this should happen. It made sense that I should struggle. I knew that this being-Italian meant being watched and wanted. No matter what I did. No matter how much weight I gained. How much I tried to hide. This happened again and again. My uncles. Men on the streets. Boys at school. This being-Italian meant that others, that men, saw something under my skin, something invisible to me but desired by them. Something dangerous. Embarrassed and scared, I pulled away, running to lean against the brick school wall where the kitchen door opened.

This being Italian meant a different thing once my family went rural, did the seventies white flight from the inner city to the suburbs. Only my immediate family — my mother, brother and I — ran even farther. We ran to a land without strip malls. To a newly planted house surrounded by an ocean of mud. My family, my German and Indian mother and her half-Italian children, her children raced as non-white by her brother, our uncles and cousins: our coloured white family joined the national white flight and moved to a land of very white people. Of people mostly German and Anglo. With generations of farming this little piece of land, generations of this Ohio earth the only darkness that stained their palms.

It wasn't my uncle anymore. Even when I went back to the city, to the little barricaded white section of inner-city Cleveland where most of my family remained, when I went there for wedding showers and communions and my uncle leaned against me to whisper his verbal warning, he didn't have the same effect. As I grew older, he didn't have to remind me that I was Italian. He didn't have to worry that I would forget.

I knew that this passion inside could burst out at any moment. And that this passion was dangerous. That this passion was something that seethed in my blood, had something to do with sex and darkness, and had a power that existed largely because it was invisible to me. After all, if I could see it, I could erase it, could become as white as my Indian grandfather with the Anglo name and the Irish alias.

But the colour of this passion was closed to me. All I knew was that I was Italian and this was dangerous. Wasn't this what the kids at school were responding to? Something inseparable from who I was? Something I couldn't hide?

* * *

My father's mother, my proverbial Italian grandmother, didn't visit us much after my father died. She came once a year when we, her grandchildren, were still young. I remember missing her, even when she was there. Distant and watchful, she started to cry at the mere mention of my father's name. In the course of eighteen months, my grandmother lost her mother, her husband, her first-born son and her first-born grandson. Her tethers to a past and a future were cut and let loose. Those of us still remaining held the frayed ends and tried to weave together some kind of history.

When I asked my grandmother for stories, she cried. Sometimes she was angry. I remember her telling me in a rage that other people looked down on her family because they were Neopolitan, Napolitano. "Someday I am going to go back to Naples," she would tell me. "Naples is a beautiful city of old squares with fountains in the center." It is one of the few memories I have to trot out as a calling card when folks ask me to talk about "being Italian," something that sounds legitimate, that has nouns and cultural placing. Once I tried to tell my grandmother that Naples had become a polluted industrial city with a port hanging over a coast line of sewage. She wasn't interested.

* * *

I hated college. In class, the students talked about poetry and novels as though they had written them. I listened and wondered how they had discovered those secrets of meaning that were closed to me. Once, after reading William Faulkner's *The Sound and the Fury*, I had a moment of great bravery. Leaving class, I ran to catch up to the Star Student, the one who always had something to say that made the professor lean back and look interested. I asked this student if he had read the book before. When he said no, I asked him how he knew the things he knew about them. He started talking about schools and metaphor, about poetry and history and then he stopped: "Where's your family from?" I told him my family lived in Ohio. "No," he said, "Where's your family *from*?" It never occurred to me to refer to my mother. We never talked about her as being from somewhere in the way that this boy meant. I told him, without a pause, that my father was Italian. "Oh," he said, very sure of himself, "that's why. You aren't really white. Not all the way white. You wouldn't get stories like this. It isn't your culture."

Italians in the US are the southerners, the dark ones, the ignorant peasants who carry statues of the Virgin Mary through their neighbourhoods and faint with religious passion. They are not the Venetians or Florentines, ancestors of the deMedicis, the Michelangelos or daVincis. No, those are Europeans. Historical moments that eventually led to the creation of democracy. Italians, well, they are something different. They came in large and dirty numbers to

Curaggia

Ellis Island. Too many of them really. Not all the way white. Certainly not white enough, rich enough, or intellectual enough to understand Faulkner.

This is not about race. This is about class. About culture and history. And then it is about race.

* * *

What is so interesting to me is that I am the one who has tried to convince friends, Italian and otherwise, that I am not really Italian.

"Oh no... really," I say, "my father died when I was young. My mother's family did most of the job of raising me. All I have are the genes."

"But you look Italian," they shoot back.

I pause at the mirror for this look-Italian. I peer close to my face and look for my father, for Al Pacino and Sophia Loren. What is it to look-Italian? What would happen if I had inherited blue eyes from my grandmother? A lighter kind of pinkish skin? If I looked Italian but not the darker kind, the brown eyes and brown hair kind? Would my uncle still feel an urgent need to warn me about my blood if the blood had not expressed itself through the straight line of my nose, the light olive of my skin, the brown darkness of my eyes? Would I suddenly be not-Italian? Does my face give me a license that overcomes my lack of cultural printing? What the hell is this look-Italian? And does everyone see it?

* * *

How can I sit here and tell you that when that kid in college told me I was not "all the way white," his words had meaning for me? That I understood what he meant? That I knew he didn't think I was "coloured" but that he told me my white was different from his? Not as pure? What still fascinates me and I have yet to place is the way my whiteness, as configured by my uncle and by the kids at school and in college, was not-all-the-way white, it was white with a problem, white with a hidden secret, a hidden darkness. My whiteness was a white they used their racism to define.

* * *

I am Italian. And a lot of other things. I only buy two kinds of identity t-shirts: queer-based and Italian-based. I always say this is a real test of outness on any subject. Are you willing to wear a shirt that says so? I am sometimes assumed to be Italian by others that I meet. Or, I am assumed to be something different, something other. I have been asked if I were Jewish, Native, Latina. At other times, I am just assumed to be white. It depends on who is talking to me. My face stays the same. It's their perceptions that change.

My brother has been stopped at airports because they thought he was an Arab. We look at each other and laugh. We're boring old white folks from Cleveland, we say. My brother is a union organizer. He used to organize in rural Kentucky. When he was there, he found out the Black and Mexican workers he organized assumed he was Black. His skin colour, eye colour, and hair texture were read by them as a quarter or an eighth African-American. By the one-drop rule, this would make my brother Black. They were surprised when he explained that he was Italian. He was surprised they were surprised. Their context for people who look like him is a specifically racial one. It's a Black and white thing.

After this, my brother continued for awhile to organize unions in the South. He learned to expect white and Black people to assume he is Black. He still doesn't know how to walk the line between honesty — his recent blood is Italian, Native American and German but not African — and respect — he does not want anyone to think he is offended when they read him as Black. He's not sure how to talk about the racism he experiences at the hands of some of the white workers he organizes. He's not sure how to write this along his white — however sometimes brown — skin.

* * *

I am white. Never let it be assumed that because I question and wonder about all of these experiences that I am trying to be something other than white. I am not on a personal crusade towards colourization; the Ted Turner of white folks. I am not attempting to be special, different, other than what I am. I am not trying to deny what privileges my skin and social placing have given me. I am not trying to craft a new and seamless identity. One with no holes and no places to challenge.

* * *

What is an identity without the firmness of culture to back it up? Is it possible to be anything at all without the cultural reinforcement of detail: the smell of food and the sound of a language? Or are individuals only a composite, a collage of experiences eagerly threaded together into an indexed outline, tagged with a name and applied to the individual bodies? Like this essay, a weaving together of memory and thought, I am still wondering about these things, about the meaning of identity, of culture, of race.

A central thing about identity is that it is flexible, it grows and changes with history and experience. Its context is never the same.

Curaggia

* * *

To be Italian-American at the cusp of the 20th century is a very different thing than it was three or even two generations ago. So many have moved to the suburbs, have left their urban Italian communities, their immigrant neighbourhoods. So many do not know about the quotas in the 1920s, the quotas when Southern Italians and Jews were raced as "other" and no longer allowed into the United States. In the 1990s we have Bill Riccio as the name of a white supremacist recently released from prison in Alabama. The photograph I see of him is insolent, his straight black hair and thick peasant face, he looks like a posterchild for Ellis Island used-to-bes. Now he is called "the driving force in the Skinhead movement in northern Alabama." He probably doesn't even know his own history. That it is only recently he would have been allowed to be a white supremacist. That there are still places in the country where he would be laughed out of an Aryan meeting. He would never admit to the terror that drives him to use the burning cross of racism to whiten his olive skin.

To be Italian-American in the 1990s is not just about the stories that our grandparents tell us but it includes these stories. To be Italian-American in the 1990s is rarely about purity of blood and mostly about conflict of identity. There is nothing essential about this identity. Hardly anyone grows up in completely Italian/American communities anymore.

It is estimated that within the first two generations of immigration, 40% of Italian-Americans from the turn of the century immigration wave were marrying other than their own ethnicity. By now that is much higher. I know people who are only one quarter Italian but who know best the stories of their Italian grandparent. I know people who look in the mirror for some kind of facial detail that will mark them as Italian, searching for the dark moles, the dark eyes, the shadows on the face. I know people who are Irish, African, German — American and who want to be Italian, really and truly want to be Italian. Why? What does this word "Italian" mean? What does it symbolize? The safeness of the Italian brand of darkness, white but shadowed?

What is identity but a brief moment in time — a moment when we tie ourselves to some kind of history or community and say "I exist here," What are the pieces of our lives that we pull out and listen to, that we set in patterns to remind us that we have a place, that it is understood that we came from somewhere, that we are of something. What do we do with our identity when it co-exists with an experience of oppression, of being disallowed, unsafe, scorned? What is an identity when it doesn't exist alongside any oppression at all?

Who is the real Italian? Is there such a thing?

* * *

There is something in Italian-ness for some people that is about darkness and shadow. And there is something about Italian-ness for other that is of assimilation and whiteness. Being Italian-American is the interplay of these things: the village history and the suburban present, the grandparents named Vito and Gina and the grandchildren named Ashley and Jonathon, the home-made pasta with the Prego bottled sauce on the top, the peasant roots in Sicily and the fake brick ranch house in the modern development.

It is dangerous to assume that Italian-Americans are the same as German-Americans are the same as Anglo-Americans. It is equally dangerous to assume that Italian-Americans share something fundamental with African-Americans, have something in common with Jewish-Americans, are close to being the same as Latinos. The complications of Italian-American identity are not about oppression, they are sometimes about cultural discrimination, they are more often about assimilation.

Assimilation for Italian-Americans means the tension involved in covering up, in concealing. It means waiting until enough time and generations have gone by that we, the white ethnics, the new immigrants, are as ignorant of the complexities of our past as those who came before. Assimilation is a cultural sharing of denial, an aspiration to a symbolic norm. Molding bodies, shaping voices, changing hair colour, the shape of a nose, the sound of a name. It says that with a little bit of work, there will be no differences to get in the way. If we assimilate we will get somewhere, get ahead, make a mark, belong, belong, belong. If we assimilate, we, too, will have the house in the suburbs and the American dream.

It's a lily white lie. And it's only offered to those with the potential of passing for and then becoming white. Those who can cross the colour line.

* * *

In the second and third generation after immigration, the grandchildren, the great-grandchildren, and the great great grandchildren of immigrants look at themselves and say "who are we?" The grandparents and great-grandparents are from a past with no resemblance to the present. There are some stories handed down, maybe a few rituals at major holidays and the smell of a kind of cooking: but there is rarely cultural cement. The ties that keep each successive generation in the same neighbourhood, cooking the same dishes, and shopping at the same stores is slowly withering into something different.

How Italian can a third-generation child possibly be? Would their great-grandparents recognize them?

* * *

I forget to talk about belonging. I forget to talk about fear and isolation, about the fact that many of us want a space to fit into, a space that has meaning and sensuality. We forget that the problem with trying to belong to a thing, a place, an identity, is that in our attempts to belong we often veer into romanticism.

As Italian-Americans, would our great-grandparents recognize us? We struggle, trying to mold ourselves into some Italian-ness that we think they would approve of. We feel such great loss through the recent generations of assimilation. We feel such loss through only having handed-down stories to stroke the concrete longings of our skins.

Deep down inside most of us know that we are not Italian enough. We know of scores of other Italian-Americans who are more real than we are. They speak the language, they cook the food, they are still in touch with cousins in Palermo, they once visited their great aunt in Bari when they were small. They have something we don't have, something we believe makes them secure. We are afraid to tell them how much we fear we really aren't Italian. Afraid to tell them how little cultural grounding we really received. We are afraid that if we do, they will laugh at us. They will tell us that we know nothing. That we don't belong. That this space we seek, this place of historical connection, is not ours to claim.

We are afraid they will tell us we are nothing but Americans.

Because we are afraid of these things, we get romantic. We find ways to create props, to reinforce our connection to an Italian past and an Italian-American present. Sometimes we know more about the village our grandparents emigrated from than the town in which we were raised. We can track the line from name to name, the blood that dripped from vein to vein to end just beneath our skins. But we don't always know the people who live two doors away from us or what happened to the girl we had cared about in sixth grade.

We talk for hours about the wonderful communal aspect of Italian and Sicilian culture. We talk about how important the family is. How this makes us different from other white Americans. We tell each other funny stories about zio Vinnie and zia Connie, do you remember the time Vinnie made wine with those strange wild grapes? Do you remember the grape stains like bruises that clung to his arms for days afterwards? How nonna thought he had been bleeding and she refused to believe the marks were from grapes?

We talk for hours about how important it is to recognize our Italian culture, how it makes us different. We talk about this and we forget to ask each other questions. To challenge each other as we write our histories. We forget to look at all the stories we were handed down. We forget to examine all of the things that our grandparents told us.

We forget to confront the fear of the outsider that has sometimes made southern Italian communities so terrifyingly racist and closed. We forget to talk about the struggle that our aunt Connie had when she wanted to go to college. How grandmother told her she had to stay home and care for Vinnie, her husband. We forget how much Connie cried, trapped between two cultures she felt, not wanting to hurt her mother but wanting something different, something she had learned to desire.

* * *

For Americans who are the children of European immigrants, and particularly of the immigrants who came in huge and impoverished numbers at the end of the 19th century and beginning of the 20th, there are some hard questions to consider. I think to myself, how Italian can I possibly be? I talk over the summer with a friend from England who still lives in England. She has only visited the States once. I tell her about this essay, about the line of my thinking. She is amazed. "Italian?" she asks. "You aren't Italian. You're American." She thinks I am engaged in a huge and joyous mindfuck. For her, Italian is about a country she has visited. It is about passports and conversations about the European community. I try and explain how the same word can have different meanings. How, in the United States, Italian refers to immigrant. And that this flavour of immigrant is marked with assumptions and stereotypes that have then marked me. I try and explain that being Italian-American has little to do with Italy and everything to do with imaginary Italy, a place left behind, of sun and history, of family. That this absence of a concrete Italy has generated a strange cultural hold over Italian-Americans. A kind of psychic Diaspora. She is still sceptical.

* * *

In 1985, James Baldwin wrote in *The Price of the Ticket*, "As long as you think you are white, there's no hope for you." So what does this say about whiteness? Is there such a thing? Are Italian-Americans members of the whiteness club? In an interview in the May 13, 1994 issue of Entertainment Weekly, Queen Latifah laughingly said in response to the comment that if she sang country music, she could be like Reba McEntire, "Nah. If I was white, I think I would have to be Italian. But then again, that would make me part Black, wouldn't it?"

One of the downfalls of identity politics has been a sometimes over-simplification of complicated issues. Politically, in the context of race politics, all Italian-Americans — aside from the extremely small number of African-Italians living in the US — are white. Those of us who are darker-skinned might experience prejudice from strangers on the street but we are still politically white. As a dark Sicilian friend of mine said, "Once I explain to whoever asks that I am Sicilian, their attitude towards me changes. They don't treat me like I'm "coloured" anymore. They might give me shit about the Mafia but they don't see me racially any longer. Now it's about cultural difference." Even if we are raised in families and communities with a fierce sense of ethnicity and culture, we are not raised within an experience of racism, neither the racism of individuals directed against us nor the institutionalized racism that affects our visions for the future. By leaving southern Italy or Sicily, we have left behind the land that remembers the history of our oppression. We have chosen to leave.

We know that we are Sicilian or Neopolitan or Abruzzian or generic Italian. We learn what this means in a larger national context. We are Europeans, tied to European history, however much we might be the poorer and darker aspects of this European-ness. We have been on the side of the colonizer. Is it any wonder that so many Italian-Americans embrace Christopher Columbus with such eagerness? That Portuguese-Jewish-Genovese pup? What symbol is being embraced? The symbol of being the ones who got here first? Not the poor bedraggled peasants who arrived in the States recently and with such little social clout? Being on the side of the one who took the land rather than the side of those who came because they had nowhere else to go?

* * *

When I was a child living in Cleveland, Ohio, we raced each other differently than I watch urban folks race each other now. On one end of the race/colour scale were the WASPs, the White Anglo Saxon Protestants. They had names like Smith and Williams. Most of them had been here for many many generations. They hung together in groups of matching clothes and light coloured hair. They stuck together because that is what they did.

On the other end of the race/colour scale were African-Americans. They had names like Smith and Williams. They hung out together in groups of matching clothes and straightened or braided hair. They stuck together because they knew it was the best way to deal with our racism. They stuck together out of choice. They stuck together because they had no choice.

In the middle were the rest of us. Arabs. South Asians. Puerto Ricans. Italians, Poles, Jews, Slavs, Greeks, and Chinese. Some light-skinned African-Americans: either the children of white and Black parents or the children of generations of light-skinned African-Americans.

It wasn't that the groups never interacted. They did. Outside of school time, a lot of us played together. Hung out in that blissful child place before our racism completely determined the lines of separation. At school, though, we had already begun to mirror our family lines of solidarity.

Her Tongue the Culprit   207

The way we all raced each other had something to do with skin colour and something to do with class. It had a lot to do with Cleveland at this period of time. The WASPs knew they were probably college material, probably moving out, certainly not connected to any of the rest of us by interest or history. The African-Americans, many who were first and second-generation Northern raised, already knew about the precarious and dangerous reality of living among white people. How we could turn in a second. How we couldn't be trusted. How different were the social possibilities for all of us. The middle group, the white/brown mixing of completely unrelated cultures, had more to do with immigration than it had to do with race. WASPs and African-Americans were a part of an American conversation about race, culture, and position that the rest of us were still learning. Still trying to figure out what side of the line we fell on, coloured like African-Americans or white like the WASPs.

Some believe that whiteness did not become an option for white ethnics until the racial integration of inner city neighbourhoods in the 1950s and onwards. Suddenly, Italians, Irish, Poles, and others saw themselves united against the perceived threat of Black neighbours. Where before there was cultural difference and competition, suddenly there was shared identity: whiteness.

"Whiteness" is not a safe and static position. It is an identity born of paranoia. With desperation, whiteness can never relax. It must be ever vigilant, scouting its borders, measuring skin tones, last names and political values.

* * *

When many Italians — specifically Southern Italians and Sicilians — came to the United States, they came with a tradition of poverty and oppression. They came to the United States because they wanted to survive. They wanted the possibility of a better life. Many moved first to urban environments. In the earliest days, most immigrants interact little with other cultural groups, except when absolutely necessary. For immigrant Italians, there was no such thing as "Little Italy." Identity and home were much more specific than that. Neighbourhoods were settled by people from the same family and village or at least, the same province. An immigrant from Petralia in Sicily would not have sought neighbourhood with immigrants from Gesualdo, outside of Naples. "Little Italy" neighbourhoods happened with later generations. "Little Italy" grew as assimilation grew. It was, for some of the older immigrants, a giving-up, a way of becoming American. Now, "Little Italy" is dying out. The few times she still exists, she is a run of restaurants and markets, places for Italians living in the suburbs and urban everyone else to visit, shop, and

Curaggia

eat. She represents the last cultural hold-out, the piece that usually changes last if it changes at all: she is food. Nutrition for a changing culture.

* * *

I am Italian-American and this has meaning for me. This places me. It places moments of my life. It places moments of my present. I was told that I was Italian as a child. I was told that this was meaningful. Some of the meaning was born with the prejudices of my uncles. Some of it grew alone and isolated within the walls of my skin, only to be noticed when contradicted. The meaning did not have a lot of music and food, it had very little language. But it did and does have meaning.

* * *

Recently I have started to connect with my father's family. I did not see all of his extended family after his death. A few came, reminded us of who we also were, while others lived far away from us and besides, we were well wrapped up in survival and my mother's people. I have started to write letters, to plan visits, and to exchange stories. I am overwhelmed at how completely I am accepted, at how I am loved. I didn't expect this. I forgot this part of the picture. A few listened as I told them what I heard as a child, about how being Italian was portrayed. For them this surprising. They are Italian and because they live in Italian community, they never think about it. It just is. And because I am family, so am I.

This part of it is going to take awhile to get used to. This is not hearing about the danger and darkness and then making it powerful. This is not about being pursued, followed, and wanted, sexualized. This is not about being cast or typed or defined. This is not about being asked: which side are you on? Are you one of us or one of them? This is the part that I didn't get and I am eager to feel.

And this is the difficult part. What I feel fiercely and intellectually is that identity can not just be. As someone with white — in terms of racial — privilege and light-skinned — in terms of colour — privilege, I feel a responsibility to question what I mean when I say culture, identity, race, and whiteness. I feel accountable to the times I am silent. I also know that part of this intensity of focus comes out of an experience of not-belonging, of being seen as different by both my mother's family and then later, and only sometimes, by the white people around me. It is not unusual to make a politics out of family dysfunction.

What I experience with my father's family is acceptingness. Their gaze and their conversation says: you belong here. You are one of us. This is the piece about identity, politics, race and community that we don't spend enough time talking about. What it feels like to be told you belong. Unquestionably. That your fear of being seen as an imposter is groundless. That the identity you have always been told is problematic is actually, in the new group's eyes, unproblematic. It is expected. It just is.

This is the fine line that we Italian-Americans walk. As people who come from a history that knows oppression based on culture and ethnicity. As Italians who have settled in a land that knows us as white and gives us privilege because of it. As Italian-Americans who still sometimes experience that whiteness as complicated. As Italian-Americans who are often called upon to make a choice. Which side are you on? Which side are you on?

Excerpts from a Letter[*]

Denise Nico Leto

I always had a distinct sense of my own cultural and ethnic identity, although it took some years for me to develop a political context and awareness for the felt experience. Sometime in 1984, I started taking Italian language and history classes. The focus was on the language and culture of Northern Italy. Southern Italian or Sicilian dialects were not discussed, or worse, were openly derided. I remember the teacher going around the room asking all the students in Italian where their families were from. When I answered, he laughed and called me a "dirty" Sicilian. It was unforgettable and helped shape my understanding of *exactly who I was and where I came from*. It was during this time that I took notice, painfully, that there were no Sicilian or Italian Americans in my own writing. *Why?* I had generic people and generic voices. They were sometimes clearly lesbian, but never explicitly Sicilian or Italian. This disturbed me greatly. At the same time that I was developing a keen awareness of what was missing in my work, I was confronted with the grim reality of the death of my immigrant relatives.

In the 1980's I lost two great aunts, a great uncle and my last living grandparent. Up until that point, I had always been conscious of being Italian, of my olive skin, the different ways of my family — and proud of where I came from. My own research and exploration into Sicilian and Italian American culture (combined with the death of these key immigrant relatives) changed my awareness into an actual, articulated cultural and ethnic identity. I had moved from self-awareness into the beginnings of developing a politic of identity, for the first time, around my ethnicity and culture and not just my sexuality.

Why I do not identify as white is clear. It is a background, a heritage that is not my own. I am not Anglo. My parents are not and their parents were not. Why I identify as a woman of mixed-heritage is also clear to me: that is what I am, where I come from, *who* I am. Why I do not identify as a woman of colour is more complicated. It has to do with how I think about the identity of colour itself. It has to do with the genesis of that identity in the location I find myself: California, the United States, North America, in the 1970's, 80's and 90's. Women from many different cultures and races claim colour as an identity. And here, in the United States, that identity has its roots in specific geographical, cultural, and political contexts and histories. Women of African American, Native American, Chicana, Latina, and Asian descent articulate at various points similar political analyses of race, class and gender inequities, but then each group renders an additional analysis that retains the integrity of its own unique experience.

Although I can and do make comparisons with my own and the experience of people of colour in this country where necessary and to illuminate the insidious nature of oppression among and between different groups of people, it is nonetheless an identity I cannot claim as my own. That is not because I do not feel that a political identity for my Sicilian and Italian heritage is not appropriate, but because that isn't the identity that *tells the truth of my experience best*. It's about a definition of terms. It's about the nexus of language and empowerment. "Woman of colour" is inaccurate for me. Because of the specificity of what that term has meant in this country, it fails to define me, it fails to embrace the full depth and breadth, the full accuracy and specificity of my experience and identity. It stops somewhere outside of who I am. It is close, very close. But it isn't true. It misses. And, when it comes to identity, missing by a narrow margin can feel the same as missing by a wide margin.

So what is my identity? What do I claim proactively as my own? What is empowering for me? To say this: I am, first, a third generation (my parents were born in the United States and are the offspring of immigrants), half Sicilian, half Southern Italian North American, a woman of mixed-heritage, and a working class lesbian. I am neither Anglo nor a woman of colour. I am something else and because I don't have the exact language, the perfect word, doesn't mean I'm not claiming a truth that is apparent to me. It means I am deeply in search of this truth — even as I know it, utterly, I am also searching. I am in a place that is new and unknown, a place of clarity and of pain. A place where the language, the words are in the process of being shaped in order to somehow embrace exactly how I feel and who I am. It is a birth and a naming all at once. And so I name myself Sicilian, I name myself Southern Italian, I name myself a woman of mixed-heritage. In that naming, my experience comes to life.

In any discourse about race, ethnicity, or culture general terms are flawed, but often used with a recognition of their fallibility. There are a myriad of experiences under the terms we now use. I don't know what the answer is except a continued, honest exploration of peoples' right to self-define. For instance, there are other Sicilian or Italian American lesbians I know who do identify as women of colour for complex reasons I find well thought through and particular to their history and experience. That they identify differently is not problematic for me, although I realize it raises a multitude of intricate and important issues. It is, however, an identity they claim and stands boldly in the truth of their lives as they experience them.

I do, most passionately, claim the experience of being a descendant of an olive-skinned and poverty class group of immigrants. Italy, and especially

Southern Italy and Sicily, has a unique history — geographically, politically and culturally. Italy was not unified until 1861, many years after major European powers had already developed into unified nation-states. Sicily itself has a separate and compelling history as an occupied and conquered land by the Normans, Spaniards, Greeks, and Arabs.

The Italian and Sicilian experience in the United States, then, has certain particularities that deserve voice and examination. The confluence of ancestries from the Arab, North African, Semitic, Greek, and Spanish bespeaks a compelling mix of ethnic and cultural forces. Transport those forces into North America and it gets even more complicated. This means, concretely, that Italian or Sicilian Americans can alternately "look" like Greeks, Spaniards, North Africans, Arabs, Germans. We can have tight black curly hair, dark skin, olive skin, light skin, red hair and freckles, blond hair and blue eyes. But this is not solely an issue of skin colour or skin privilege, it is a blend of complex issues regarding language, class, cultural values, perspectives and history.

Self-determination for Italian or Sicilian Americans can involve basic, comparisons with other oppressed groups and with the mechanisms of stereotyping and prejudice. Although this point of view must be carefully and intelligently articulated, Italian or Sicilian Americans do not need to make it with guilt or apology. This argument, as far as I'm concerned, contains within it a perspective grounded in fact and history and does not smack of "metooism." I have attempted to articulate this crucial journey of self-definition in a country wrought with institutionalized oppression, divide and conquer mentality, and colossal pressures to assimilate. The Italian Sicilian American need for self-determination is not meant to be a censorious stab at the body of other group struggles; particularly women of colour. The development of Sicilian Italian American consciousness and identity is itself a celebration of multiculturalism, of diversity, of self-determination as a cornerstone of freedom.

So even though there are levels at which I can personally and deeply resonate with some aspect of the experience of women of colour in this country, and even though I can draw some political and historical similarities with people of colour in terms of the infra-structural oppression faced by ethnic immigrants and their descendants in this country, I do not claim that identity and I acknowledge the vast differences that exist between us.

At the same time, to point to similarities, to dialogue about the systemic socio-economic and political conditions faced under patriarchal capitalism is, I think, an appropriate and valid response. I can further assert my distinct ethnic and cultural experience without violating or detracting from the experience of other oppressed groups. It is simply one more truth among many truths, seeking to be heard. It is not an appropriation of the history and culture of others' to claim my own.

It is important to understand the experience of Italians and Sicilians in this country, as they experienced it. Not as the media or the dominant Anglo culture or any other group interprets it. I and members of my family have experienced instances of prejudice and discrimination because of anti-Italian bigotry or classism. This has come in the form of damaging stereotypes, name calling, invalidation, violence, verbal harassment, lack of opportunity or voice, alienation and cultural annihilation. There is a language, a middle to upper-class Anglo lexicon in which I have not been immersed and which I do not speak. This means entire opportunities fueled by a certain way of thinking are, by their very nature, exclusive of my working class and ethnic values and perspectives. Because of my ability to articulate and write, there is a presumption of a middle-class, Anglo background. I am constantly confronted with this assumption of a privilege that the world I lived in did not, in reality, bequeath to me. Although I am keenly aware of the privilege I *do* have in this society, I am also painfully aware of that which *I do not* have as a result of my class background, my ethnicity, and my lesbianism.

I consider myself a feminist. The mainstream feminist movement has not addressed some of my specific needs, ideologies, or politics simply by virtue of the fact that Sicilian Italian Americans are often invisible or assimilated within this movement. On the other hand, I have been able to extract a deep meaning and value for the construct of my life from feminism particularly radical lesbian feminist thought and activism.

A few years ago some women I know experienced intense anti-Italian sentiment at an anti-Columbus protest, and it was horrible. If it is not realistic to expect any organized protest to be sensitive to the diverse populations supporting it, then call me idealistic. I am one of many Italian or Sicilian Americans who have rejected Columbus as a hero (and everything he represents), and still expect to confront people on their ignorance or vilification of Italian Sicilian Americans. All at the same time.

Columbus is no friend of mine nor is racism or colonialism. But any attempt to silence a woman's right to self-definition is reprehensible and should be pointed out. Suggesting that Italian Sicilian Americans have two choices — either march and be quiet about the complexities involved for us and ignore slights, or speak out about our perspective and be slammed as racists or opportunistic parasites shopping for an identity — leaves us with, at best limited, if not completely spurious options. Juxtaposing these two options, in and of itself, is a fallacy. I believe we have a range of options available to us as Italian Sicilian Americans. The former are one; mine is another and in no way are we representative of all the possible perspectives. What I need is for people to examine the static paradigm through which they are evaluating issues that are currently undergoing a radical transformation.

There is a difference between being of Sicilian descent and being from the North or South of Italy. In general, the agricultural South of Italy and the island of Sicily are impoverished compared to the more solvent industrial North. The people in the South and in Sicily are not always but often darker-skinned. It is common to hear racist slurs regarding Sicilians from other Italians, even in Naples. Sicily is a unique world encompassing a different language, different food and different customs. Italy also has a range of influences and in the South they are similar to that of Sicily, but in the North there is a more pronounced influence from other Western European countries, Germany, France, and Switzerland. I experience a profound bond with my Northern Italian sisters, especially if they are willing to acknowledge and grapple with my Southern Italian, Sicilian roots as different from their own. Then if I am willing to acknowledge the truth of their experience, we can at least talk. I believe our differences, on all these various levels, do not preclude discussion but rather necessitate it.

---

* *This is an excerpt from a much longer letter and originally germinated from telephone conversations and written correspondence with Nzula Angelina Ciatu. Some ideas were taken from my response to a survey on identity conducted by Roseanne Lucia Quinn for her doctoral dissertation on Italian American women writers.*

Go To Hell*

Nancy Caronia

What is Italian American? John Gotti, the Teflon don, saying stupid shit like my wife is the boss of the family, I don't know what any of youse is talkin' about, now a major made for cable TV motion picture starring Emmy-nominated Armand Assante? Or Mario Puzo, writing words proving Italians are criminals, but loyal to their family even if they do gotta whack each other once in a while? I have friends that will argue for hours over which was more realistically portrayed, the spaghetti Paulie cooked when they went to the mattresses in *The Godfather* or the sausage and peppers Paul Sorvino stuffs into his face in *Goodfellas*. I'm confused. I keep thinking our ancestors tried to leave this shit on that island in the Mediterranean years and years ago for a better life. They left poor *not* rich, they left power*less* not with any firepower in their hands. They thought they'd get a better deal in that new country that was about a hundred years old, the French built a statue to liberty and they came by shipfuls to see this lady in the harbor. Lincoln had signed the Emancipation Proclamation, but the money men, not used to having to pay for their labour, were looking for willing slaves to work long hours for little pay and they opened up Ellis Island to welcome yesterday's boat people, didn't turn none of those disease-free ancestors of ours away.

Those poverty-filled men and women who left Sicily did not envision becoming the very thing they thought they left behind. The old country, the land of olive oil and figs, had landlords who robbed the little money they slaved for, barely enough to put food on the table and while these Dons, a feudal title whose meaning has been skewed today, stole from these peasants, the peasants had to thank the Dons for leaving them their lives. Willingly they gave up what little they had, not thinking, not knowing they had other choices. The end of a gun or a swinging machete the deciding vote in their survival. And when these same ancestors dared to leave poverty and fear and terror, which streaked their hearts the colour of dirt, they were told they betrayed their homeland and the criminals they hoped to leave behind shouted to them across the sea, "traitors, you are all traitors." And their tongues were cut out. And they tried to forget where they came from. In vain they tried to beat back the echo in their heads by beating their children.

My father and his brothers were no exception. Their parents beat them, told them in a broken dialect from the old country, "you're in America, speak

English." They beat their sons until my father forgot how to speak his parents' language. They beat him until he understood fear.

Don't nobody know that yesterday's mythology is today's religion; that yesterday's Helen of Troy is this decade's Princess Di. My confusion grows when I see actresses like Michelle Pfeiffer play Italian American women, madonnas who get out of the mob scene unscathed and find nice 'straight' white boys in the process. When Italian American females actually win Oscars it's for portraying tarts and prostitutes. They receive their awards, smile sweetly, say, "thank you" pretty as you please, "without daddy, I couldn't of done this, it's all due to him." I'm crying too even though her father played his own version of a mob boss in a *fucking great, really true film* about the mob, because I wish I could thank my father for something besides putting his hands down my pants.

I wonder sometimes what he thought he was doing with me in my bedroom in the middle of the night. I wonder when I wake up sweaty, my breath shallow and hard, fear lurking in the corners of my mouth, the taste of metal on my tongue. The room is red. My eyes are open wide. The room is bloody red. I wonder if he knew I'd carry this with me for always. I wonder if he knew what would haunt my nightmares and fill my daydreams.

Maybe if I were a man I would do something different. I'd become a mobster, or direct a movie about mobsters, or write a couple of bestsellers about mobsters or play a mobster in every single major motion picture I ever act in, get my aggression out by playing the aggressor. Better yet, I'll become like Rudolph Giuliani, a one-man demolition team, shutting down what he calls all 'mob-related operations,' until his son Andrew's head winds up in his bed one morning or more realistically, he just doesn't get re-elected. Italian politician as fascistic government official, now there's a new twist to our history.

How do I get off the romantic train of Italian American criminal wealth? Where is the stop that doesn't have Francis Ford Coppola seducing me, making love to me while he's sticking a knife in my heart. Or the seduction of Marty Scorsese's *Goodfellas*, which is slightly more palatable to my senses because it's just a fuck, a good old-fashioned fuck. Surprise, surprise, Marty only wants my body. He says, "I want to fuck you," and in my rage I'll give it to Marty, I'll lay on the kitchen table for him, hike my skirt up, spread my legs to let him get a good look at my cunt because I know he can't have my soul, he's not even asking for it. Mario and Francis, they want souls, they gave away our souls. I can't do that. I can't say it's okay. The truth I experienced is painful enough without putting machine guns and piano wire next to the lace collars and doilies on the table.

I want to be different. I want an Italian American film without guns and guys talking out of the side of their mouths, but the only picture of Italian American neighborhoods I see in this country, besides the *stellar* portrayal of mobsters in the movies, is the beer-swilling ginzos and their big hair and nail wives yelling "niggers go home" when Al Sharpton gets stabbed leading protesters through Bensonhurst after the murder of Yusef Hawkins by a bunch of Italian American teenagers with baseball bats and a gun. I want to give these assholes a map and say, "doesn't anyone realize we have 'nigger' blood in us? Can't you see how close Africa is to Sicily?" Growing up, my relatives said shit like, "oh, he's a real mulengnan" and I'd ask, "what's that" and they'd laugh, "an eggplant" and I'd go, "but I like eggplants" and some dimwit with the smell of cigars and espresso on his breath would say, "oh, not that kind you better not." It never changed.

When I moved back home after being away at college for four years, I was in my bedroom one night with Donovan, a high school kid I was directing in a play for a local community theater. I had cast him as Jesus in *Godspell* and we were talking about acting technique. The door was closed, but my father didn't knock, just barged in and said, "whatta ya doin' here?" "We're talkin'," I answered. He said, "well, keep the door open." I didn't get it, I thought my father had lost his mind, I was 24-years-old, not some little girl. I turned and looked at Donovan and when I saw the expression on his face I realized my father swept into my room like that because Donovan was Black. Which was kind of funny when you knew my father and our next door neighbor, Max, who happened to be Black, were thick as thieves. They were always talking tools and helping each other out with problems in their gardens. There was this one day, my Grandma Dooley, my mom's mom, the Irish side of the family, was out for a visit. The two of us sat on the front porch drinking iced-cold Nestea, our glasses and our bodies sweating in the July heat. She turned to me, "is that Raffaello's brother?" I looked at her and laughed, "Grandma, that's Max, our neighbor." The two of them were standing on our front lawn, examining my father's lawn mower in minute detail. That was when I first noticed they were exactly the same colour, the colour of Hershey milk chocolate bars. "Oh my god," she wiped the bottom of her iced tea glass, then her upper lip with an old tissue she had hidden in the sleeve of her dress, "they look like brothers. Jeez, yer father gets so dark, he could be a nigger."

So is that how the Mafia became a respected part of our culture in the U.S.? The bottom rung of an endless ladder your legacy, making less than a living wage, treated as if you are feeble-minded, treated as if you don't have a brain. Is that what happened? The same as in the old country they tried to cut from their hearts, only *this* time they became the perpetrators, establishing their own version of the protection that almost killed them.

That's why I argue with anyone who hails Mario Puzo's *Godfather* as a great piece of literature. My father read the book when it first came out in paper back. He read it for two weeks straight. When he was finished, he closed the book, said, "that's the greatest book ever written and I'll never have to read another book again.'' As far as I know he's kept his word. I too have read the book and I've seen all three Godfather movies and what I can't ever get my head around is how we began life in this country as gardeners and construction workers and wound up on everyone's favorite ten most wanted lists and according to Mario and Francis, we're proud of that climb up the justice ladder. It doesn't make sense. Except if you choose to forget where you come from. Except if you choose to romanticize your own beginnings. What I resent most though is the seduction. I am made love to. Promises of protection and the whisper in my ear tells me blood of my blood come closer, I know the secrets. My guard is dropped, but then I see Talia Shire as Connie Corleone on her knees to Al Pacino's Michael Corleone, sister and brother in an incestuous circle of killing hate, begging to be allowed to come back and take care of him. Connie says she knows she was wrong. She knows Michael was only trying to protect the family. What family I want to shout at the screen? What family I want to know? One of his brothers killed, the other with a Sicilian kiss on his lips *from* his brother. Her first husband murdered, all the children without one parent or another. What family? What horror is what I wanna say. Connie on her knees, saying what Michael did was for the family's good is like a knife in my heart. Women as madonnas or whores. Women closing their eyes to what is happening. Women having their womanliness ripped out and leaving them empty fuck and pasta maker machines. Their purpose only to make more babies and feed the males in their quest for legitimacy in an unclean world. Is that our history? Is that our only history?

Grandma Caronia turned a blind eye to my grandfather's ways the way Connie Corleone did in that Coppola classic. Grandma became a silent perpetrator. She stayed when she could have gone. My grandfather's siblings went to her when my father was a baby, ''please, leave a 'im, he's a crazy, we'll take a care a you. We'll take a you an' a yer four sons in. Don'a worry.'' She stayed, let him beat her and her sons. Let him abuse them, his grandchildren and his children abused their children. Maybe I'm looking at it the wrong way. Perhaps Puzo is ''right on the money,'' as my father might say. Protection of 'family honor' is everything to the Italian, even sacrificing their own blood to maintain that stringent code of silence.

It wasn't until Grandma was in her 70s and Grandpa too old to hurt her anymore, in and out of hospitals, that she decided to leave him. She could take his beatings, but she couldn't take his helplessness. She went to her sons and asked them to take her in. But it was too late, or was it merely revenge for all those long ago years of abandonment? All her sons had excuses, they weren't able to take her in, the most famous being, ''my wife, she just can't handle it right now.''

I saw Grandpa for the last time in a hospital bed. He was a stubborn son of a bitch, held on for eight months when other people would have just gotten it over with and died. I went to the hospital with my godfather, daddy's brother, Uncle Ed, and his wife, Aunt Mimi, a born again Charismatic in the Catholic Church, and their daughter, Bernadette, the one they said would be a beauty queen, but wound up marrying a womanizing salesman instead. My two sisters looked like Bernadette as little kids. It was remarkable when you put their three photos together, anywhere from the age of six up until about thirteen they all looked exactly alike, but how come she was the only one that was beauty queen material, that's what I'd like to know?

Grandpa was curled in a fetal position, his arms wrapped around his head. He was sleeping when we first walked in. Aunt Mimi and Uncle Ed went up to him and kissed him on the head. Uncle Ed spoke loudly to him, "how ya doin' Pops?" Grandpa woke up from the sudden noise, "what, what, I can't hear ya, what are ya sayin'?" Uncle Ed laughed said, "the old man's deaf" and walked out of the room, left the three women alone with his father. Bernadette went up to Grandpa then and put her arms around him and kissed him hello, all gentle and soothing like. Me, I hung out in the background not wanting to get too close, pissed that his son left us alone in the room with him. Grandpa must have noticed my separateness because he shouted out to me, "yer Raffaello's daughta, ain't ya?" "Yeah, Grandpa," I replied as Uncle Ed walked back in the room. "C'mere," he said, "I wantcha to tell ya fatha' somethin' fa me, I wancha ta tell 'em... . Hey, c'mere I wanna talk ta you," he shouted across to me when I didn't make a move. Uncle Ed stood next to me and suddenly pushed me forward, taunting me as he pushed, "Well, go ahead, don' be afraid, he's not gonna bite you." I went to Grandpa's bedside glaring at Uncle Ed. I put my face close to his, smelled the death on him and was glad, glad he was almost gone, glad he couldn't hurt any of us anymore.

When I was about seven-years old, my cousin Maddie burned herself on my grandparents barbecue grill at a backyard party they had at their house in Woodside, Queens, late '60s suburbia. Some of us were playing tag and she ran right into the hot grill that Grandpa had placed in the middle of the driveway after he'd cooked all the sausages on it in the backyard. The kids had been playing in the driveway the entire day, but he'd insisted on placing the hot grill in the middle of our playing field even after our fathers, his sons, told him it wasn't a good idea. "What the hell do any of you know anyway," he shouted at them. "Leave me alone and let me do what I want. It's my house," he proclaimed. His sons shrugged their shoulders, walked to the small backyard and opened up fresh bottles of Rheingold. Grandpa laughed when Maddie ran into the grill. She was running backwards away from our other crazy, but cute cousin Joseph, who was 'it' in our game of tag. Grandpa cornered Maddie between the grill and the house, teasing her, "serves ya right for playin' rough, ya wanna play rough ya gonna get burned" and he laughed louder as he pushed against her arm where the second degree burn was beginning to blister. All the cousins were yelling at him to stop, but

Maddie was defiantly silent, not shedding even one tear as he taunted her. Finally, Aunt Helen, her mother, came running from the kitchen where all the women were washing the dishes and pulled Maddie away from him, "leave her alone Pops. Jeez, she's only a little girl." Grandpa reached out for my aunt and said, "don' talk ta me that way, I'm not yer husband, I'll smack ya." And he picked up a nearby broom and tried to swat her with it, while his sons drank their Rheingolds and watched quietly from the backyard.

I was about to walk away from his hospital bed when Grandpa placed his arm around me in a chokehold, a position in my younger days he enjoyed administering. He was too small now, too weak, but his arm lay heavy on my back. I gave into his weight and leaned in closer. I waited for words that would change the way I thought him. Words that would erase the past.

I turned to look at Uncle Ed and Aunt Mimi hoping for some help. Grandpa wasn't speaking, just looking at me and he began to caress my hair. I felt suffocated. It felt strangely familiar and my impulse was to bolt from the room without looking back, but it was more important at the time to stay and get the message for my father. The message that would make sense of my grandfather's cruelty. I would be the receptacle, tell my father Grandpa, "didn't mean it. He never had." I tried to cut off the death that surrounded him and waited for the sacred message. "Grandpa, what do you want me to tell my father? You said you had something you wanted me to tell him. What is it?" He stopped playing with my hair, "tell ya fatha…," he started then stopped, hesitating for only a second, "you sure yer Raffaello's daughta, right?" I was losing my patience with this old, smelly man and my voice came out short, "yes, Grandpa, what do you want me to tell him?" And then he spat it out, surprising us all, "tell ya fatha go ta hell." He laughed loudly, "tell em go ta hell." He repeated it over and over singsong, like a nursery rhyme. "Tell em go ta hell. Tell em go ta hell." I lifted his arm away and stepped back across the room. My Aunt Mimi shook her head back and forth, "Pops don't mean it. He don't mean that." Uncle Ed said, "you'll have to tell ya fatha."

I remember sleeping at my grandparents' house only one time in my life. I'm sure I must have more than this incident, but it's the only time I have any recollection of and I didn't even remember the whole picture until after that last time I saw him in the hospital. My grandparents had an apartment in Coney Island on Avenue U after they sold the house in Woodside, which means I had to have been about eight-years old. My sister, Stephanie, and I slept over on a Saturday. We were supposedly helping Grandma do the shopping for the big Sunday dinner she cooked in those days. The menu consisted of antipasto, soup, macaroni, roasts of lamb and beef, lots of fried vegetables, like zucchini, cedona or cauliflower and salad with fruit, cheese-cake and cannolis for dessert. We shopped all day walking up and down Coney Island Avenue, the deli men giving us slices of salami and the bakers handing us cookies. That night after dinner we sat in the kitchen asking questions on how to make the sauce and what did she put in her meatballs that made them taste so different than our Irish American mother's. "Well, yer mother she jus' don' know how ta cook. She won't listen ta me, so you two betta watcha good so you canna teach her." I don't understand people who exchange written recipes. All I ever needed to learn about sauce I got from watching Grandma. "Throw alittlea this an do this," she always said when I wanted to know how much of something it needed. And then it was always, "but it changes wid how many people ya are, so ya jes gotta do it a fer yourself eacha time ya make somethin'," she advised.

That night, Grandma put the two of us to bed in their extra room where we'd have dinner starting at noon the next day. "Be good and go ta sleep. We gotta get up early to get a ready for evahbody," she admonished as she closed the door. Stephanie and I were squished in the same bed, something we didn't like and were talking to each other when Grandpa came in later that night. He came over and since I was on the outside of the bed, I was older and less likely to fall out, he grabbed my arm and said, "ya wanna play?" I told him it was too late, but he didn't hear me or he didn't care, I don't know which and next he unbuckled his belt and opened his trousers. Stephanie tried to get him off me, but she was just a skinny little kid then, and no matter how hard I kicked him with my legs he held my arms above my head with one hand and pushed my head into his crotch with the other. Finally, Grandma heard the noise and opened the door, yelling at Stephanie and me, "I tole you to go ta sleep. Whatsa matta wid you two?" She screamed Grandpa's name when she saw what he was doing. He pushed me away fast, buttoned his trousers and the two of them started yelling at each other in dialect. Grandma sighed and called to me. She wanted me to go to her, but I couldn't move. I didn't want to go past Grandpa. Stephanie took charge and pushed me forward squeezing the two of us past him. The three of us went into the kitchen and Grandma wiped my arms and face with a dish towel. Stephanie sat at the other end of the table and made faces at me to try to get me to laugh. When I didn't have any reaction, she became antsy and said she needed to go to the bathroom and that she could do it by herself. I screamed out, "no," and she plopped back down into her seat. I was, after all, still her older sister. Grandma looked upset, "what's wrong, you wan' somethin' to eat maybe? Yeah, that'sa good, I'll make you somethin' ta eat." I shook my head yes. I didn't want to disappoint her. She took out a saucepan and pulled out a box of farina from one of the cabinets over her head. I didn't pay close attention to what she was doing, but when she took the pot off the stove and I saw the white stuff in it I started to choke and said I wasn't hungry. She threw up her hands, "Wha'sa matta' wid you? I made this fa you and now you don' want it? You kids. What am I gonna do?"

After the hospital visit, Uncle Ed drove us back to my grandparents' apartment. I sat silently in the back seat, next to Bernadette. My father greeted us at the front door. I hadn't seen him in about a year. He looked older and heavier than I remembered. He also looked worn out, something I never remembered about him. Grandma yelled from the kitchen, "what kep' ya so long? I ben waitin' ta put the macaronis on." Uncle Ed made a bee-line for my father. True to form, first thing out of Uncle Ed's mouth was, "Raffaello, ya daughter has somethin to tell ya." "Jeez, Uncle Ed, can't you even let us say hello." I kissed my father on the cheek, "Grandpa didn't say anything. Don't listen to your brother. He's as crazy as your father." "What did he say? C'mon," my father rubbed the back of my neck as he questioned me, "what did Pops say?" "Nothing," I sighed, "you're all crazy, you know that." Uncle Ed laughed. He knew he'd aroused my father's curiosity, "Pops gave a message to you through yer daughta." I shot Uncle Ed a nasty look and didn't look at my father when I said in an angry voice directed at my godfather, "you don't want to know. Trust me." I wanted to protect my father from the unprotectable. The way he never seemed capable of protecting me or my siblings. "What was it?" he asked. I was silent as I turned toward him. My father looked down at his feet, rolled back and forth toe to heel, his hands deep in his pockets. He broke the silence by saying softly, "my fatha' tol' you to tell me go ta hell, right?" I looked directly in his eyes. I was surprised and shook my head in assent to the truth he already seemed to know. My father blushed. He knew the joke was on him again and he had to play along.

As the youngest, my father was the brunt of their jokes for years, but he learned to see where the next assault was coming from and always beat everyone to the punch. His nickname from birth was Chubbs and that was usually where the abuse began and ended. My grandmother fed him proudly when he was child. She made him eat and eat and eat. Her baby, the youngest, would prove there was no poverty in their house. Where there was girth there was wealth. "Eata somamo, ya so skinny," I still hear Grandma's voice accusing my mother of not feeding him, always telling my father he was too skinny even when he was too fat, always measuring how they were doing against his size.

I stood in Grandma's kitchen, watching his face go through the same fight for control that mine does when I try to ignore a hurt. It's this look in the pupil of the eye that says I know, I want to kill, but instead he eats another piece of roast beef, another plate of pasta. His weight is no longer a sign of their wealth, but of a rage unexpressed, violence committed, poverty of the soul and ignorance of the heart.

"I know, he says it ta me all the time. Everyday I go ta the hospital, he tells me go ta hell. It's like a joke," he laughs to accentuate the last point. His laugh turns to a shrug when I don't join in and look like I'm going to cry. Uncle Ed laughs with my father, pats me on the back. My father rolls his eyes toward me as I slink away from my uncle's hand. He picks up a cookie on the counter top, puts it in his mouth. My grandmother yells at him from her place at the stove, "Raffaello, we gonna eat now, wha'dya doin'? Yer not gonna have an appetite. Lookit all the food I made fer you." He picks up another cookie, pops it quickly in his mouth and says, "don't worry, ma, I'll eat. You know me. I always got an appetite. You don't gotta worry about me."

After that hospital visit to my grandfather, my memory was jarred but good. I could never look at any of my relatives the same way again. And once I remembered about him, it was like the flood gates opened onto the memories that had kept me frozen inside my own life for so many years.

When my mother called to tell me Grandpa was dead eight months after I last saw him, I whispered, "good" into the receiver. Not sure if I wanted my mother to hear my word or not. She either didn't hear me or didn't want to hear me because she plowed on with her own agenda, which, in all fairness to her, I didn't pay much attention to either, "well, he's bein' waked on such and such days and I'm goin' on this day and the funeral is on this day, you better plan with work..." I cut her off, "I'm not going." She let out an impatient breath, "wha'daya mean yer not goin'? Oh my god, how can you not go? It's yer father's father, for chrissake." "Listen. I don't care. He wasn't a nice man and he made a lot of people miserable." I was tired from the conversation. She changed the subject when she realized I wasn't going to join in the adrenalin rush of her newest drama. I could hear her taking a puff off her cigarette as she said, "well, do ya wanna at least talk to yer father?" "Is he there?" I asked. "Yeah, I'll put him on," she was curt. "Well, no ma, I don't. Not right now. I gotta go," I stammered out and hung up the phone.

Funny, but no one called to find out why I didn't go to the funeral. No one ever said anything. It was like this wall came tumbling down only they continued on as if the wall was intact, and for them, I guess, it was. At least that was what I believed until Aunt Mimi wrote a note to me a year later begging me to reconcile with my immediate family, "everyone misses you. Jesus loves you and so do we." She sent a religious greeting card along with a green plastic rosary and a bunch of prayer cards with Saints' pictures emblazoned on them. I wrote her back and told her I had nothing to reconcile and for the first time I let a blood relative know what my grandfather had done.

Aunt Mimi and Uncle Ed surprised me by calling and inviting me to lunch at their house in upstate New York. "We'll have take-out, praise Jesus," she says when I surprise myself by saying yes and ask for directions to their home.

The three of us sat together around their white formica 1950s kitchen table, Chinese take-out spread before us. Uncle Ed barely touched his chicken

Curaggia

and broccoli, tears formed in his eyes as I recounted as much of the story about Grandpa as possible without giving them a heart attack. He looked at me, "is it true?" I wasn't angry when he questioned me, simply answered, "yes, Uncle Ed, I have no reason to make any of this up." "We always knew Pops was crazy, but this, we never thought he was sick. You know we asked Betsy (their oldest daughter, not beauty queen material) and she says it never happened to her," his voice pleaded with me. I kept quiet, because I thought well, she just doesn't remember that's all. My uncle said, "well, look at me, I'm fine. He beat us, you know, but I'm okay. Well, I am afraid of the dark, but I have Aunt Mimi stay up with me at night until I'm ready for bed. If the hall light's off I won't walk to my bedroom. I get scared. So yer Aunt Mimi stays up with me until I'm ready for bed." I listened silently to this 65-year-old man with two daughters and four grandchildren. I have my answer. We sit quietly until Aunt Mimi breaks the stillness by gathering up the leftover Chinese food and packing it away. "Lunch tomorrow, praise Jesus," her voice tinkles through their kitchen, "praise Jesus."

* Names have been changed.

A Minority in All Seasons

Maria Barile

The political and personal experience of growing up a woman living with disabilities from Italian background in Canada can be like a maze. It resembles a state of weather collision, between warm winds coming from the ocean and mountains in Calabria, Italy and the cold icy winter winds of Montreal. The result of this is a compound not easily identifiable.

Most social movements have raised the question about self-definition: Is society reflecting onto us some predetermined view, or do we mirror into society a carefully thought out view of how we wish it to see us?

In reflecting on this dialectic and the impact it could have on me as an individual, I consider that since one cannot separate the personal existence from the political one, and since I cannot identify myself as a whole, in any single path, I am a "minority in all seasons." Coming from a linguistic background other than French or English, in Quebec, I am known as allophone. I am a disabled person in a non-disabled person's world and a member of the working class in a capitalist society; where great value is placed on "health and wealth" as if these were self-made and self-deserved states of being. I am a woman in a patriarchal society, with a male-oriented system, in which male-oriented values are built and passed on from one male to the other. Men are still predominantly the heads of family, business, and politics. Yet, everyone talks about equality for all, as if it were reality. When one is overwhelmed by multiple-dimensional states and points of view, one can easily confuse personal choices with the apparent choices permitted by the system. Feminist standpoint theory holds that:

> people's positions within a historical network of social and political relations, i.e. gender-specific perception, are determined by their status within that network.Therefore, systemic differences are determined by all of the individual's characteristics. Likewise, their view of the world is shaped by their complex position in the social framework. One subordinate layer of social relations both includes and explains the surface or appearance and indicates the logic by means of which the appearance of events destroys the deeper reality. (Light, 1989).

In other words, one sees and/or hears the world from where one stands or sits, and develops her\his reality from there. Being a woman with disabilities from an ethnic (Italian) working class-background, my realities developed from a variety of minority positions.

La Stagione: Season 1

Immigrants that arrived in Canada from Calabria, Italy quickly realized that "la casetta in Canada" — the little house in Canada — was just a nice song, but nothing more!

They arrived in the new country with lots of hopes and dreams. However, reality soon shattered their dreams. The systemic rules of the dominant groups often ridicule the values, beliefs, and costumes that immigrants cherish, ranging from the way one dresses to the life choices they make. Moreover, Canadian policies dealing with integration of immigrants indicate that to survive here, immigrants need to become like the majority, otherwise they will face isolation.

Yet, immigrants abide by values that are part of their upbringing and in which they are deeply rooted. They bring these values with them when and where they immigrate. In effect, these values represent an inveterate cultural state.

Much like flowers under a winter frost, this state remains frozen in time.

The inveterate cultural state, was the basis for choice immigrants made. As a result, immigrants view the world with nostalgia through those values and very few will change their views significantly, let alone completely. The people who remained in Italy would have progressed with time, while immigrants because of the "inveterate cultural state" tend to remain faithful to old traditions.

Children who immigrated to Canada with their parents as youngsters, or those who are born here soon after their parents immigrate, grew up in contentious cultural realities, and learned to negotiate with each culture. At some point, they came to the realization that their peers in Italy and in Canada were progressing at an equal pace. Nonetheless, their family and community in Canada, progressed like a sunny day in February, taking one step forward and a few steps backward.

I was born in Calabria. Being an allophone, in Quebec I am subjected to ethno-cultural values on the one hand, and stereotyped ethnicity on the other. At one time or another, I experienced the double binds between Italian and Canadian / Quebecois values. The English Quebecois territory has many contradictions of its own adding more ingredients to my mosaic identity.

As a teenager I expressed certain ideas regarding foods, family, ways of acting or reacting that differed from those of my peers and family. These were elements of the counterculture and identity crisis happening in me simulta-neously. Evidence of differences was also clear in the academic sphere. For example, during an I.Q. test, when I was asked who Robert Frost was, I did not know, but I loved poetry. Maybe if they asked who Dante was, I would have known. My Anglophone, Francophone friends could date at an early age with their parents' blessing. For Italian teenage girls, dating conflicts with

Italian family values. Furthermore, Canadians of Italian origin also perceive disability and the role of woman differently than our Anglophone\Franco — Canadian counterparts.

The value systems of each group has an impact on how each group defines 'facts'. For a young woman who is just beginning to identify factual realities, these divergences can be contentious. For me, it was very confusing to see how English, French Canadians and Italian define the same facts differently.The confusion of dual or triple values was so strong that I often risked not knowing what I, myself, really wanted. Indeed, like others in the same situation, I abided by one choice or another. I can't help but wonder what makes certain values prominent? Who creates the values and what purposes do they serve? In the decision-making processes, do I really choose or are choices made for me?

Years later, as an employment counselor working in an agency for people with disabilities, I found it imperative to encourage and increase ethnic participation in the agency. Here the cultural bind manifested itself as my employer and co-workers scrutinized my motives, and they ridiculed me for my passion regarding the issue. "Italian passion" as they called it. In addition, I spoke Italian with those clients who felt more comfortable in that language. This action was like adding rain and hailstorm to the slippery-slopes of a linguistically divided Quebec. Later still, when I became Quebec'srepresentative for DAWN Canada, my Italian background remained an issue. Some federal bureaucrats felt that I was of the wrong linguistic group to representQuebec. I remember asking one of them: "Why am I from the wrong ethnic group? I am from the same country as Senator Rizutti." The Senator was the only Italian senator from Quebec. The difference (as I perceive it): he was rich, non-disabled, and a man.

Being of a cultural minority group one is often compelled to perform simple life tasks by someone else's standards. These standards may be either those of your minority culture, which go against the flow, or those of the majority, which conflict with the minority way of doing things. Then we have multi-cultural policies whose practical purpose, I have yet to understand. What good are these to the ethnic teenage girls who cannot attain post-secondary education, equal employment opportunities or decent pay? These young women are, on one hand, ridiculed by peers for doing things differently and not assimilating. On the other hand, their families punish them for attempting to integrate and assert themselves in a new culture. In the Canadian working class, being Italian is a political gamble. For me, it never did work. I like being Italian, and I do not want to give up that part of me.

But like the year that has four seasons
Do all inequities have their reasons?

Curaggia

The "inveterate cultural state" keeps the same view of disability that the Italo-Canadian first generation brought with them when they immigrated. Thus, through 1970 and 1980, the perception of people with disabilities, in the Italian community, reflected an understanding of disability rooted in the Italian 'mind set' of the 1940s, 1950s, and 1960s. At that time, everyone used the word "ammalato" (sick) to refer to disability.

We all internalize socially transmitted ideas to varying degrees. Some ideas expressed in specific words, influence the way we think and this thinking in turn shapes our actions. Given that there is no equivalence for the term "disability" in our Italo-Canadian community, the majority of first generation Italo-Canadians still call people with disability ill or sick. In fact today, the Italo-Canadian media still uses words such as "bambini malati" (sick children) when in English the reported expression is "children with disabilities."

Personally, I had a few mortifying encounters with people who run services in the Montreal Italo-Canadian community. As a college student, I applied for a summer job at La casa d' Italia. I recall the cold and piteous look in the eyes of the man who said, "no," to me. During our conversation he kept his eyes focused on my left side, (I have hemi-dystonia, a disorder that produces spasticity). This experience repeated itself in three other Italian service agencies. I succeeded in finding work in mainstream service agencies, and there I tried to service people of Italo-Canadian community in their language. My community would not hire me directly. They hired people with my same academic background, but not me. I assumed that my disabilities kept me from serving my community. Therefore, I quit applying for work in the Italo-Canadian community.

Italian and Canadian cultures share the medical rehabilitation points of view about disabilities. That is, both believe that either, one finds a cure for the 'problem' or that the disabled person must integrate into society with as little help as possible from any technical aid. In addition, people with disabilities need to achieve the appearance of being non-disabled without assistance, despite the physical or psychological consequences to him/herself.

My mother had moved to Canada hoping for a cure for me. Immigrant children with disabilities often have to become self-advocates, because their parents are unfamiliar with the language and customs of the new country. As well, often parents of disabled children are far too overwhelmed by their biases and their own guilt about disabilities. Consequently, they cannot fight the new, unfriendly and over-extended system.

The way we act or react, is cultural to some extent. However, the ways in which we respond, act or react, can also be sub-cultural. Living with a disability in a world not equipped for it creates difficulties on a daily basis for most people. Most of us learn somehow to get around these difficulties by finding creative ways to accomplish the same tasks.

One of the greatest things that happened to me in my twenties was coming across the disabled consumers' movement/Independent Living movement. This movement advocated a progressive point of view about people with disabilities. It validated the view that as people with disabilities, we know our needs best and that we have the right to self-determination. Through this movement I learned to redefine both the term and notion of "sickness" instilled in me by the Italo-Canadian culture and as well as by the medical model (Enns, H. 1981). I no longer viewed myself as something bad and diseased that needed to be cured, or for which I had to apologize.

Through the consumer/Independent Living movement, I began to talk about my disabilities as a state of being, which is different from what society accepts as "normal." With further personal growth and political under-standing about disability, via social model (Oliver, M. 1996). I began to differentiate impairment — parts of me that had limitation due to biology — from disability barriers caused by socio-economic inequity and disabling environments (e.g., too many stairs, no elevators, biased attitudes and socially promoted myths.)

Identity crises are part of a young adult's life. For me, as a woman with disabilities from Italian background the crisis was multifaceted. The changes in my self-perception shook up my parents' realities about what I wanted and who I was becoming. I no longer wanted to play the medical model game of trying one experimental pill after another.

The view of disability promoted by the medical\Rehabilitation Model is an example of the non-disabled culture's imposition of its values on people with disabilities. Lack of accommodations and understanding by the non-dis-abled persons constitutes handicapism.* In looking at physical limitations and culturally imposed norms, I have learned that most often it is the non-disabled cultures and its imposed norms that create handicappism. The dominant culture demands that we jump every hoop without questions. The only way to surpass these barriers, I have concluded, is to ignore them. One needs only to learn to differentiate between the cultural norms, and the non-disabled norms.

> Then like the sun that shines from between the clouds
>> One's self-determination is awakened aloud.

The Women: Season 3
Very early in my life, I started reacting to socially-imposed differences between genders. I recall wondering why all those who had decision-making power over me were men. At the time I expressed it as, "All the people who

Curaggia

tell me what to do are men: doctors, priests, my uncles." My dad, who I barely knew, worked in Canada while we lived in Italy until I was eleven.

Biological factors influence the primary role of the Italian and Italo-Canadian women of my generation. Our grandmothers grew up under Mussolini, who praised and rewarded women for childbearing. Those generations of Italian women put aside the fight for the rights to vote and to serve the nation (Greenspan, K. 1996). These women internalized what the regime wanted them to learn and in turn taught their daughters that their role was to produce future generations. Our mother's, like our grandmothers, believed that their roles were that of having children and being homemakers. This notion became part of the "inveterate cultural state" that came with women who immigrated. However, once they arrived here, economic reality forced most of them to work. Most women could only work, in factories, as housekeepers and at jobs consisting mostly of unskilled labor. This meant that they were underpaid and most of them had to endure humiliating experiences in silence. After eight to ten hours of work at their paid jobs, they went home to do housekeeping as was culturally expected of them.

Some, like my mother, did not join the labor force. They stayed home and took care of their children, as well as children of relatives' and friends. The views held by these women, more than those of others, remained frozen in the yesteryears. The motherland as well as adoptive land neglected their needs, hopes, and frustrations. As a result of their isolating circumstances, they barely learned the languages of the land and rarely integrated into society. Nonetheless, these women contributed to the wealth of both the motherland and the adoptive nation. They made sure that we the children learned our native language and customs, as well as the official languages of this land. They also ensured that somehow most of us earned university degrees. These women's concerns are not part of the Canadian Women's Movement's agenda, and the Ethnic Women's Movement cannot find the time to help them. They are like autumn, everyone relies on them to adapt themselves from one type of weather to the next but all soon forget.

> As we go, from the summer's sunshine to winter's snow
> They protect us, always from the wind that blows.

The Disabled Women's Thunderstorm: Season 4

Women with disabilities are members of two socially disadvantaged groups, disabled and women. The social roles assigned to these two groups are concurrently pejorative. Society assigned passive roles to both non disabled women, and to persons with disabilities.

Although women both in Italy and of Italian origin in Canada have been successful in all spheres of life, their accomplishments are not considered on par with those of men. To avoid misconstruing the issues of women with disabilities from Italian background living in Canada, one must analyze these components one by one. At first glance, one may assume that there are no differences between the issues of disabled men and that of women with disabilities, and those of non-disabled women. This view point, would be like looking out the window in April, and assuming that the sunshine means a warm day; only to step outside and find it to be stiffly cold.

Women with disabilities make up the highest numbers of the unemployed and the lowest paid at all economic times. Statistics show that in Quebec, among women with disabilities of working age 81% had a yearly income below $15,000. Some 34% lived under the poverty line (OPHQ,1996). Similar statistics can be found for women with disabilities in other parts of the world. The system has failed to allow these women socially-acknowledged roles. For men with disabilities this differs since, historically, their role was that of providers. So, when men become disabled, both the rehabilitation system and society in general are better prepared to provide them with a job.

There are two contradictory misconceptions about women with disabilities. On a personal level, like most women with disabilities of my generation, I have heard both. Some people including professionals, on the one hand, would suggest that we find a man and get married. Others would, candidly suggest that marriage, romance, sexuality of any kind and motherhood, were not dreams that we should pursue. Confused? So were most of us.

Prior to 1980, the academic world had not theorized on the effects of womanhood and disability to explain what seemed unanswered by one or the other on its own. Still today, disability theories with an understanding of women-centered issues are relatively unknown in the social sciences. Furthermore, feminist theories of disability as proposed by a few feminists with disabilities are "avant garde." None of these theories however, are inclusive of the 'triple jeopardy experiences' of women with disabilities from ethno-racial backgrounds.

Our Italo-Canadian family and community gave us some rather ambiguous and pejorative messages about our physical reality. These messages were very different from what non-disabled girls were getting. True, for the most part, we were not subjected to overt sexist stereotypes, but we had dosages of paternalistic comments about our appearance. Paternalism, unlike racism and sexism, appears a gentle and "stainless" form of power play. Whenever, teenage girls with disabilities rebel they are labeled, ungrateful and their punishment ranges from isolation to not having their immediate needs met. When girls\women with disabilities complain about paternalism, (i.e., having people do for you more than you want) no one listens or understands how this can affect one's dignity. This is a very ambivalent situation. For how can you fight those who claim that they are doing things "for your own good?"

Maybe with all good intentions, our families overprotect us and set rules for what they thought were "our own good." The clash came nonetheless, for once we grew up, we found ourselves having to fight handicappism, cultural norms in addition to social norms thus, the challenges tripled.

To understand ourselves, those of us from ethnic backgrounds living realities of being women with disabilities, we must peel off the three layers of social and cultural norms. Thus, every time I attempt to sort out my experiences: as a woman of Italian background with several disabilities and limited resources, I feel overpowered by an "emotional hurricane."

Internalized oppression causes self-doubt. Women with disabilities of ethnic background, experience this both within the family, and in the society. These oppressive conditions are imposed by social rules and reinforced by individuals in position of authority. One such example is the suggestion that one must move out of the parents' home at a certain age. Italian customs are that women should stay home until they get married. These norms were indefinable for women with disabilities. When receiving counseling at the rehabilitation center, the questions of living arrangements always pop-up like a rainy day. In my personal experience, if I would say that it's OK for me to stay at home somehow, the assumption would be that I stayed due to ethnic or religious coercion. No one ever accepted that some of us made the decision to stay at home to pursue other goals. This is not to say that the merger of Italian values and economic needs does not play a role in the final decision.

Many Italian and Greek women with disabilities that I know live in their parents' home for various reasons. This situation could become contentious. Immigrant parents, who overprotected their daughters due to gender and disabilities, suddenly find themselves confronted by women with a will of their own. Consequently, conflicts arise.

At a DAWN Montreal meeting, a Greek woman, who lived with spina bifida, and was a few years wiser than most us, gave us the best of all advice. She said, "Fight with your parents on some issues, like your autonomy, make sure you win these arguments. You let them win nother ones. The key is that you always decide which arguments you win, and which ones you let them win. As for the non ethnic people that annoy you, let them think what they will!" This blended advice avoids thunderstorms in and out of families.

To survive architectural, technical, and attitudinal barriers, women with disabilities must become strong, self — determined and sometimes aggressive. They must identify their realities for themselves. In the 1990's through my feminist consciousness, I started wondering how and if the description of the independent women's choices stated by Simone de Beauvoir's, was applicable, to me? The women's movement has taught me that there are choices.

Yet, if I have the choice of many seasons
Why would I choose only one, and for what reasons?

La Piazza

In Italy, la piazza, is an open space where people meet. There are a multitude of people and a variety of ideas, creating a human mosaic. I vividly remember all kinds of different people in the piazza of our town, where I grew up as a child. This merger of opinions would sometimes start political and personal arguments, and other times, these old political and personal arguments would intertwine and find solutions. I am a bit like that at this time, with interrelated parts, contradictions, and different layers of reality. My personal and political realities are intertwined: as a woman living with disabilities, I am to be passive and grateful for everything people do for me. The disabled person in me must be strong, determined, and often aggressive to surpass the barriers.

The messages, passed down to Italo-Canadian of my generation are equally contradictory: work hard, reach for the sky, be gracious, but be careful not to overpass those of the English and French groups. You are still the immigrant's child. Your leadership qualities must be those of subordinates.

Feminism tells me that as a woman, I must be independent strong and self reliant. The old socially predominant medical model promotes the same idea. It further stresses that the non-disabled world will be more receptive if I do it on my own. In reality, people living with disabilities know that disability makes us interdependent on others, and on technologies. The only way we can be independent is by acquiring the socioeconomic means that allow us to be independent. All these components are so paradoxical. Then of course there are the other questions. How is it for Italian women with disabilities? What must I give up to earn the power to make choices?

All these clouds hide the sun that I so much would like to see.
But when the sun finally shines, what will it mean for me?

I am not sure that there is only one answer. However, from Feminist stand point theory I have learned that everything in life is continuously changing, nothing including choices, are static. This brings us back to the dialectical question as to whether society reflects onto us it's pre-determined image or whether we mirror out into it a careful view of how we wish it to see us. For me, the question remains one of interrelated relativity. This is like the year with all seasons in place. The constellations that make up the woman with disabilities from Italo-Canadian background remind me of a multicolor rainbow. These rainbows are like the one I used to see in the piazza with all colors emerging simultaneously and at the same time each of them remaining distinctive.

Curaggia

* *Handicappism*: A set of assumptions and practices that promote the differential and unequal treatment of people because of apparent or assumed physical mental or behavioral differences (Bogdan and Biklen, 1977: 14).

References

Bogdan, R., and D. Biklen. Handicappism Social Policy (1977, March/April, 14-19).

Enns, Henry. *Canadian Society and Disabled People: Issues for Discussion Canadian Mental Health* (1981) 14-17.

Greenspan, Karen. *Timetable of Women's History: A Chronicle of the Most Important People and Events in Women's History.* Toronto: Simon & Schuster, 1996.

Maggio, Rosalie. *The Bias Free Word Finder: A Dictionary of Nondiscriminatory Language.* Boston: Beacon Press, 1991.

Oliver, Michael. *Understanding Disability from Theory to Practice.* New York: St. Martin Press, 1996.

Offices des Personnes Handicapées du Québec. *Potrait socio-économique des femmes ayant des incapacités: Collections statistiques.* Drummondville, Quebec: Offices des Personnes Handicapées du Québec, 1996.

olive story #4

Vittoria repetto

```
sophomore year
a group of kids at the next table
   talking about puerto ricans
   don't shave their armpits
              their legs
   tufts of hair under nylons
i'm fresh back from italy
  my cousins
        young women
        don't shave either
        only bad girls
              puttane
                 shave
```

Americanization

Elizabeth Palombella Vallone

The little girl with the long Italian name who began school speaking her parents' native tongue is now a well-educated suburban matron married to a prominent executive. She and her standard all-American family of one son and one daughter live in a cavernous colonial in Westchester County. She is employed as a teacher.

Things hadn't always been this way. I remember when her parents, three siblings and she were all stuffed into a four-room apartment in Hoboken, New Jersey. This is where she began, let us say, her "Americanization."

How dutifully she studied and learned her lessons at St. Columba's School. Along with her ABCs she was taught that her name, Serafina, would not do. So that first week of school, she became accustomed to the name Sara, just as her sister, Filomena, had become Phyllis the year before. Sara was a bright girl and usually managed to get placed in the "A" group, the above-level section of the grade. That is, except in seventh grade.

I remember what happened very well, because I was seated in the first seat of the first row and could hear the entire discussion taking place in the doorway. We were all sitting in Sr. Maura Anthony's homeroom when the principal and Mrs. O'Brien came to the door. It seems that little Kathy O'Brien had been placed in the "B" group instead of the "A" group this year. Mrs. O'Brien was very upset — and well she should be. Everybody knew the "A" group was for the bright students and the "B" group was for the WOPS or dullards.

Sr. Maura explained that she already had forty students in the class. There was nothing she could do. She didn't even have a spare desk for Kathy to sit in. As Mrs. O'Brien's complexion turned redder and redder she glared at the principal, Sr. Assumpta. The principal sputtered, "There must be a way!" Exasperated, she pushed past Sr. Maura Anthony. As she stepped into the room, we sat there with our hands folded, staring straight ahead. Her eyes methodically scanned the rows of children until Sr. Assumpta's gaze came to rest on Sara. Suddenly a resolution to the problem came to her. She swiftly turned on her heel and squarely faced Sr. Maura. Pointing to Sara, Sr. Assumpta said, "That girl over there, the one by the window, move her to Mrs. Carroll's class. Kathy will be in here from now on." That was the only year Sara was placed in the "B" group that I can recollect, and we go way back together.

One summer day, she invited me to a Sunday picnic with her family. "By the sea," Sara said. I couldn't wait! Anything to get off the hot, grimy streets of Hoboken. I kept imagining all the barbecued hot dogs, potato salad, cole slaw and dill pickles. Can you believe her mother brought eggplant parmesan and meatballs instead. She heated them on the GRILL! I couldn't believe it. There I was, all day long, dying for potato chips and all her mother kept giving me was a banana. I told Sara her family was weird. My parents had warned me they were R-E-A-L Italian.

Don't misunderstand me, my family is Italian too, but not like these people. We were Italian-Americans! My father even fought in WWII and no one spoke a foreign tongue in my house. I don't know exactly where in Italy my family came from. Come to think of it, when nonna died the obituary mentioned she had immigrated from a place called Giovinazzo. My mother assured me that it was somewhere in Northern Italy. I guess that's why my nonna spoke perfect English and cooked American food.

Sara's family ate octopus, squid, and clams. For dessert every night all they ever had was fruit and nuts. I was afraid to eat in their house. Imagine what they might put in the ragu — yuk! Anyway, even if I would be able to get through the meal, I couldn't live without my pretzels with ice cream for dessert.

I'm sure Sara does not eat squid anymore. She married "an Irish" you know. He's a very successful stockbroker. You should see her. She wears designer clothes now instead of those outfits her mother used to make. No more homemade stuff for her. Her husband laid down the law early.

For her first wedding anniversary they threw a big party. Sara's mother gave her a sewing machine for a gift. She said it would come in handy. Well, her husband made it perfectly clear that he could well afford to purchase his wife clothes and curtains. There would be no homemade goods in his home. Over the years he provided for her and their children handsomely. At least they always looked great, whenever I saw them, which became more and more seldom.

This year during Labour Day, I happened to see Sara walking up Third Street as she was returning from the "Muffie" Feast of La Madonna dei Martiri. Sara's family was "Muffie." That's what you call immigrants from Molfetta, Italy. Their three-day feast dedicated to La Madonna dei Martiri has been held in Hoboken since the beginning of the century. "Muffies" hoist a statue of the Madonna on their shoulders and parade it around town.

I used to enjoy the feast and seeing lower Hoboken festooned with ribbons and lights. I especially liked the food stalls, with sausage with peppers and zeppoles, playing the wheel of fortune and having my palm read by the mechanical gypsy. They even set up a stage and singers would perform. One year Julius LaRosa sang or maybe it was Lou Monte. I wonder if they are "Muffies" too? This one opera singer would sing a song called Granada every year. I guess it is some place in Italy, because the crowd always seemed to like it.

This year a little Irish fife band lead the procession which was smaller than previous years. Thank God too! The columns of matrons carrying lighted candles and wearing thick blue ribbons with a gold medallion around their necks would stretch the length of a city block. They would be followed by rows of first communicants, a large band dressed in black, the representatives of the town council and an assortment of soccer club members.

But enough about "Muffies," let me get back to Sara. As I said, she was coming up Third Street so I invited her to sit on the stoop and catch up on old times. My husband, Joe, had just gotten back with lemon ices and I offered her one. She seemed to like it so much. You would think I gave her something special.

As we sat reminiscing, she rambled on and on about exploring her roots and having visited Molfetta for the first time. She revealed her regret at having been away from the feast all these years. She hadn't attended since she had gotten married. She was saddened that the procession was a third its previous size and that it was no longer full of vibrant and proudly strutting Molfettesi. Instead, she described it as a hodgepodge of meandering adults with a smattering of youngsters dispersed among small groups of octogenarians.

She exclaimed tearfully, "How could it be that an Irish fife band lead the procession?" Then she really began to exaggerate. "It's all my fault! How could I have cast off my heritage just because I married. How could I, and the hundreds like me in my generation, have contributed to the gradual erosion of a beautiful tradition." I told her to lighten up. "What was the big deal? You're American now!"

The Story in Her Bones
(Anna Camilleri)

My Mother Mine

Francesca Roccaforte

Violent, Sad and Drugged
She walks in rhyme to the dirges inside her head
Bitter and Self-Denied she screams
"Going to the hospital is like going to the funeral home...put that camera
down!"
My Mother Mine
Her lives flash like pages in a book
Abandoned and pacified by her men
Giving them life, they take her beauty
My Mother Mine
Losing her fire, I watch her glow
She teaches me what I need to see
I silently *watch* with *one eye above*
Virginia is My Mother Mine

This photograph is part of a body of work that I produced while in art school in N.Y.C in the mid 1970s. Photographing my mother when she was having her second major "nervous breakdown" was dangerous but yet revealing. It taught me about my own sanity/insanity, my own theatrics and melodrama. As serious as crazy may seem, my mother taught me how unproductive and self-indulgent it can be. Taking these photographs was like therapy for me. Later on when she was able to look at them, she realized what had happened to her and me. She was once a beautiful and vivacious woman caught in the web of Italian co-dependency, alcoholism, and violence. My mother never recovered from these breakdowns and spent the next thirteen years in severe depression and died at the age of 62 in 1988. She did however apologize to me for taking out her frustrations on me and scapegoating me in the family. She realized I was her ally, friend, and only loving daughter in her circle of women-hating men.

The Story in Her Bones

Veal

Anna Nobile

Every few months we would go the *macello*, the slaughterhouse. Our families believed in bulk buying, so my mother and her sister, Claudia, would split the cost and buy a cow. Not just a side of beef, the whole animal.

We always went to the same place, Casa del Vitello, located just downwind of the stockyards and the Swift packing plant. There were many such 'casas' in that area catering to the European taste for selecting your own carcass, but my mother and my aunt enjoyed an open flirtation with Tony, the proprietor. He was an immigrant from a village not far from where they'd grown up, and the three of them would talk about old times and all the people they'd known.

Tony was tall, fair-haired, with large welcoming brown eyes and fine long lashes. One of his front teeth was missing, putting a black spot on his easy smile. Whenever we came into the store, he always treated us as though we were his best friends, called zia Claudia and my mother his favourite customers, no matter who else was standing around. He'd usher them to the front of the line regardless of the dirty looks thrown his way by other loyal customers. Tony had charm and a warmth and hospitality that reminded his mostly immigrant clients of their old home. He always gave me and my cousin Flavia lollipops, and when we got older, chewing gum, and he always threw in a couple of free chickens for my mother and zia Claudia.

The hottest, most humid, August on record was the last time I went to the slaughterhouse. Flavia and I had survived our first year of high school, though I'd met with more success in the classroom. Flavia's interests had turned to boys and her best subjects were accessorizing and eye shadow application. She used to wash her make-up off in the school bathroom before going home, but I grew impatient with her, constantly having to wait so we could walk home together. Finally, one day I dared her to go home with her blush and eye shadow still on.

"You're old enough to start making your own decisions," I said, using my English teacher's favourite line in her attempt to advance us toward maturity. "Stand firm and people will respect you," I continued, not believing a word of it, and not for one moment thinking Flavia would take me seriously.

To my amazement and subsequent guilt, she looked at me and said simply, "You're right, Sonia," and led the way, while I wondered what the outcome would be.

She was beaten, as I'd suspected. Not severely, we were older now, but badly enough to remind her, and me, that what is a sign of growing up and sophistication in one setting, is still taken as evidence of loose morals and prostitution in another. No one, not even Flavia, blamed her father for his outburst.

"It's just the way he sees things," she explained. "He believes its for my own good."

So when Flavia and zia Claudia arrived at our door, already puffing and sweaty from their climb up the hill in that stifling heat, there wasn't a trace of cosmetics on her face.

There were the usual ceremonies over whether coffee should be consumed before the trek to the slaughterhouse, but zia insisted it was too hot to really enjoy an *espresso*, so we headed off. We walked in pairs, Flavia and I retracing the route we had travelled so many times since childhood. We ducked into Jan's corner store to buy chocolate popsicles for the walk ahead.

"Don't be long," my mother warned.

"We'll catch up," Flavia said.

"*Alla svelta*," zia agreed.

"But Ma!"

"*Basta parole!* You know why I don't want you in there."

We knew. Jan was supposedly having an affair with Renzo, the baker across the street, but nobody had any proof, it was all just talk. Renzo was married with two kids and didn't live in the neighbourhood anymore. When my father teased him about his new reputation, Renzo only smiled secretly, but neither confirmed nor denied the rumours.

My father laughed as he told my mother about it.

"*Non vedo*," my mother began. "What is so funny?"

"*Renzo con quella donna*," he chuckled. "I didn't think his wife ever let him out of her sight."

"*Pauvera*," my mother sighed sympathetically at the mention of Renzo's wife. "Its the fault of that woman!" she said with distaste. "She should control herself. *Putana*."

"Flavia says Jan called Renzo a fat pig not good enough to lick her shoes," I offered, hoping to get in on the conversation. "*Perche*," I wanted to know, "would she sleep with him if she doesn't even like him?"

"Ha!" my mother exclaimed. "Just trying to cover her tracks, *sporca Canadese*." She stopped short suddenly and seemed to be thinking something over. "*Ma guarda*," she said, giving me a whack on the head. "Mind your own business. You're too young to know about such things." My father only laughed.

The neighbourhood wives tried to stay away from Jan's store but it was the closest one where milk and cigarettes and last minute groceries could be bought without having to drive to the supermarket. I didn't know any mothers who would buy anything there anymore unless it was an emergency. Even then, they usually sent us kids.

Jan always gave you the feeling she couldn't wait to get you out of her store. She hated it when we went in to look at magazines or if we took too long picking out the things on our mothers' lists. It was hard to imagine her in a passionate embrace with Renzo. I always pictured her struggling to get away from him so she could breathe or pulling away as soon as it was over to have a cigarette.

"You watch too many soaps," Flavia said.

I paid for the popsicles while Flavia studied some women's magazines, looking for ideas.

"Ideas on what?"

"On what to wear this fall, dumb-dumb. Your clothes say something about you," she advised, giving me the once over.

I compared. She was wearing a light blue, knee length skirt that showed off her waist and a pale yellow tank top that revealed a promising cleavage. I was wearing the usual denim cut-offs and white t-shirt with Mickey Mouse on it.

"It's okay," she said generously, catching my eye. "Its summertime and its hot."

She put the magazine back on the shelf and, making sure Jan didn't see her, tip-toed up into the back row and pulled out a *Playboy*.

"Flav!" I hissed, alarmed. "What're you doing?" I turned and saw Jan ringing up Mr. Foster's milk and eggs. "You'll get us in trouble!"

"Relax," she said coolly. "Look."

She flipped through the magazine slowly. The pubic area was of interest only because most of the women sported so much curly hair. I couldn't help it, but I was reminded of scouring pads. The few wisps I had grown were still fine and very straight. More important, though, were the breasts. Or so it seemed since they always got such attention in the magazines. They were like over-filled water balloons out of which came long jelly bean nipples.

"They're huge," I whispered. It didn't seem possible that either Flavia or I could grow so much — certainly not from the pudding lumps we were starting with. Our mothers weren't that big. Even Jan wasn't that big.

"There are exercises you can do," Flavia said.

"Do guys really like women like this?" I asked pointing to one woman whose tongue arched upward toward her nose, legs spread and breasts hanging.

"Well," she hesitated. "They don't want a slut."

"What about Jan? People say she's a slut and she doesn't look like this."

"My dad has ones where they show the men too and everybody is...touching each other and...making love."

"Really?"

She laughed at me. "Well what did you think?"

"No! I mean you father has magazines like this?"

She nodded. "I found them under his workbench with the old paint."

I could feel myself blushing and let Flavia think I was embarrassed by the pictures, but I was thinking of when I'd found some dirty magazines looking for sewing scraps for Home-Ec class. They were buried in the rag box in the garage. They showed men and women, sometimes three or four of them together, touching. It never looked like love to me. I never said anything because I didn't want anyone to think my dad was a pervert. But if they all looked at them, then maybe it was okay. Still, I didn't want to explain how I'd found them or that I knew what was in them. It was easier to keep quiet.

"Buy it or put it back!" Jan shouted at us. "No readin' in the store."

"We were just leaving, thank-you," Flavia called and slipped the *Playboy* behind some copies of *Seventeen*.

Back on the street we had no trouble catching up to our mothers, who plodded along, gossiping and exchanging news received from overseas. The heat of the concrete sidewalks penetrated the soles of our shoes, making the bottom of our feet burn, and the asphalt roads gave way slightly under our weight. The air was thick with moisture, like the bathroom after someone had showered. Only this was coarser because of the black, gritty smoke emitting from passing cars and trucks. As we neared the slaughterhouse, the air became heavy with the odor of overheated animals, manure, and what I imagined to be burning hides and blood. I'd often ask my mother what it was like in the back, where the cows hung, but her answers were vague and never told me what I wanted to know.

"Ten minutes to the abattoir," Flavia calculated, sucking on her popsicle. "We could de-coagulate by then."

"Abattoir? De-coagulate? Have you been reading the dictionary again?"

"Its a good way to learn new words."

"Who are you trying to impress?" I said laughing, "Because it ain't working on me."

"You really ought to pay more attention to yourself," she countered. "Then others might too." She let the sting of her words sink in. "I bet you don't even know what de-coagulate means."

"Its what's happening to your popsicle," I said as some of the sticky brown ice hit her foot and slid to the pavement.

We reached Casa del Vitello just before noon. As my mother opened the door of the shop a slab of refrigerated air hit us and the sawdust on the wooden floor swirled at our feet. The staff always looked so bulky since, even in summer, they wore sweaters under their blood spattered white coats and gloves with the fingers cut off to keep warm. My mother began praying she wouldn't catch a cold, zia joined in begging for protection from pneumonia. Flavia crossed her arms in front of her and motioned for me to do the same. I furrowed my eyebrows at her and she looked exasperated, then bulged her eyes out at me, looking in the direction of my chest. I followed her stare and saw that my nipples seemed ready to burst from my shirt. I blushed and quickly folded my arms over them hoping no one had seen.

"*Buon giorno, buon giorno paesani!*" came Tony's greeting from the doorway that led into the freezer area. "*Vengo subito.*"

My mother and zia began inspecting the specials of the day in the display cases. Tony went back into the freezer, his upper body visible through a thick pane of glass. Beyond him were the stripped, red and white bodies of countless veal hanging from giant meathooks, waiting to be chosen and cut to order. He seemed to be arguing with one of his employees, waving one blood smeared hand in the air. He began hitting the back of his hand into the palm of the other, quickly and repeatedly, causing blood to spit into the woman's face and chocolate coloured hair. Impatiently, he waved her away and when she turned, he slapped her behind. She looked back at him angrily, but he laughed it off. I looked away, ashamed at having seen something that was not meant for me.

Whatever he'd been upset over seemed quickly forgotten, since when he came out to the front counter, he was all smiles.

"*Come va? Come va?*" he asked, nodding his head for no apparent reason.

"Antonio," my mother said, tsking. "Haven't you put that tooth back in your head yet?"

"Oh, what for?" he replied, grinning broadly, showing the missing tooth. "Who would recognize me then? *Ma Signora,* answer me something," he leaned on the counter confidentially, putting his hands together as if in prayer. "Why do you always wait so long between visits, eh?"

Zia Claudia giggled. "*Ti piacherebbe,*" she began, "you'd like us to visit more often, would you?"

"*Sicuro,*" he replied, winking at me. "Who wouldn't want such lovely ladies to visit?"

"*Da vero?*" asked my mother, laughing. "Is it our smiles you miss?"

I snickered. "And our money," I said, meaning only Flavia to hear, but all the adults turned to look at me.

"Sonia Fedes Angelotti!"

My mother only used my middle name when she wished to scold me in public. 'Fedes' is a name peculiar to the region of Fruili, Italy, and means faith, but it is so ugly and abnormal a name, that's its use as punishment is especially effective.

I was quite red faced. *"Mi scusi, Signor Tony,"* I apologized as everyone waited.

"Di niente," he replied, straightening up, his manner suddenly business-like. "What can I do for you today? The usual?"

My mother glared at me, promising further punishment later. For the moment, the three of them nattered on in their native dialect, as Flavia and I looked on. Although it appeared I had offended him, Tony was trying to include me in the conversation. He winked and directed comments at me, and sometimes Flavia, as though he expected us to reply. Flavia, however, took an interest in the boy who was wrapping cuts of beef at the far end of the counter. Discreetly, she made her way along the display case, feigning interest in chicken livers and pigs feet.

"Your daughters are growing more beautiful everyday," continued Tony. "Becoming women like their mothers."

Zia heard this as a compliment, but my mother took it as an opportunity to go on about the difficulties of raising teenage daughters in the city.

Tony nodded sympathetically. *"Non si puo aver fiducia di nesuno,"* he warned. It wasn't possible to trust anyone anymore.

When it came time to head into the freezer to pick the cow, Tony invited me along.

I hesitated.

"Dai," my mother prodded, overlooking my previous misbehaviour. "Here's your chance to see the back for yourself." I followed her through the cold fog that surrounded the thick, insulated locker door.

On the other side was a close-up view of the carcasses, a healthy layer of fat covering them, the purply-blue *Grade A* stamp clearly visible. The freezer was a large warehouse of dead livestock hanging suspended from the ceiling, forming a maze of aging flesh. My mother walked on ahead, following Tony and asking his advice. I saw the woman with the chocolate hair and two others slip out the back door with their lunches. How could they eat when they'd been handling dead meat all morning? I lagged behind, repulsed yet fascinated. I tried to reconstruct the cows, to return to them their legs and feet and heads, but that made them more hideous to look at. That was like giving them an identity, a personality, like Delsey the Borden cow. But not like Delsey, because she was animated and cute, wore a daisy petal collar and told us to drink our milk everyday. These cows weren't even cows anymore. They were just beef. Baby beef. Baby cows that would provide us with dinners over the next six months.

Slowly, I put my hand out to touch one, just to discover what it felt like. But before I could do so, Tony appeared and took my hand.

"*Cosa fai?*" he asked quietly. I thought I was in trouble again, that I shouldn't be touching the meat.

"*N-niente,*" I replied. I wasn't sure if I was stammering from the cold or because something in his expression had frightened me. His eyes were suddenly sharp, focused. He seemed intent on something, as though he expected something of me. His chapped lips parted and I thought he would finally tell me what he wanted. Instead, they remained still, his mouth partly open, his grip on my hand tightening. Suddenly I knew, with the terrible certainty that comes from knowing a thing intuitively, I knew I was in danger. I looked around quickly — just in time to see my mother and zia slip through the mist and back to the store, rubbing their arms for warmth. There was nothing but row upon row of silent, hanging flesh without even eyes to witness what would happen.

Tony was not watching me, but looked only at my breasts with their still hard nipples. I started tugging at my arm and backing away, but he held fast and took a step forward to keep his balance. He twisted my arm and pushed me into one of the carcasses, its cold, plump surface slapping against me, knocking into another one, until three or four of them were swaying on their great hooks. Tony didn't seem to notice.

"*Cosa vuoi?*" I shouted at him, trying to keep from panicking. "Leave me alone!"

I looked toward the window where I could see my mother, between the rows of veal, chatting with someone up front, unaware of my shouts.

He smiled his jack-o-lantern smile. "You want to feel something, little girl?" he asked in a hoarse whisper, a voice so different from his usual cheerful tenor, that for a moment I thought it wasn't him. "Then feel this," and he thrust my open palm underneath his bloodied white coat, forcing me to feel his private part, long and hard, warm and slightly moist.

"No!" I cried. "*Basta!* Stop! *Auito!*" Still, no one heard.

I tried pulling away, but he gripped me tighter, telling me I was pretty and how I would soon be popular with the boys. I was horrified as he led my hand up and down, stroking him, still cooing compliments, then instructions. He set the rhythm, expecting me to keep it, Maybe that's what set me off: that he didn't doubt for one moment that I would do as he demanded or that I would do anything to stop him. I thought of my mother and zia Claudia, the way they flirted with him; of how we all thought of him as a good, kind man. That man was no longer here. In front of me stood a panting, red faced stranger, yet familiar, his trousers at his knees, one hand groping a veal for support, the other still clasping my hand, methodically leading it up and down, down and up, his head thrown back, waiting.

I didn't know how to get him to let me go. He was squeezing my wrist and hurting me. I tried punching him, wringing free, but he only held on tighter, more frantic and rough. I was afraid, afraid of what he might do. And

Curaggia

say. Was this "making love"? Would he tell people I wanted this and then they'd think I was a slut? I remembered how no one believed Jan was innocent even though she seemed to dislike Renzo and how everyone thought it was her fault — even my mother. I didn't want to be a slut, but I had to get away and had to get him to let me go.

I took up the pace. Gratefully and with a smile, he let go of my hand and I continued stroking him until he trusted me not to stop, his moaning growing more audible, white puffs of breath escaping him. Then I squeezed it as hard as I could — twisted and pulled, intending to hurt him as much as I could, to make him feel as small and ashamed as I did. His face contorted as it slid from surprise to pain. He bit his lip, and like me, stifled his instinct to cry aloud.

He fell to his knees. "*Vigliaco! Porco!*" I hissed at him between sobs. "You pig."

I stopped. Words were useless. I spit in his direction trying to get the taste of fear and disgust out of my mouth and left him there, crouched among the hanging veal, gasping for breath.

I wiped my hands, took a deep breath and went back, through the mist, where Flavia met me at the door with a broad grin. She didn't seem to notice anything different.

"Guess what?" she said, barely able to contain her excitement. "I've got a date for Saturday afternoon!" She sounded very proud of herself.

"Sonia!" my mother called. "*Dove eri?* What took you so long?"

Red Dress

Anna Camilleri

By the time Vierra was sixteen years old, she had nothing left to lose. She knew emptiness well and risk meant little. He pushed the door open at three o'clock in the morning, when her three younger brothers and mother were fast asleep. His belt, undone. His motivations, clear. As he had done since she was five years old, he came, with a broad grin running the width of his square face. Vierra lay still in bed, pretending to be asleep or dead or away somewhere. She became so good at going away that it didn't require much effort and really, she was no longer pretending. "Away" became a place where she spent most of her time. Separate from the rest of the world, and everyone in it.

That night, Vierra forced herself to stay in her body. To feel all the rage and fear that she usually kept hidden away. She forced breath and life into her bones. She had grown tired of being a prisoner; of the echo bouncing back, tired of the weight that bore down on her not only at night when everyone was fast asleep, but always.

He staggered in the doorway like a drunken bull and hesitated, as if to announce himself. She had witnessed this entrance many times. Sometimes she imagined him collapsing from sudden heart attack, or the chandelier falling, swiftly and efficiently cracking open his skull, or a lighting bolt striking him dead. None of this ever happened. Like clockwork; he appeared in her doorway, as he had done, three times a week for seven years. No catastrophe would stop him from coming; nothing had.

Vierra was long past wishing for her mother and brothers to hear. She had taken to sleeping with a kitchen knife, tucked safely between mattress and box spring. It had already been there for one year. No one would find it. She alone changed the sheets and made the beds. Vierra didn't intend to use the knife, in fact, she hadn't touched it since she hid it. That night, though, she needed to feel its cool steadiness in her shaky hands. He stepped toward her. Before she felt her feet on the ground, she was standing, poised and ready. He laughed.

As surely as she found her feet, she found her tongue, "I'll hurt you if you come any closer to me...you're not my father anymore," knife and shoulders pointed squarely, "I'll kill you."

For one long minute, they froze in a tableau. The silence, thick. He knew that Vierra was serious. She had never spoken back to him. Never so much as looked directly at him for fear of catching the back of his hand on her cheek. At the sight of his daughter, a fully formed woman, he reeled. He had been so sure that there was no fight left in her, that she would always be his little girl. He stepped back, "We'll see. Just remember - you're my ragazza. Remember whose roof you're under, Putanna." And with that, he left. She stared into the blackness beyond the empty doorway. From that night, Vierra lay awake, gripping the knife, just under the sheets. He didn't return to her room again.

* * *

One year later, age seventeen, Vierra married a young man named Philip. On their wedding night, she returned the knife to the kitchen drawer. No one had noticed its absence.

Within a year of marriage, she gave birth to a five pound, colicky girl, and two years later, a bright eyed boy. Vierra solemnly swore on her grandmother Rachaela's grave that no one would ever harm her children. And with that vow, the sea of silence grew.

* * *

1972. The cultural revolution was in full swing... free love, peace, sex, drugs, long hair and harmony. Vierra longed to experience life beyond her small Italian neighbourhood; beyond tragic family stories that felt like inevitable destiny; beyond her own story. She loved music and wanted to dance into the night, to forget the stories in her bones. Sometimes when Philip and the kids were asleep, she put on red lipstick, tuned into the the top forties, shut the lights off and spun the flashlight around. It was her own private disco, and she, the diva.

Vierra ironed her curly hair into long, straight tresses and peroxided it orange. She wore white go-go boots and mini skirts that made her shapely legs stretch out for days, but the revolution passed her by. Her new home was across the street from the house she had grown up in. Vierra continued to tend her mother's house; cook, clean, shop, manage the finances and avoid her father. The eyes of the whole neighbourhood were still on her. "Exactly what is a married Italian woman with kids, doing with those skirts and that hair? Dio mio!" There was always talk and the only things that would put it to rest would have been the Pope's death, suicide, or nun hood. The neighbourhood signoras sat on their separate porches, waved hello, and whispered over red geraniums in white planters. They fastidiously counted the days between Vierra's marriage and the birth of her daughter. According to Signora DiFrancesco, Vierra must have gotten pregnant, and then married to save face. Signora Rossi boasted a sighting of Vierra buying condoms. Signora

Perrino and Signora Di Matteo crossed themselves and kissed their rosaries. Vierra knew they were whispering about her and also knew that gossip's wind changed quickly and fiercely. Next week there would be a new scandal and she would be just another woman trying to make ends meet.

* * *

Vierra picked out defective chocolates on an assembly line that moved too fast. The job provided a regular pay cheque, she reminded herself. In the daytime after getting off shift, Vierra tended her children, napping before and after their lunch break.

While chopping vegetables, she listened to the radio and imagined wearing an expensive red dress and sipping scotch at her leisure. The DJ interrupted the countdown, "I have some shocking news people. We just received a bulletin. Elvis Presley died today at the age of forty-two..." Vierra was heart-broken. Tears fell onto the cutting board. Her son tugged at her pants to ask what was wrong she said "Mommy's ok. It's just the onions, they make my eyes water. Now go play. I'll call you when lunch is ready." Elvis was an army brat from a poor family, who had made it. Why couldn't he hold on? She kissed her kids good-bye, "Come home right after school...and don't talk to strangers. If your nonna comes to pick you up, give her a big kiss, but come straight home. I don't want you there alone. I love you. Be good." Vierra slept for a couple of hours, tidied the house and went back to work.

She punched in exactly on time, walked through the security gate and checked in her purse. Vierra was never late and she sure as hell was never early. Some of her co-workers arrived half an hour early and had coffee and donuts in the cafeteria. Vierra thought they were crazy- it was like being sentenced for twenty-five to life and showing up early to make a good impression. As far as she was concerned, her supervisors could kiss her sweet Italian ass. She wasn't planning on staying longer than she needed to. She worried though. She knew the factory was a trap. It paid better than most other shitty jobs.

Sometimes she spoke aloud on the line, sure that no one could hear her over the machine noise "Well, I'm not a fool. I know I'm spending the best years of my life in a *stinking* factory, but at least my kids'll be safe. What other choices do I have? If I worked day shift the kids would need to go somewhere for their lunch break — they would go to my mother's house and my father would be around because he's always around- drinking in the cantina. What would I say to my mother? "Ma, I'm sorry but I can't leave my kids here because your husband messed with me for seven years while you were sleeping." Oh god, I'd rather slash my wrists than say those words to *anyone*. And what would I say to Philip? "Philip, I forgot to tell you about

Curaggia

my miserable childhood and that's why I hate my father and that's why I don't want the kids anywhere near him — OK?"

At the end of each shift, Vierra took off her cap, washed up and applied some lipstick. Then she'd stand in the long line with all the other workers and wait for her turn at the routine security check. On the bus ride home, Vierra tried to stay as far away from the other passengers as possible; she was sure she smelled of chocolate and grease. She sat at the front, where the pink and lavender hair ladies usually were. Her body throbbed from toes to head. The driver scanned stations on his portable a.m. radio and settled on CBC. A crackly voice reported "Women rally at Queen's Park today for equality and choice..." Vierra nearly jumped right out of her seat. She mumbled quietly,"Who do they think they are — talking about equality? Bet none of them work in a factory. And they probably all say 'Eye-talyin!' Sisters...my ass. Liberation in what...a burning bra? My bra is the only thing that holds me together on a Monday. They should step into my sweaty boots for a day..." The driver chuckled and looked over at Vierra, "They're probably all dykes. They should go live on an island, eh?" Vierra said nothing. It was her stop.

When Vierra quit the chocolate factory, her daughter, Mary, was seventeen years old. The same age that she had been when she married. They couldn't talk for longer than a minute without it turning into a screaming match.

"Mary, don't dry the dishes with that towel. I used it to wipe the counter. Sit down." Vierra pats the chair. "Do you want some espresso?"

" No, I need to go out." Glancing furtively at the clock.

"Just sit for a minute. Where are you going?"

Mary sits reluctantly. "A meeting." "What meeting? School?"

"I told you already — the International Women's Day committee."

"Oh, *that* group."

" It's a collective, mom."

"What do you mean? Isn't there a boss or leader?"

"No, it's a collective."

"Well, it sounds disorganized to me. No leader, no bosses- just a bunch of women talking. How do you get things done? Anyway, I'm worried about all the free work you're doing. Can't they pay you?"

"Mom, it's volunteer work. Feminist volunteer work."

"Feminist or not, it's work. Don't feminists need money? Don't you want to be paid?"

"It's volunteer. That means no money."

"I know what volunteer means. I used to volunteer on your school trips sometimes. Remember?"

"No."

"Oh come on Maria! That was only a few years ago. You're not old enough to be forgetting things."

"I forgot."

"Ok, so you forgot. Listen Mary, those feminists keep calling you to do more work...and they're rude. Don't even say hello. How much does it take to say hello? If they can find your number, they can find money. Or do they only pay the ones with six initials after their names?"

"Mom, you can't always be paid for what's important to you." Clipped, enunciated words.

"Don't you talk to me in that snotty voice...I've heard enough of that in the factory to last me a lifetime. And why do you think you have all that goddamn tim to run around doing free work anyway? Have you thought about that? I haven't asked you to pay any bills have I?" Trembling.

"No mom! You haven't asked me for a thing. I have it made. Life is a bed of red fuckin' roses."

"Don't raise your voice in my house!"

"You know what? I'm tired of being your pain in the ass. You won't need to make any more sacrifices for me 'cause I'm moving out!"

"You're what? Who do you..."

" You heard me. I'm leaving. I've been saving my money."

"Well leave then...let me help you pack your bags if you're so independent! Leave me!... Just like a Canadian. Go."

Mary stormed out of the room. Vierra forced herself not to chase after her. This wasn't what she had planned. Everything was supposed to be better. She didn't know what *better* would look or feel like, but she was sure it existed.

* * *

For as long as Vierra could remember, she had been wishing for the winning lottery ticket and praying for her father's death. She pleaded with God to take her father, but he lived, as did her memories. Vierra had one recurring dream that she dreamt both at night and during the daytime: Her father suffers a long and painful cancerous death. No one goes to the funeral because they know he is a terrible man. Not one tear is shed on his behalf. Everyone, even the priest, is happy to be rid of him. When the casket is lowered into the ground, Vierra is sitting on a stool, in a piano bar, wearing a gorgeous red, satin, designer dress- sipping scotch. Men make advances, offering to buy drinks. She says, "No thank-you, I'm buying my own drinks," and abruptly looks away, clearly ending the conversation. Very Sophia Loren, very in-control, very sexy.

Curaggia

* * *

True to her word, Mary moved out, one month later. Vierra didn't want to let her go, but wouldn't stop her. She wanted to hold her daughter and tell her how much she has always loved her. Vierra was afraid that if she started to talk everything would spill out indiscriminately. And where would she start? Would she tell Mary about the nights her father came to her room? Would she disclose that she has not had a good night sleep since she was five years old? No, it was too much to sew together on a thread. Too many years. Too many expanses of silence to bridge in a moment. Vierra watched her daughter walk away. Mary had become a beautiful, head-strong woman. The spitting image of her mother- eyes that flashed like lightning, an easy laugh that was all at once guarded and a walk that placed her firmly on the ground under foot.

Conserve

Stefania Vani

The Motorcycle

Toni Ellwand

The dust on the dirt road was shiny and wet. There had been a short rainfall that morning and now puddles on the road reflected the sun's bright golden rays. Steam was starting to rise from those puddles. The day would soon be too hot, in the small Sicilian village where Kristina lived with her mother and father. Kristina was six years old.

On this particular morning, Kristina's mother had just finished giving Kristina one of her bi-monthly baths. During the storm, she had sat Kristina down between her legs and with a sharp comb had painstakingly combed and separated her thick curly hair in search of lice. Periodically she would drag something from the root of Kristina's hair all the way down to the end of the strand. Then she would take whatever it was between two of her nails, rub them together and after a few seconds Kristina would hear a little grunt of satisfaction rise from her mother's throat.

After the lice hunt came the bath. Which was done in the everything tub. The everything tub was used for dishes, laundry, hair and baths. Kristina was too big to sit in it now so she would stand while her mother sponged her from head to toe. Afterwards, she would crouch down as far as she could while her mother filled a bowl with warm water and poured it over her entire body.

Now, the bath done and the sun out, Kristina was ordered to sit in a chair in front of their one room house. Kristina sat with her head leaning against the wall of her home, enjoying the morning sunlight as it dried her wet head. A towel was wrapped around her shoulders so that her wet hair wouldn't soak her clean, dry clothes.

"Psst, psst, Kristi, come here, come for a visit."

Kristina opened her eyes. It was the gruff voice of the motorcycle man. He lived a few doors away from Kristina and her family and to tell the truth people rarely saw him. He spent most of his time in his house, tinkering with his motorcycle and only when it grew dark did people hear the roar of his machine as he drove it out of his house and out to wherever.

He was a mystery. But he knew everyone on the street and everyone knew him.

"Kristi, vieni qui, come and look at my motorcycle."

Kristina was stunned by this invitation. No one had ever seen the motorcycle man's vehicle in broad daylight. But they had all wanted to. Especially the kids on the street. If she saw it first, she would be the envy of her gang. She could tell them all about it when they gathered together that afternoon, in the bombed out ruins of the old church, to play hide and seek. But she was a little bit afraid of the motorcycle man.

He looked like a little ferret, with dark greasy hair and slanting brown eyes. His old mother lived above him and he supposedly spent all his time taking care of her.

"Kristi, I'll give you some candy after. Come on, su!"

Candy! What kind? She wondered. Chocolate maybe or lemon candy with a soft syrupy filling. This was too much to resist. Standing up, and making sure her mother was nowhere near the open doorway, Kristina made her way up the still soggy street towards the motorcycle man's door. Something told her that her mother wouldn't like her going over there by herself. But she would only stay for a minute, look at the bike, memorize the colour, red she hoped, take some candy and run back home.

When she got to the door, it was ajar so she cautiously stepped inside. He must have been behind it because he shut it quickly behind her. Her heart started pounding and she thought maybe she should leave right away but then she saw the bike. It was standing right in front of her.

It was enormous and the silver chrome shone magnificently in the little light that filtered into that dark room. It was silver and blue, not red as she had hoped, but the blue was the bright blue of the sea. And the wheels were huge and pure black, with deep grooves cut into them. That bike took Kristina's breath away. She had never seen anything so majestic.

"Do you want to sit on it?" The motorcycle man asked. Kristina just nodded. She couldn't speak. He lifted her up and placed her astride the great monstrous thing. The seat was long and narrow and the black leather felt soft and pliant against her childish thighs. The motorcycle man smoothed her dress which had worked itself up close to her underwear. He pulled it down and straightened it out and stroked it down the length of her upper legs. Kristina wasn't sure about this but then he stopped. He seemed a bit out of breath.

"I'll get you some candy," he said in his low, gruff voice. He went into the darkness of the room and rummaged around somewhere and finally came back with something that looked like it had been sat on.

"Here," he said, handing her a piece of the flattened candy.

"No, grazie," answered Kristina in a little quiver of a voice. She was beginning to be afraid again.

"Go on, have it. It's good. Go on." He unwrapped it for her and forced it into her mouth. It was a caramel. As it started softening and melting in Kristina's mouth, she felt better.

"Why don't you play horsey on the bike. Just rub yourself back and forth. You'll like it." Kristina smiled. This was fun. She pushed herself back and forth on the bike, jumping a little up and down, the kid leather giving in to her assault. It felt so good.

Abruptly, she stopped. The motorcycle man was sitting behind her on the bike and he had put his hands around her waist.

"It's alright," he whispered, close to her ear. "I don't want you to fall." He popped another candy into her mouth. Her cheeks were now bulging with caramel. Hot caramel juice started trickling down the side of her lips. She wiped it up with her finger and licked it back into her mouth.

She felt the motorcycle man's hands on her buttocks. He was smoothing her dress again. Maybe it was time to go home. She tried to speak but her mouth was engorged with candy.

"Hold on to the handle bars for a better ride," he said. She grabbed onto the black rubber handle bars and started moving back and forth again on the bike. The rubbing against the leather had made her inner thighs all soft and warm and a trickle of hot liquid just like the caramel juice was oozing out of her fiore, her flower, as her mother had called it.

She'd felt moist down there, before, at night sometimes when her hand had secretly explored her inner being. But this was different. The back and forth movement on the motorcycle and the wetness that it created sent a pleasurable hotness all through Kristina's body. She loved the sensation so much that she increased her motion to the point where she was almost lost in a frenzied dance on that big blue bike.

Then, in the midst of her pleasure, she felt two fingers, quickly inserted under her loose cotton underwear and into her fiore. She froze. The fingers did not. They were not hurtful, in fact, their gentle exploration and insertion increased the secretion already started by Kristina's gyrations.

But then, she felt something else, something hard — a stick? It was trying to prod her from behind.

"Go up and down a little on the horse, Kristi, please." Something wasn't right. The motorcycle man's thick, caramel voice made the acrid juices in Kristina's stomach jump up into her mouth. The stick was prodding harder from behind and the fingers had become more insistent, less gentle.

"Ha...ha...ha!" The motorcycle man was breathing so hard. Kristina's ears were screaming. Her face, once flushed with pleasure was now burning with fear and pain. Her heart was exploding inside her small chest, her breathing had turned into the panting of an injured animal. She wanted to scream but she was frozen in fear. Meanwhile, the motorcycle man's body had turned into a roaring engine against her, the stick, the fingers, the breath driving at full speed.

"Kristina, Kristina!" Her mother's sharp commanding cries broke the spell and the motorcycle man came to a full stop.

"My mother. She's calling me." In the second of pause, Kristina some-how slid off the forbidding bike and ran for the door.

"Kristina, Kristina!" Came her mother's voice.

"Mama!"

"Sssh, Kristi, quiet please, here, here, have the candy, take it, go on. I'll open the door for you, but quiet, please."

Kristina nodded solemnly. She knew that she could never tell. He didn't have to say it. The motorcycle man opened the door slowly. She saw a slit of dirt road in the bright light of the day.

"Kristi, quiet, ha?"

"Si." He pushed her out with a sharp slap of her behind. She stood still for a second, blinded by the sudden blaze of sunshine. She reached for her towel, her comfort. It was gone. And this is when Kristina started to cry

Her Garden
Asks for Water

(Francesca Gesualdi)

I am the Woman Who Cries

Mary Russo Demetrick

I am the woman who cries
        in my sleep
I am the woman who wonders
        what makes me sad
I am the woman who works hard
        and at times   not at all
I am the woman who knits
        instead of writing
I am the woman who throws out
        what I knit   or
The woman who unravels what I knitted
        and rolls it into balls
I am the woman who always rewrites
I am
        the woman

Closing Speech for YOUNG, LOUD & PROUD

Boa

For Shannon Sallisbury avec amour

The following speech was given at "Young, Loud & Proud," a conference organized by young queers through LYRIC, set in San Francisco on July 13 and 14, 1996.

I picked up an announcement in the lobby the other day for something called "Young Tongues" and it got me thinking. I have seen some pretty nice young tongues here this weekend. The dignity and power of these tongues is not lost on me, speaking, signing, sparkling and spitting to the rhythms of our languages. Each one telling stories, survival tales, even glamour tips and gossip. There is a young butch or a fourteen year-old trainee adjusting their laughs to match their voices and this is how we begin to become heard. First, to those close to us. Young people in an adult world are rarely heard but to those close to us.

Few of the adult men of my very privileged origins as a euro-quebecoise, white, middle-class, able-bodied gentile, who control the majority of power have ever listened to young people talk to each other, particularly young people living in the margins, speaking in versions of our own languages. I assure you, they have not listened to a group as diverse as this one.

The dominant gay movement has been no different when it refuses to look at our lives with all their variations-including age and the difference this means in terms of services, needs, cares and power. It must ally itself with different movements yet to successfully combat things such as electric shock therapy and homophobic/transphobic family violence as child abuse, queer abuse and sometimes woman abuse and ableist and racist abuse. It must push itself to the front edge of the fight against poverty that oppresses many, many young queers, particularly the homeless, the HIV+ and some in the sex trade already stigmatized, particularly those who can't make it to wonderful places and events like this one.

It makes me think about how we are reinventing this struggle every second to keep each other alive. It is about stretching and learning to embody what this society sees as contradictions. It is about being allies to each other and traitors to the system of privilege. Ironically, I know, as I stand up here, I would say to other people of privileged backgrounds similar to my own, this sometimes means our silence is powerful when it leaves a space many times stolen by our people for more oppressed and silenced people to speak.

Now, I had all this on my mind as I flipped through a floral encyclopedia back home and fell on the definition for a flower called "Painted Tongue." It read: "this flower's tongue is veined or 'painted' in a contrasting and contradictory colour. It is planted in beds and borders. It is often used to replace other flowers that cannot survive a cold and harsh climate. It is shaped like a trumpet." In many ways, this is how I hear us. I think each tongue here is a contradiction to hateful governments and people. We are the contradiction that young people have a sexuality of our fucking OWN, that young people can claim desire that is neither white-washed nor parentally-acceptable. It is our own and we shock people by owning it despite adult exploitation, abuse and appropriation. In the words of Minnie Bruce Pratt: "If we dare claim our lives as our own, we must read all the poems we write with our bodies." This flower is planted in beds and borders. I think of the commonalities between beds (as in wherever you lay your head to sleep), borders and young queers-we are everywhere.

To us, beds and borders are sites of struggle and strength. Beds, when we are young can be the only secret place we acknowledge our queerness and internalize our hate for it. They can be places of passion and danger, places to lie in and be loved in, and places to lie in to recover-or maybe not to.

In beds, we tumble over borders, sometimes between bodies, across worlds. We take in. Sometimes borders are forced on us or broken. Abuse in and out of our communities exists and betrays us when these borders are trespassed. Then, there are the borders imposed. The borders where we are stopped and carded or tested. Sometimes we are asked to have sex to prove our queerness to gay adults or we are pressured to try heterosexual sex by straight people who whine; "All you need is a good dick!" These days, I have taken to answering, "what makes you think I don't have a dick of my own!"

These borders imposed between male and female as Leslie Feinburg points out, are viciously and violently guarded much like the colonial border between US and Mexico or between Us and Canada that cuts up the First Nations lands of the Iroquois into two provinces, one state and two countries. making these connections is necessary and cannot be the burden of only people many times oppressed.

And then, there are the fences known as borders. I have been told I sit on them by many people. There was the psychologist this year who said something to that effect as she ticked off "sexual orientation" on the diagnosis sheet. However, I have been called a "fence-sitter" many many more times by conservative gays and lesbians. This year, the queer youth group I facilitated led a purge of all bi and trans members. To these people, as a pansexual, I would say in the words of Rebecca Kaplan: "Your fence is sitting on me!"

Powerful people enforce borders until we plant our own, not necessarily as labels. We do not need to adopt Anglo eurocentric labels but it is one way. Calling ourselves "young and queer" is one way we have done that here.

This flower, like young queers, is planted in a climate cold and harsh-and survives. I look at this audience and we have so far survived. I know it hasn't been easy but we have survived.

This flower is shaped like a trumpet that blown with the breath of each person in this room would shatter the windows of the whitehouse and leave Jesse Helms, among others, gasping for breath.

Yes, imagine what we can do as YOUNG, LOUD & PROUD.

Curaggia

Blending "Literary" Discourses

Helen Barolini's
Italian American Narratives

Edvige Giunta

"Though she didn't know how to read or write, when it came to cooking she knew everything there was to know." (Laura Esquivel, *Like Water for Chocolate*)

"One could read the progress of her life in the spills of mysterious substances that now obliterated her favorite recipes.... this dripping and this dribbling had been Helen's way of making history." (Louise DeSalvo, *Casting Off*)

"If books did not tell me who I was, I would write those that did." (Helen Barolini, "Becoming a Literary Person Out of Context")

The scarcity of writings by Italian American women in 1979, the year of publication of Helen Barolini's *Umbertina*, places this novel in a problematic position with regard to issues of tradition, genre, and authorship.[1] In *The Dream Book*, an anthology of writings by Italian American women edited by Barolini and published in 1985, Barolini, assuming the role of the critic rather than the fiction writer, explores the issues underlying her own emergence as an Italian American woman author. In the long introduction to this book, she indicts a literary market that is blind and hostile to Italian American women:

> That Italian American women have been underpublished is undeniable; just as exclusionary, however, is that the few who are published are not kept on record and made accessible, even bibliographically, in libraries and in study courses. Not only do Italian American women writing their own stories publish with great difficulty ... but once in print, they must confront an established cadre of criticism that seems totally devoid of the kind of insight that could relate to their work. (44-5)

Although she does not include her own work in this anthology meant to legitimize the writings of the authors included, posing as a critic, Barolini adds another feature to the authorial persona that she has been painstakingly constructing.

In "Becoming a Literary Person Out of Context," an autobiographical essay published in 1986, Barolini refers to *The Dream Book* as an *"apologia pro vita mia"* (BLP 267), and maintains that "an Italian American woman becomes a writer out of the void. She has to be self-birthed, without models, without inner validation .... She is perceived as a stranger both to literature and in literature" (BLP 263). Barolini's defiant claim that, in the absence of books that would tell her how she was, she would "write those that did" (BLP 265), becomes especially poignant when one tries to define exactly what kind of writer Barolini is and to identify what niche she has created for herself in the literary market. Examining the interconnections between textual experience and extratextual elements in Barolini's work sheds light on the ways in which gender, genre, and ethnicity intersect in the process leading to the creation of her authorial voice. An intertextual analysis of Barolini's works, that weaves fiction and life, poetry and criticism, recipes and autobiography, will identify the forces shaping her development as an author while also pointing to the role played by discourses on ethnicity in the process of authorial self-fashioning.

A search for books by Barolini in a large bookstore in the northeastern U.S. proved fruitful, to my delight, since, besides Barolini's *Festa*, only one other book by an Italian American woman author was kept in stock (Dorothy Bryant's *The Kin of Ata Are Waiting for You*). But as I made my way to the Fiction and Literature section, the bookseller competently steered me towards another part of the bookstore, a more exotic one: "Cooking." Even bookstores, I thought to myself, have managed to keep Italian women in the kitchen. As I browsed through Helen Barolini's *Festa: Recipes and Recollections of Italian Holidays* (1988), I could not help thinking that there was something subversive about the presence of this book in a bookstore that had exiled Italian American women. Had she not written *Festa*, Barolini would not have entered this place.[2] And wasn't Dorothy Bryant's book kept in the Science Fiction section? Could it be that this was a decoy, a strategy for survival devised by Italian American women writers? Could it be that in order to survive Italian American women authors did not have to revise only the male literary tradition, as Adrienne Rich astutely advises *all* women writers to do,[3] but also to "revise" themselves — to hide, to disguise under anglo-sounding names or to turn to genres that seemingly have no direct connection with their ethnic tradition (science fiction) or that have more acceptable connections with that tradition?[4]

Criticizing Scorsese's *Italianamerican* (1974), Barolini argues that this autobiographical documentary offers yet another stereotypical representation of Italian Americans:

Curaggia

the scene opened on his mother and father at the food-laden table, eating; then he [Scorsese] directed his mother to go into the kitchen and show him how she did the tomato sauce. Doing the sauce, of course, is *the* metaphor for being an Italian American woman. (BLP 272)

Barolini rejects this oversimplified view of Italian Americans, alert to the fact that such a view is deeply ingrained in American culture.[5] Yet she writes *Festa*, a book of recipes that presents her as *the* Italian American woman "doing the sauce" rather than attempting to become a literary person. The title of her autobiographical essay, "Becoming a Literary Person Out of Context," clarifies the literary and autobiographical nature of *Festa*. "Context" is the key word. Barolini creates herself as an author "out of context," that is, because she has no context, she utilizes diverse spheres, even non-literary ones, as spaces for authorial expression. As domestic texts, cookbooks have always been an accessible genre to women, even Italian American women. This is one genre in which they are authorized: Marcella Hazan, Cathy Luchetti, Anna De! Conte, Biba Caggiano, Anne Casale, Viana La Place — women with Italian names make it in this specialized section of the publishing market.[6] And *Festa* fits the genre: the recipes are there to initiate aspiring cooks and refine the skills of experienced ones. But *Festa* speaks in other voices and languages that are at least as important, if not more, than the dominant voice of the experienced cook: from the autobiographical introduction to the introductory sections that combine accounts of the customs and festivals of Italy with more autobiographical tidbits, *Festa* strives to create a language and a story, moving beyond the declared purpose of the cookbook.[7]

   The genre of *Festa* is not new. Other cookbooks are complemented by subtexts, such as photographs, cultural histories, and biographical anecdotes.[8] Viewed in the "context" of Barolini's literary work, however, this book further problematizes her status as an idiosyncratic author — one who does not specialize. She is a novelist, a critic, a translator, a reviewer, an anthologist — *and* the author of a cookbook. Writing of a time when she had "receded in the shadowy recesses of translation and ... camouflaged [her] voice with another's," Barolini recalls the fragility of her "hold" on her work and the fear of being pushed "into the morass of self-doubt" (SDS 555). Recounting her emergence as an author, Barolini herself calls attention to the variety of her literary production, which is linked to her struggle towards authorial self-creation:

   I wrote about the Italian poet, Lucio Piccolo, and about *Giacomo Joyce*; I wrote stories about displaced Americans in Rome and this time the displaced people were Anglo-Americans, not Italian Americans.[9] (*BLP* 269)

Her Garden Asks for Water   271

Fascinated by displacement, Barolini writes about that experience in her fiction and in her criticism, and vicariously examines the implications of existing on the margins. The heterogenous quality of her "literary" production sheds light on the displacement of Italian American women authors in the literary market, which is directly linked to their absence from the curriculum.[10] In his discussion of Barolini's literary production, Gardaphé argues that the autobiographies of Italian American women are characterized by "an intense politicization of the self ... [which] emerges in combative voices, representative of the intense struggle Italian American women have waged in forging free selves within the constraints of a patriarchal system" (20-1).[11] Barolini's blending of genres and writerly personas articulates the extremity of Italian American women authors' exclusion and their willingness, as a result, to explore diverse routes in order to become authors. Through a process of self-authorization, Barolini fashions a multiplicity of voices, all participating in the creation of a decentered authorial voice. Trying to establish her "voices" in canonical genres in which her gender/ethnicity is absent, such as fiction and criticism, Barolini resorts to a subversive transformation of the genre in which her gender/ethnicity *is* present.[12] Opening *Festa*, one reads, "Other Books by Helen Barolini," with *Umbertina*, *The Dream Book*, and *Love in the Middle Ages* listed below. Facing the title page of *Festa*, this list defies the circumscribed literary space that the genre of *Festa* may seem to ascribe to its author. At the same time, adding *Festa* to these titles, Barolini sanctions her diverse authorial experiences, which both reflect and challenge cultural definitions of Italian American femininity. Indeed, as Gardaphé puts it, Barolini transforms the stereotypical image of the Italian woman by turning "the woman's room, the family kitchen, into an embassy of cultural tradition" (24).

Food as a literary subject matter is a staple of Italian American literature. In the writings of women, this topic takes on an especially poignant significance, as it articulates both a perception of the domestic space as oppressive and an awareness of the ways in which women empower themselves within that space. Not only does food provide a language through which to express such an ambivalent view of the domestic space, it also becomes a vehicle through which to articulate ethnic identity. In Louise DeSalvo's novel, *Casting Off*, the Italian background of the overtly Irish Helen MacIntyre emerges through lavish descriptions of food and in the use of the recipe as an autobiographical text of sorts:

> She thought about how one could read the progress of her life in the spills of mysterious substances that now obliterated her favorite recipes, the one for pecan pie in an old Good Housekeeping cookbook that was now out of print and that she held together with rubber bands. (28-9)

Curaggia

The "dripping" and "dribbling" that covers Helen's cookbooks repre-sents her "way of making history," while through the "splotches" and "spills" she inscribes her signature on the text of her life, a life from which she feels disconnected (29-30). In a similar fashion, the poet Rose Romano proclaims that she can "write" her "life/story with different shapes in/vari-ous sizes in limitless patterns of/pasta laid out to dry on a thick, white/table-cloth" (*The Wop Factor* 57). While neither DeSalvo nor Romano turns to the cookbook as a genre, they demonstrate the interconnectedness of food-writ-ing and life-writing. Writers such as Romano and DeSalvo, but also Tina De Rosa, Sandra M. Gilbert, Phyllis Capello, and Kathy Freeperson, to mention just a few, have variously used food as the necessary ingredient to subvert popular views of Italian American ethnicity pervasive in American culture. For these writers, ethnicity, as Romano puts it, is not something to "drag out/of a closet to celebrate quaint holidays/nobody heard of" (*The Wop Factor* 57). Barolini turns to the cookbook, the text that American culture deems the recognized token of Italian American women's identity, to create a much more complex story, one that the reader must learn "to read."[13]

The intersection of gender and ethnicity magnifies the conditions that stifle the authorial voice and restricts the choice of genres available for the creation of Italian American women's literary discourses. This shrinking of the literary space replicates the narrowing of the walls of the domestic space that have historically circumscribed and shaped female creativity. Exploring the ambiguities of the domestic space, many women writers endow the language of domesticity with a poetical function, and thus fashion an aesthet-ics of domesticity. Barolini herself draws an arsenal of literary strategies from domesticity, paralleling the strategies employed by other women authors who inscribe the narratives and objects of domesticity in their works.[14] Gender, genre, and ethnicity all play a role in Barolini's creation of a poetics of domesticity. The cookbook represents a literary occasion for Barolini to explore her relationship to each of these cultural forces. By asserting the author's "cultural specificity" and "ethnic difference," a cookbook "pro-vides the self with authority to speak" (Goldman 179). As a "form of writing," a recipe is a "culturally contingent production" (Goldman 172): *Festa* thus functions as a narrative through which Barolini negotiates her position between American and Italian culture, but also as a text that furthers her authorial assertion as a woman who cooks *and* writes. Like a ventrilo-quist, Barolini speaks through her "recipes." The introductions to each month — "chapter" — in *Festa* rely on subtitles such as "Strambino: In My Italian Kitchen" (*F* 115), and intertwine memories of the Festival of Spoleto and descriptions of menus, quotations from *Childe Harold* and prices of food, conversations with artists *and* with cooks. "Mother, parents, family — they all merge in the festas that are so much a part of Italian life" (*F* 260), writes

Barolini, and in a similar way, disparate elements "merge" in *Festa* to forge the author's voice and authorize her stories.

Festa is much like the "feast of tongues" in Sandra Mortola Gilbert's poem, "Still Life: Woman Cooking" (*Emily's Bread* 65). Even in the title, Gilbert reverses the paralyzing implications of the domestic space by turning it into art — "a still life" — but she also critiques the creative paralysis caused by the rhythms of domestic life. Barolini's own literary transformation of domesticity involves a re-vision of *the* domestic genre *par excellence*, the cookbook. Such a re-vision challenges the criteria that define "literary" texts and "'fine literature'" (Ling 742) and critiques the conditions that limit access to the literary space — as a public space — for groups that are victims of social and cultural discrimination. Discussing the possibility of defining a female poetic, Jane Marcus focuses on a "model of art, with repetition and dailiness at the heart of it, with the teaching of other women the patient craft of one's cultural heritage as the object of it" ("Still Practice" 84). Marcus argues that this is "a female poetic which women live and accept. Penelope's art is work, as women cook food that is eaten, weave cloth that is worn, clean houses that are dirtied. Transformation, rather than permanence, is at the heart of this aesthetic" (84). And "transformation" is "at the heart" of Barolini's *Festa*, a book that transforms recipes and cooking into a newly created literary experience. Susan Leonardi argues that in a literary text a recipe can function as "embedded discourse" and "narrative strategy" (340): "Like a narrative, a recipe is reproducible, and, further, its hearers-readers-receivers are *encouraged* to reproduce it and, in reproducing it, to revise it and make it their own" (344). Thus the recipe simultaneously empowers the author and the reader, erasing hierarchical distinctions between the two. And through *Festa* Barolini gives "a version of the Italian American house" that, as Gardaphé suggests, presents the "kitchen" as the space for female storytelling (26).

Barolini resorts to a wide spectrum of creative vehicles and models to empower herself to speak different languages and tell different stories. In *Festa*, she writes about a book of recipes she has inherited from her husband's grandmother, written "in her own beautiful hand" (*F* 12). A recipe indeed works as "an apt metaphor for the reproduction of culture from generation to generation" and "the act of passing down recipes from mother to daughter works as well to figure a familial space within which self-articulation can begin to take place" (Goldman 172). Barolini entitles her anthology of Italian American women writers after an actual "dream book" that Italian immigrants consulted and shared:

> On a front page, in awkward uphill handwriting was the Italian notation of one Angela Zecchini who, with many misspellings and an incorrect date for the inception of World War I, recorded this terse account of her life....

It was ... a book the Italian women of Telluride [Colorado] used constantly, the Baedeker of their dreams....

The original tattered and much-thumbed dream book was the companion of those displaced women. (*DB* xii-xiii)

These writings, produced within a culturally constructed private space, deprived of access to the realm of "public" discourse, and seemingly addressing a self-selected, "private" audience, represent the cultural heritage of marginalized groups. They are indeed literary artifacts, women's early literary production, formulating notions of art, authorship, and audience not sanctioned as "literary."[15] *Festa* subversively crosses the bounds of female privacy and speaks in a "politicized" voice (Gardaphé 20), claiming an authorial space that legitimizes its narratives. In *The Languages of Patriarchy*, Jane Marcus questions traditional methods of literary history and claims that:

> ... in the case of Virginia Woolf, very often the drafts and the unpublished versions seem "truer" texts.... Perhaps it would be true of all women writers. Perhaps it would be true of all oppressed people's writings, of blacks and lesbians, that the published text is *not* the most interesting book. (xii)

Marcus contends that the ways in which different forms of censorship intervene on texts often camouflage the authorial voice. Constructing the literary history of "oppressed people" necessitates a search for unofficial texts and sources.[16] Women's autobiographies, letters, memoirs, and other non-"literary" texts, such as cookbooks — and "dream books" — represent a repertoire the critic must draw on in order to construct a marginal author's history.

The process of authorial self-birth (BLP 263) lies at the core of Barolini's literary production. Her entire opus aims at the creation of an "autobiography as piecework" (Gardaphé 19), a fragmentary and discontinuous narrative which nevertheless brings forth the author's voice. Barolini's novel, *Umbertina*, self-consciously examines the history of its creation as an ethnic female bildungsroman *and* kunstlerroman.[17] Questioning the conventions of these genres, the novel traces the Italian roots of Tina Morosini, an aspiring scholar of Italian literature. As Anthony Tamburri argues, *Umbertina* departs from traditional representations of Italian American femininity: "The novelty of *Umbertina* lies precisely in Barolini's treatment of women as individuals, who, at one point or another in their lives, become aware of their true plight — the duality of gender and ethnic oppression — and ... attempt to free themselves from the prison-house of patriarchy" ("Gender/Ethnic" 42-3). By telling the stories of Tina's mother's (Marguerite's) lifelong and seemingly unsuccessful search for a talent, Tina's decision to become a scholar of Italian literature, and Tina's "encounter" with her great-grandmother Umbertina's bedspread, Barolini examines the diverse routes leading to, or thwarting, the creation of an Italian American woman author. From an autobiographical perspective, Barolini portrays herself both as Marguerite, the unrealized artist who dies pregnant with an unwanted child — a metaphor for her aborted artistic creativity — and as Tina, who succeeds in becoming a literary scholar. Marguerite's tragic death captures Barolini's perception of the fragility of her position as an aspiring artist. Marguerite's possible suicide, an event the narrative hints at without ever asserting with certainty, symbolizes Barolini's own self-doubt.

Marguerite's unfulfilled search for her artistic talent emerges in her "restlessness" (*U* 181), her moving from place to place, and her inability — or unwillingness — to define a "domestic" space.[18] Marguerite's houses are characterized by "this visible edge of impermanence, of things falling apart" (*U* 304). "I don't care where I live" (*U* 305), she used to say, but her daughter knows that "she did care. She cared enormously for place, and each one they came to and claimed, she worked at to make beautiful. And then moved on" (*U* 305). Tina thinks how "curious" was her mother's attachment to "drawers and boxes and to the idea of having everything contained, in place; she who tore it all apart so readily, ready to move on, sending them winging like birds of passage on the flights of her inquietude" (*U* 306). Marguerite's "care" for "place" represents her search for her space "in the world" (*U* 182), but she cannot find this space because she focuses her intellectual energy on her husband's professional and personal success (Tamburri, "Gender/Ethnic" 33). The juxtaposition between personal "place" and public "world" articulates the author's critique of the historical dichotomy between private and public and of the effects of such a dichotomy on an author's self-fashioning. Similarly repressed in her artistic aspirations, Lily Bart, the protagonist of Edith Wharton's *The House of Mirth*, dwells on her unrealized aspiration to redecorate her aunt's drawing room, which would provide an ineffectual outlet for her creative talent.[19] Like Lily, Marguerite is displaced, and her displacement is illustrated through her relationship to places: constant moves, attempts to mark the places with her presence, simultaneous attachment to and disregard for the domestic space.

Marguerite's displacement figuratively reflects Barolini's own awkward position on the Italian literary scene, in which her husband, Antonio Barolini, much like Marguerite's husband, found himself perfectly "at ease":

> He was supremely at ease with the fact of his calling as an Italian poet and author, confident of being a literary person without having to question his right to be one, or whether he was odd to be one. Literature was his unquestioned patrimony and privilege. (BLP 267)

In an oblique exploration of her own conflicting and ambiguous relationship to the literary world, Barolini portrays Marguerite as muse, translator, spectator, amateur artist striving to articulate a speech for which she finds no words. After hearing of Marguerite's death, her mother wonders, "What did she want? What was she looking for? ... All that moving around. All those homes she set up and then tore down. And moving those girls around so they had no normal life at all ... What was it all for? To punish us?" (*U* 286). Marguerite's expatriation and marginality are linked to and express her cultural and historical entrapment as a third-generation Italian American woman raised in America in the 1950s, a period that did not encourage the emergence of female or ethnic voices.[20] Marguerite remains on the margins, a spectator even of her own life. However, her daughter will begin to articulate the cultural disconnection from which they both suffer.

Both Marguerite and Alberto Morosini, Tina's poet father, influence the professional direction taken by Tina. In many ways, they legitimize her literary career by establishing precedents for her: Marguerite through her struggles, and Alberto through his confidence in his position as an Italian poet. Tina's ambivalent attitude towards Italian culture — and specifically Southern Italian culture — becomes apparent while she is travelling in Calabria and feels torn between being a tourist and being a traveller. The image of Tina as a "tourist" of her "heritage" (BLP 270), a phrase Barolini elsewhere uses to refer to herself, is recalled in the description of Tina's visit to the Museum of Immigration. Tina's role as a passive spectator seems to undergo a change when she stops in front of Umbertina's bedspread:

> Tina stood before the glass drinking in the beauty and warmth of the old spread. Its colors irradiated her spirit; the woven designs of grapes and tendrils and fig leaves and flowers and spreading acanthus spoke to her of Italy and the past and keeping it all together for the future. It was as if her old ancestor, the Umbertina she had fruitlessly sought in Castagna, had suddenly become manifest in the New World and spoken to her. (*U* 407-8).

Tina intuitively understands the poetical language spoken by the bedspread, both a domestic artifact and the epitome of her past. The bedspread contains its own kind of writing, "woven designs" which speak to Tina in a language that she begins to comprehend. The history of the bedspread, its acquisition, its loss through sale, and its donation to the Museum of Immigration by a Northern Italian woman symbolically capture the turbulent history of Italian American — specifically southern Italian — ethnicity. The artifact that represented Umbertina's connection with her heritage is deviously appropriated by Anna Giordani, the Northern Italian social worker whose name enters the annals of immigrant history at the cost of erasing Umbertina's. The unspoken story of the bedspread raises the question of the need for corrective stories and histories that will trace, reclaim, and record the life stories of marginal figures such as Umbertina.

Tina's search for her great-grandmother represents her search for a poetical subject, though this search does not actualize into a life choice. Taking a Ph.D. in Italian, Tina begins to write *about* Italian authors, but she has not yet learned the language to articulate her own *italianità*. The bedspread, an embodiment of the ethnic subject matter, remains in many ways inaccessible, displayed in the Museum, not revivified in poetical language. But if Tina does not become a poet, Barolini does become a writer. The novel thus captures the struggle of the authorial voice of one Italian American woman, trying to extricate itself from cultural paradigms that prevent it from being born. Barolini's work provides an account of her experimentation with different mediums for artistic expression. Although fiction and criticism appear as mutually exclusive in Tina's career, Barolini's entire literary production expresses a struggle to reconcile and "merge" the two as well as other genres. "Becoming a Literary Person Out of Context," for example, compresses the undertakings of the critic, the fiction writer, and the autobiographer. In that essay, the third person pronoun, used in reference to the Italian American woman writer as a figure whose creation in process risks being aborted, is soon replaced by the first person pronoun, an "I" voice that, though "besieged by doubts" ("BLP" 263), speaks confidently, telling a story — *her* story — that claims its right to be heard.

A history of disguises, male pseudonyms, unrecognized collaboration with male partners, and censorship characterizes the emergence of nineteenth- and early twentieth-century women authors. The illegitimate status of the woman author caused emerging authors to experience an all-consuming "anxiety of authorship," a gender-determined "dis-ease" which Sandra Mortola Gilbert and Susan Gubar juxtapose to Harold Bloom's "anxiety of influence" (51):

> In comparison to the "male" tradition of strong, father-son combat ... this female anxiety of authorship is profoundly debilitating. Handed down not from one woman to the other but from the stern literary "fathers" of patriarchy to all their "inferiorized" female descendants, it is in many ways the germ of a dis-ease or, at any rate, a disaffection, a disturbance, a distrust, that spreads like a stain throughout the style and structure of much literature by women. (51)

Gilbert and Gubar find that the anxiety of authorship does not afflict with equal intensity twentieth-century women authors who, having become legitimate creators of literary discourses, free themselves from that form of anxiety and embrace the anxiety of influence.[21] Conversely, the absence of literary foremothers and the unrecognized — and thus illegitimate — status of Italian American women authors places them in a position in which they are still

Curaggia

stifled by the "anxiety of authorship." Italian American authors experience a sense of belatedness, magnified by their connection with the celebrated literary tradition of Italy,[22] and various ethnic, multicultural "renaissances," including Jewish/American, African/American, Chicana, and Asian/American among others.[23] Mapping out the territory inhabited by Italian American authors, especially women, one finds the names of small publishing houses and unknown literary magazines, and titles that quickly go out of print — which brings us back to Barolini's comment on writing "out of the void" (BLP 263).[24]

Barolini's work captures the position of Italian American women authors who, rather than benefiting from the debates on multiculturalism and gender issues, find themselves still on the fringes. Ironically, even their marginalization has not yet entered fictional or critical discourse.[25] A letter from a reader of *Umbertina* comments directly on the absence of Italian American "literary" women, both as the creators and as the created: "I've never seen the name of an Italian woman on a book cover before, so I had to buy your book" (BLP 271). Have things changed over the last fifteen years? The publication of Mary Jo Bona's *The Voices We Carry: Recent Italian American Women's Fiction* (1994), a special issue of *VIA: Voices in Italian Americana* (1996) devoted to women, several books by authors such as Rita Ciresi, Louise DeSalvo, Marianna De Marco Torgovnick, Diane di Prima, Maria Mazziotti Gillan, Daniela Gioseffi, Cris Mazza, Carole Maso, Mary Saracino, and Agnes Rossi, to mention just a few contemporary authors, and also the reprints of Tina De Rosa's *Paper Fish* (1996) and three of Dorothy Bryant's novels by the Feminist Press (1997), and Diana Cavallo's *A Bridge of Leaves* by Guernica (1997), represent a step forward in the making of a tradition of Italian American female authors. However, there has been no concerted effort on the part of the literary market and the academic world to allow the "dream book" to enter the realm of literary reality. The placement of Barolini's and Bryant's books in the "Cooking" and "Science Fiction" sections reflects the still-existing displacement and marginalization of Italian American women authors, women who might be relegated to the kitchen or forced to travel to utopian lands to achieve recognition. But while the terrain remains still largely uncharted, Barolini's and other authors' subversive strategies forge alternative territories that have begun to legitimize Italian American women's voices.

Notes

1. The author acknowledges the Purdue Research Foundation for granting permission to reprint this article. An earlier version was first published in the *Romance Languages Annual 1994* Vol. 6. Eds. Jeanette Beer, Ben Lawton and Patricia Hart (West Lafayette: Purdue Research Foundation, 1995): 261-66. The following abbreviations of Barolini's works will be used in parenthetical documentation in the text: *F*: *Festa*; *DB*: *The Dream Book: An Anthology of Writings by Italian Ameri-*

can Women; BLP: "Becoming a Literary Person Out of Context"; SDS: "Shutting the Door on Someone"; *U: Umbertina*.

2. Significantly, as of March 1996, *Festa* was the only book by Barolini still in print. Since the original publication of this article, Barolini's *Chiaroscuro: Essays of Identity* (West Lafayette, IN: Bordighera, 1997) was first published, and will soon be reprinted in a new edition by University of Wisconsin Press. Umbertina will be reprinted by The Feminist Press (New York: The Feminist Press, 1999).

3. "Re-vision, the act of looking back ... of entering an old text from a critical direction, is for women ... an act of survival" (Rich 35).

4. Dorothy Bryant is the author of many books, some of which focus on Italian American ethnicity, such as *Miss Giardino* (1978). While science fiction is only one of the many genres Bryant has turned to, it is significant that *The Kin of Ata Are Waiting For You* is, among her many books, the one that can be easily found in bookstores. In "Where Are the Italian American Novelists?" Gay Talese speaks of the pressure to anglicize Italian names to gain access to the literary market (29). Unfortunately, this is a familiar story that many, besides Talese, can tell. For example, Francesca Vinciguerra, a popular Italian American author of the 1940s, anglicized her name and called herself Frances Winwar (*DB* 6). Sandra M. Gilbert reduces her Italian name, Mortola, to an "M," a cipher that captures the diminutive status of Italian American ethnicity: "I am really Sandra Mortola Gilbert," Gilbert wrote to Barolini, "and my mother's name was Caruso, so I always feel oddly falsified with this Waspish-sounding American name, which I adopted as a 20-year old bride who had never considered the implications of her actions!" (*DB* 22).

5. Barolini writes of the response of the students at Sarah Lawrence College, where the screening took place: "Viewing Ms. Scorsese's life as spectators, they could indulge in sentiment and nostalgia for a life they'd never have to live. Being liberated from imposed roles, they could romanticize the heart-warming Italian Americans who were represented as living confining roles. And so it is in literature: Italian American characters serve the function of picturesque peasants for the tourist-reader who doesn't have to be them" (272).

6. "Write an Italian cookbook, author Nives Cappelli was told when she tried to market an ethnic novel, but don't write about Italian Americans because they don't read" (*DB* 44-5).

7. For an analysis of the cookbook as a cultural and literary text see Leonardi and Goldman. On food in Italian American culture see Gardaphe, "Linguine and Lust: Food and Sex in Italian/American Culture."

8. A book by Gabriella De Ferrari, *Gringa Latina*, contains recipes to accompany the autobiographical narrative.

9. *Giacomo Joyce* must have been an especially significant text for Barolini, because of its idiosyncratic nature and thinly disguised autobiographical subject. Barolini must have also been intrigued by its author's self-imposed exile, reminiscent of all those "displaced" figures who fascinated her, as well as of her own displacement. Joyce's creation of an Italian persona also captures Barolini's own struggle between two cultures.

10. For a discussion of the historical exclusion of Italian American authors from the canon see Chiavola Birnbaum, "red, a little white, a lot of green, on a field of pink: a controversial design for an Italian component of a multicultural canon for the United States" in Tamburri et al. eds, *From the Margins* 282-93. See also Barolini's Introduction to *The Dream Book* (3-56). For a broader critique of the canon, see Robinson and Lauter.

11. See Louise DeSalvo's memoir, *Vertigo*. Also Diane di Prima's *Memoirs of a Beatnik* and her autobiography in progress *Recollections of My Life as a Woman*..

12. Sandra Mortola Gilbert's reputation as an established critic of English literature contrasts with her reputation as a poet who writes about Italian American topics. In an interview, Gilbert comments: "I don't feel myself to be a tremendously established poet. In fact, I'm always interested when people even know that I write poetry" (Hongo and Parke 99).

13. In the concluding line of "Ethnic Woman," after claiming that her life is written in "limitless patterns of/pasta laid out to dry" on her bed, Romano challenges the reader," "Must I teach you/to read?" (*The Wop Factor 57*).

14. See Geyh's analysis of Marylinne Robinson's *Housekeeping*. The poetry of several Italian American women abounds with domestic imagery. For example, Gilbert's "The Dream Kitchen," "Parable of the Clothes," "Still Life: Woman Cooking" (*Emily's Bread* 19-20, 26, 65) and "Doing Laundry" (*DB* 349-50), Anna Bart's "Ravioli" (*DB* 326), and Kathy Freeperson's "Italian Bread" (*DB* 303-4).

15. It is through the consideration of what Homi K. Bhabha describes as a "cultural hybridity that entertains difference without an assumed or imposed hierarchy" (4) that the multicultural discourse can shape a cultural space in which "the 'right' to signify .... is resourced by the power of tradition to be reinscribed through the conditions of contingency and contradictoriness that attend upon the lives of those who are 'in the minority'" (Bhabha 2).

16. Many feminist critics have re-written literary history, embracing wider criteria that validate the specificity of female literary experience. In *Women of the Left Bank*, for example, Shari Benstock recovers the work of the women who participated in the creation of Modernism in ways that are not recognized as legitimately literary.

17. See Tamburri's two essays on *Umbertina* (one of the essays appears in Tamburri et al. eds., *From the Margin*, 357-73). See also Beranger, and Gardaphé, "Autobiography as Piecework" as well as the section on *Umbertina* in "The Later Mythic Mode: Reinventing Ethnicity Through the Grandmother Figure" in *Italian Signs. American Streets*, 123-31.

18. Tina thinks of her family as "campers on the move, vagabonds with aristocratic baggage and topnotch pots and pans to drag behind them as they traveled" (*U* 305)

19. On Lily Bart's role as an artist figure see Dittmar.

20. "Marguerite is prototypical of Lopreato's 'second- generation' (i.e. third-generation) family, which he considers to be the first 'to make the big cultural break between the old society and the new" (Tamburri, *Margin* 359). Tamburri points out that Marguerite represents the rebellious type who even through her "mode of dress and behavior at school" expresses her "contempt for imposed roles" (*Margin* 359).

21. See Rosdeitcher's interview with Sandra M. Gilbert and Susan Gubar, 23-4.

22. See Chiavola Birnbaum.

23. Italian American women writers have creatively responded to the questions raised by multiculturalism. See Giunta, "Reinventing the Authorial/Ethnic Space: Communal narratives in Agnes Rossi's *Split Skirt*."

24. See Giunta, "'A Song from the Ghetto': Tina De Rosa's *Paper Fish*."

25. See Giunta, "Crossing Critical Borders in Italian/American Women's Studies."

An Ethnic Passage

An Italian-American Woman in Academia

Maryann S. Feola

At my Ph.D. commencement, I spoke with Gerry, the candidate in the next seat about being there. We had never met before, but we discovered that we had a lot in common. Both of us had been students in the same program and were encouraged by the department head to complete the necessary requirements and move on. Along the way we had each lost a husband. Gerry's husband had gotten sick and died; mine had turned indifferent and left. And though we never spoke about being minority candidates, we tacitly agreed that given my Italian surname and her Caribbean complexion, it was a minor miracle that we were there. Gerry had regrets about not inviting an aunt who ridiculed her "fancy thinking." I nodded and thought about what several of my Catholic relatives would think when I explained that the subject of my dissertation, a seventeenth century Quaker writer, had started out as a regicide, joined a radical Puritan religious sect, and ended up a pacifist who spent most of his final years in jail. In my mind I saw my great-grandfather Orazio, who had died shortly after my tenth birthday pleased that I could legitimately write "Dr." before my name, reminding my parents how he had prophesied that my brazen questions would lead to no good.

During the course of our discussion, Gerry and I speculated that the commencement ceremony might serve to exorcise the ghosts that had made long and painful the entry into academe. We talked about the emotional price we had paid for personal growth and about both loving and hating the distance that stood between our new lives and the past. But once the voice from the stage made us aware that we should be silent, my thoughts turned inward and I recalled my odyssey to self-realization past the Scylla and Charybdis of an Italian-American girlhood.

Growing up Italian-American in 1950s Brooklyn, I was taught to fear authority and follow tradition. I was reminded that thinking clearly and reserving judgment were desirable, but they ranked second to possessing "common sense." Both at home and at school I heard that questioning and criticism were the tell-tale signs of a "doubting Thomas." Speaking your mind was understandable; challenging the status quo, however, was not. Now with almost three decades between my entry into grammar school, and my completion of graduate school, I thought about how I came to a profession and a lifestyle that turned upside down the lessons of my childhood.

I remembered that when I was growing up there was no doubt in my mind that I was anything but Italian. The basis of that identification had little to do with the fact that most of my family had left the impoverished rural villages that surrounded Naples some fifty years earlier: it was simply who I was. It was assumed that I would become a housewife — if I lucked out, a doctor's or lawyer's wife. I was encouraged to mind my tongue and remain close to the church and traditions that secured salvation. In other words, inquiry, esoterica, and independence were tribal taboos that evoked earnest and frequent "God forbids" from the family who sought to protect me from "all the wrong things" I seemed to love.

Like many other Italian-Americans, our family life centered around the homes of my grandparents. We lived upstairs from my father's parents; everyone else lived close by. Around dining room tables that were loaded with fruit, nuts, and wine, my grandparents told story after story about relatives or *paesani* — people from their native villages — who suffered, or, who on occasion, had caused some suffering in Italy. They emphasized how these people had struggled against the forces of fate and had managed to survive. Everyone thanked God at the end of a story, refilled their wine glasses, and glanced over to give their mischievous children dirty looks that were invariably followed by expressions of love.

At these gatherings my great-grandfather presided as master story teller. He told endless stories about Italy, stories that colored my imagination with the romantic image of another time and another place. The Italy he invented with his facts and fiction sowed the seeds of my cultural imagination and defined the borders of my parochial world.

His warm-hearted chatter and the ease with which he could instigate an argument between my grandparents shaped my interest in well-informed eccentric characters. He was my earliest encounter with the old world thinking that I now sit in libraries and research. If he knew me today, I believe he would consider me as shameless as the radical writers I study, but he would brag about my work to anyone who would listen.

Great-grandpa, an incessant teacher, was particularly eager to instruct my young mother and her sisters-in-law in the fine art of rearing Italian children. Never invited to begin a lecture, he nonetheless came prepared with the power of myth and the burden of history and a walking stick which he tapped to emphasize essential points. He told these Italian-American mothers that their children must learn respect. We must learn to be careful with our money, especially it came from him. The boys should follow his example and become successful in this country. The girls, of course, must learn to keep spotless homes and know their place. They should also be taught to stop asking so many questions and only speak when spoken to. We must remain close as a family and be wary of the Americans — that is any one who is not Italian.

Our left-handedness concerned him deeply. Fortunately, neither my mother nor any of my aunts ever tied our left thumbs to our adjoining fingers as he suggested. Believing that left-handedness was an invitation to evil spirits he saw us as likely candidates for disaster. When he was a young man, two of his children died of an epidemic that ravaged the ship which was bringing them to a better life in America. He had to warn future generations not to tempt fate.

Why were these guidelines so important to my great-grandfather? How were they influenced by the transition from old world to new? How did they shape my future?

Today as a teacher at a multi-cultural university, I am fascinated with how immigrant families transplant their roots in America. I wonder how my students are reconciling new ideas and new ways of communicating with their family traditions? What will they gain? What will they lose? Like me will their movement away from the traditions of the past make them feel like strangers?

Memories of my girlhood daydreams and adventures are mixed with images of those numerous great aunts dressed in black warning me not to forget who I was. My interests, dress, and plans for the future might stem from personal taste; however, they must not break with the traditions that offered security. How I loved the spidery handwriting in the letters of my Neapolitan relatives thanking my Grandma Mamie for her generous packages. My grandmother happily translated these letters for me and filled in the details of my impoverished relatives' lives. These letters, while they may have fueled my romantic imagination and transported me to an exotic world, also reminded me of sorrow and humility not-too-far removed.

To most of my parents' generation success meant having a job. A college diploma was respectable, but they feared it would undermine the traditions of the past, or worse still, family closeness. Like them, my family admired academic learning, but they were also suspicious of it. In Southern Italy higher education had had no place in their rustic culture, and in Brooklyn the fancy ways and polished language of college-educated Americans made them uncomfortable. As for me, going to college was a mixed bag of intellectual excitement and nostalgia for the ideas and traditions that I cherished were slipping away.

The Catholic grammar school I attended, suitably named for the Biblical John who created the image of the apocalypse, had a reputation that encouraged my parents to pay tuition they could hardly afford. The priests who managed parish affairs were Italians but the ethnicity of the nuns was a mystery since their surnames had been erased. Ironically, these women, my first teachers, had assumed the names, but not the patience, of saints.

In the 1950s, ecumenical thinking was a thing of the future. With the McCarthy hearings in progress, we were told the difference between good guys and bad guys, who would be saved and who would be damned. Then our classrooms were orderly and quiet. Today elementary education gets kids to arrive at generalizations that apply across sex roles and cultures. Then we learned by rote our teachers' assumptions. When my son Mathew was eight years old, I noticed that his view of the world was expanding. When I was his age, I was reprimanded for questioning why St. Isaac Jacques continued to pursue Indians who resisted conversion: my critical thinking skills were being stifled.

As a young student, I was somewhat chagrined that Mom, Dad, Dick, Jane, and Spot were not Italian. Although the women in my reading primer were held up as role models because their homes were ordered by feminine patience, sacrifice, and submission, I had no plans to imitate them. In those days, we did not read Kate Chopin, Tilly Olsen, Maya Angelou, or Grace Paley. There were no real households for us to relate to in either the present as children or in the future as adults. Trying to preserve custom, the nuns read us stories that showed how innovation and debate resulted in tragedy — Martin Luther, for example, and Anne Hutchinson. A good cautionary tale, so my teachers believed, would prevent the evils brought about by individuation and acculturation.

In college I was awed when a fellow student questioned our professor's rendition of Shakespeare's Richard III. What motivated her to criticize what we were being taught? But to my surprise, our instructor welcomed her ideas and conceded certain points he had previously raised. Was I now free to think for myself? If so, how did I go about it? Wouldn't it get me into trouble? In the sixth grade hadn't Sister Thomas More been quite clear about the dangers of impertinence and willful pride? Did I really want to be "a true daughter of Eve"?

In college I excelled because my essays and exams presented my instructors with written affirmations of their own ideas. Then, in my last semester, a sociology teacher saw through me and threatened to withhold my A until I told him what I — not what every one else — thought about Nietzche's philosophy.

However, thinking for myself became a mixed blessing, for it created the shift in power that eventually caused my marriage to fall apart. How can the same woman who challenges myths and pursues truth in the classroom be expected to return home and subordinate her ideas and opinions to a husband who cuts off any discussion that makes him feel uncomfortable? My Italian-American marriage did not survive this question.

During my many years of graduate school, my husband spoke proudly of my accomplishments, especially in front of other people. In private, he frequently complained that I had become too opinionated, too argumentative. A few weeks before he moved out, he joked that his next wife would be barefoot and bookless.

Now I had a new question: "Where does an Italian-American single mother completing a graduate degree, so crucial an issue in her tenure decision, turn for understanding and support?" Most of my family and many old friends waxed nostalgic when my husband and I separated. Knowing less than they thought they did of the obstacles that my education had placed in my marriage, they all but canonized the wonderful cook who had "helped" me clean our house. "What does Maryann want?" was the question they offered with their condolences. Very few of my college friends understood how thoroughly academic values were in conflict with my role as an Italian-American woman. Fearing that they might consider me less than their equal, I grew protective of the very traditions that had undermined my happiness.

As I completed my degree, I often wished that Dick and Jane's mother had gone to graduate school. I needed some role model who had been in the British Museum writing her dissertation while her child was on the other side of the Atlantic in New York. Curiously, I felt like my great-grandfather Orazio crossing an ocean and hoping that *paesani* would be waiting on the other side. But few of the people I met while I wrote my dissertation were women, even fewer were single parents, and no one was Italian-American. I was all three. The string intended for my left thumb bound up my workdays with feelings of guilt, alienation, and fear. The librarian at the University of London, when she asked me where I came from, treated me kindly as I began to cry and babble about how lonely I was away from my son and how I needed to get this work done quickly, or both of us would be in real trouble. "No," I told her, "There was no one at home who knew how to help me through this." "You can't go home until you complete your research for your dissertation. After all," she said, "if you return home without it, what kind of role model will your son have? Someday he will know your story."

I often hear from my Italian-American students how much they enjoy learning and how they look forward to teaching. Using idyllic language, they also speak of the support they receive at home. Everyone is rooting for them, everyone is lending full support. "That's good," I tell them, "when you are struggling with new ideas and ways of improving your writing." But these students rarely say that what they learn in school is being discussed or explained at home with their husbands or families or at any cultural, social, or political events. In that matter, the separateness between the new ideas and the old remains. To what extent, I think, will their learning also separate them from their family traditions?

Today, when I think of my Italian heritage, I think of holiday cooking, cordial hospitality, and family closeness. But I also think of Anne Cornelisen's "women of the shadows" and wonder how long educational deprivation and the Italian ambivalence toward higher education will continue to haunt Italian-American women who brave the uncertain shores of academe.

Curaggia

Looking at the Tree and Not the Forest

Domenica Dileo

This paper on Canadian immigration policies prior to World War I: The Italian Experience was prepared for York University, Toronto, 1986

It is said that the history of Canada is the history of immigration. Aside from our native peoples, we are all immigrants. This notion has led to our present concept of Canada as a tolerant multicultural nation, a mosaic, where all groups live in harmony, learning from each other. Behind this rhetoric, however, is a history of racism, sexism and oppression of the working class. Our history of immigration, in many ways, acted as a means by which much of this oppression was enacted and maintained. The focus of this essay is the Italian immigration experience prior to World War I. But to put this experience in context, I will examine the role the Canadian state has played with regard to its immigration policy prior to World War I. Then I will attempt to engage in an examination of the formation of the social relations of class, race and gender by analyzing the Italian immigration experience during this period. And finally I will touch on how the state and capital reacted to early attempts at resistance by the Italian community.

It is necessary to begin by defining some pertinent terms. I will be using specific definitions for the term "state" and "social relations" in accordance with the needs of this essay. According to Leo Panitch, the "state" is,

> "...a complex of institutions, including the government, but also including the bureaucracy (embodied in the civil service, as well as in public corporations, the central bank, regulatory commissions etc.) the judiciary, representative assemblies..."[1]

Also included in the "state" in the Canadian context are the provincial and municipal governments, bureaucracies and legislatures. Furthermore, the state must, "fulfil two basic and often mutually contradictory functions: accumulation and legitimization."[2] Thus, the state must try to maintain or create the contradictions in which profit-making capital accumulation is possible, while at the same time, achieving the greatest degree of social harmony possible. It is within Panitch's conceptualization of state and its function in capitalism that my examination of immigration policy and the Italian experience will take place.

Social relations are the concrete practices of legitimization and accumulation within a mode of production. Dorothy Smith, in her article, "Women, Class and Family," says that,

> "The very separation, the very privatization of women's work in the home and how it is mediated by private property is a feature of the social relations of a definite mode of production."[3]

Although Smith, in this example, is discussing women's work, her point is relevant for this essay. The methodology of social formation in terms of analyzing social relation, that is, trying to understand the connections between economic, political and social forces in order to gain a better historical perspective, goes well beyond factual historical recounting. It is within this framework that I will discuss the Italian male/female immigrant experience in pre-World War I Canada.

Let us begin by looking at the state as the organizer of social relations including gender and class, and in particular the role of immigration. Any examination of the history of immigration must begin with the actions of the federal government. It is the Canadian government that has the authority to determine who should be admitted and deported, when and under what conditions.

Historically, three major factors have underlined Canadian immigration policy: "the desire to populate Canada with British people, the need to heed international pressures, and the demands of the labour market."[4] While these three factors may at first appear neutral, they, in fact, are not. Since international pressures did not become an important issue for the Canadian state until after World War II, it is the other factors that concern this examination.

British and American people were viewed as the preferable people to populate Canada because, theoretically, they would assimilate more easily, given their knowledge of the English language and Anglo-American culture. This view was reflected in immigration policy which, in 1910, established race as an official grounds for exclusion. The act stated that,

> "The government could: prohibit for a stated period, or permanently, the landing in Canada...of immigrants belongings to any race unsuitable to the climate or requirements of Canada."[5]

Here Canadian immigration policy reflected not only the racist attitudes of the Canadian state, but also of the economic and ideological system of the British Empire of which the Canadian state was a proud part.

The supremacy of white people was a common sense assumption made popular by Social Darwinist theories in the early 1900s. These racist theories provided the justification for England's practice of colonization and the expansion of its Empire. The white man saw himself as a "civilizing" force with a role to bring into Christian society the "uncivilized" peoples outside of Europe. While notions of "civilization" and "empire" provided the justification for the colonial systems, economics provided the real force, and civilization was traded for exploitation which brought great wealth to Britain and other European powers. However, the formal official policy of immigration in Canada was also determined by the need to attract agricultural workers to settle the west. The federal government tried to attract people by offering 160 acres of free land upon settlement in the west. But the population did not increase between 1867 and 1896. Thus Canada turned to immigration from Eastern Europe and China.

Unsuccessful attempts to increase Canada's population from traditional sources in Britain, generated two movements of people to Canada, the Mennonites (Germans) and the Chinese.[6]

Eastern Europeans were seen as acceptable compared to southern Europeans because they were more "advanced" than the southerners. Donald Avery states that:

"A distinction was made, however, between southern Europeans and central Europeans; the later group, it was widely believed, was superior in a racial sense, as well as, having preferable cultural qualities which were derived from their agrarian way of life."[7]

Finally, Canadian immigration policy did open its doors to southern Europeans when it was determined that they could be used as cheap labour source that could aid in the accumulation of wealth.

The first wave of Italian immigrants were Southern Italian peasants, "contadini." After the "little Italies" were established throughout North America, and the railroads were built, Italians who chose to settle in Canada were constantly being judged and appropriated in the labour force based on the common stereotype of "inferiority" and, as such, as people capable only of labour intensive work such as construction.

The notion of "desirable immigrants" embedded in the immigration policy, validated the stereotypical and racist or ethicist common sense assumptions that people had about non-British immigrants. For Italians, specifically, males were seen as criminals, undesirable, maffioso, and females as passive, obedient slaves to their husbands and children. For example, the Canadian government attempted to legitimize people's racist attitudes towards the southerners by introducing a literacy test in 1917. There was, however no contraction with populating Canada with British people were concerned. Assumption being that Canada belonged to White Anglo-Saxons and not to the aliens.

The Canadian state legitimized the British as first class citizens. For the white Canadian capitalist, and his American and British counterparts, the government offered a free hand. The law gave the right to individuals to set-up their own business as they saw fit. It encouraged investment in the building of the railway through loans and tax benefits. In order for capitalists to invest they needed to be assured that a cheap labour force was available according to the changes of the economic cycle. H.C. Pentland states that under capitalism:

> "...the employer is confident that workers will be available whenever he wants them; so he feels free to hire them on a short term basis, and to dismiss them whenever there is a monetary advantage in doing so."[8]

More specifically, in the early 1900s the building of the railroad was essential in the making and expansion of Canada as a political and economic nation. Italians and Chinese played an important role by providing cheap unskilled labour. The railroad capitalists supported an open door immigration policy because they would have access to a large labour supply and thus minimize costs based on supply and demand. They favoured the Italians and Chinese because they "ask for no light-handed work...they are obedient and industrious."[9] As much as the state had the official goal to populate Canada with British subjects, the capitalists did not want this. In 1897, Welsh workers in a construction camp organized a demonstration demanding better working conditions. The capitalists' attitude towards British workers was as follows:

> "...It would be a huge mistake to send out any more of these men from Wales, Scotland or England...it is only prejudicial to the cause of immigration to import men who come here expecting to get high wages, a feather bed and a bathtub."[10]

Also the cheap unskilled labour that the capitalists required in their investment in the expansion of Canada was not provided by the British immigration during the period between 1901 and 1911: "few of these British immigrants were in the category of unskilled labour — only 15.6% as compared to 51.1% for the European immigrants..."[11]

In order to assist capital development, the Canadian government supported short-term unskilled contract labour to fulfil the needs of the labour market. Contract labour offered a way to bring into Canada cheap labour while maintaining control over those forces which were not the product of British "civilization." The nature of contract labour was that it was not permanent, and thus, these "aliens" seemed less fearful to British Canadians because their status was carefully controlled by the state. By having different types of immigration status the state could have the control to modify the influx to the need of the capitalist, as well as using the "undesirables" as scapegoats during hard times.

The case of Antonio Cordasco provides an example of this practice. When Italian entrepreneurs were also trying to capitalize on contract labour the issue became not exploitation of workers but rather one of race. This was

Curaggia

the outcome when the government wanted to investigate the practices of Cordasco. The issue in the press was presented as a conflict in the Italian community, with Cordasco trying to undermine the Italian establishment or "prominent."[12]

As we have seen, the Canadian state used immigration policy in its functions to provide capital with a cheap labour force and as a tool of social control through a number of measures such as exclusionary laws, literacy tests and the creation of temporary immigration status's. I will now turn to the social relations practised by the Italian men and women during the early 1900s and how this experience was used by the state to manage society. Italian immigration was dominated by southern Italian peasants. They came either as settlers or male contract labourers, and sojourners. Unlike the male contract workers, Italian settlers usually came as a family unit, hoping for a better future in Canada. During the early 1900s Italy was experiencing high unemployment and famine. The family unit was based on a patriarchal structure, that is one where the man is the primary income earner, and the woman is responsible for the domestic realm and the rearing of the children.

The common form of employment for Italian men, as stated by John E. Zucchi in his article on Italians in Ontario before World War I, was in three categories: in the building of the transcontinental railroad through the province; in mining and labour for Northern Ontario's mining boom; and in the service trades; fruit retailing, street construction in growing towns and cities.[13] By this account, we can see that Italians were relegated to specific jobs within the labour market that were labour intensive, while the British were concentrated in semi-skilled jobs. This division of labour was also justified by racist assumptions about Italians as inferior to the British.

The type of work that Italian men provided the Canadian economy which was not considered valuable, and hence justified low wages and hazardous working conditions. As a result, in order to supplement the family income, Italian women would also participate in the labour force doing factory work, especially in the garment industry where women received even lower wages than their male counterparts. Women's work was not considered as a primary income either by a patriarchal economy or family organization where the man was perceived to be the breadwinner. Women contributed economically to the family in related ways. Another means by which women could make an income was by turning parts of the home into boarding units primarily occupied by migrant Italian single males. Producing some of the essentials of living was also an important aspect of women's work at home. They would engage in planting vegetables, making homemade salami, bread, and other foods in order to reduce the cost of living.

The second form of Italian immigration was the male contract labourer, the sojourner. This particular form of immigration is gender-specific: under a patriarchal family structure, the man is perceived to have more mobility, because of his limited responsibility to the domestic realm and to child-rearing. Contract labour was organized through an employment agency, usually headed by Italian entrepreneurs called "padroni." The padroni would act as middle-men between the industrialist and peasant male, the contadino. The conditions of exchange between the labour of the contadino and the wages and living arrangements provided by the industrialist varied. Contract labour was seasonal. For example, they were hired to do construction on the railroads. After the contract expired, they either had to return to Italy, or remain in the cities usually boarding with an Italian family or looking for other work.

The Italian labour force was also divided along lines of class as well as race. Thus we can see, in the immigrant Italian experience, the process described by Dorothy Smith, whereby social relations are mediated by the mode of production they operate in.

In addition to what has thus far been discussed, the state and immigration policy, and capitalism and the labour supply, as well as their effect on social relations, it is also important to note that social formations are not stagnant, and that social relations are constantly in transition. Here we should turn to Marx for discussion of the inherent crisis of the capitalist mode of production, related to the falling rate of profit, introducing a shortfall in accumulation.[14] For example, this process is most obvious in capitalism's stages of expansion and recession. As stated above, the state must also try and maintain social harmony without fundamentally harming the capitalist mode of production. I will now look at how the Italians were appropriated by the state and the capitalists to maintain social harmony, justified by racist common sense assumptions.

By muting direct class contradictions, and promoting conflicts within the working class, capital and state can thereby divide and rule, and weaken the community as a whole. For example, this become evident from the pattern of Italian participation in the process of social transformation. This often involved action by workers to secure their rights. Some of the methods used were union organization and negotiations, work slow downs and strikes. The state was able to use its immigration legislation during times of upheaval when workers were demanding their rights. Immigrants could be brought in and used as scabs to replace workers who were on strike. In 1901, for example, the maintenance employees of the C.P.R. went on strike. The Canadian government amended its Alien Labour Act so that C.P.R. was able to bring in Italians to undermine the workers' demands. Avery notes that the C.P.R. was allowed to import four or five hundred pauperized Italians from the United States in contravention of the Alien Labour Law."[15]

This kind of action was successful because of the conditions of contract labour. For example, if a person had to travel a long way and go through the lengthy process of applying for a work permit, when he arrives to his

Curaggia

destination to work, his choices are limited given that usually migrant labourers had starving families dependent on the money back home. Does he support other workers and go on strike with them, thus improving the long term conditions of the working class, or does he take care of his immediate needs sand responsibilities? Thus contract labour was used in undermining working class solidarity.

Moreover, when Italian workers went on strike, other immigrants were brought in to undermine their bargaining power. In 1907, a year after Italian workers had made moderate gains in wages, the C.P.R. waited until the new season arrived, and excluded the Italians and Greeks from working at the freight sheds. They were replaced by British workers. When the British workers arrived, the company announced they were going to lower their wages. As a result the British workers went on strike and the Italians and Greeks were brought back in. Pucci rightly observes that "the division of the working class along ethnic lines was cultivated and exploited by management."[16]

Common sense stereotypical, ethnicist attitudes about Italians resulted in the disharmony and lack of unity amongst the working class as a whole, and thus strengthened the bargaining power of the capitalist. The way this divide-and-conquer practice was manifested, was through the notion that the preferred citizens were British, whereas, non-British immigrants, while also citizens, were seen as the "other," even by his/her fellow workers, thus offering a sop to the sense of status of the British workers. The ethnicist assumptions about Italians made them "aliens," even though they shared a common experience with the working class British. This can be shown by the assumptions made in 1907 in an editorial about Italians going on strike:

> "To strike for more pay is the legitimate prerogative of any man or body of men. But for a community of British citizens to have to submit to the insult and armed defiance from a disorganized horde of ignorant and low-down mongrel swash bucklers and peanut vendors is making a demand upon national pride which has no excuse."[17]

This examination of Italian immigration before World War One has shown the way in which Canadian state used racist and ethnicist immigration policy against Italians and other "non-desirable" to exploit, exclude, control through contract labour and other social manipulation in servicing accumulations, and crushing their attempts to build resistance. Much of this action was done in the name of the good of the "nation" and economy, and perpetuated by encouraging racism. And yet, Italians and others continued to come and have continued to take part in the social transformation of Canada. Thus, in order to understand the history of this process and where the Italian community is at now, we need to engage in an analysis of the political, social and economic realities of Italian women and men at particular points in time and the factors that have contributed to their social transformation. In addition, the Italian community does not exist as a separate entity, but in relation to all the other communities that make up Canadian society, so we need also to understand the dynamics of those relationships. An analysis of class, race and gender issues and their relationship to each other is essential in understanding what is behind all the happy rhetoric about the Canadian mosaic.

NOTES

1. Leo Panitch, *The Canadian State: Political Economy & Political Power*, (Toronto: University of Toronto Press, 1977), 8.
2. Ibid., 8.
3. Dorothy Smith, "Women, Class & Family," *Socialist Register*, Summer 1983, 6.
4. Law Union, *The Immigrants Handbook*, (Montreal: Black Rose Books, 1981), 17.
5. Ibid., 22.
6. Donald Avery, "Canadian Immigration Policy & the 'Foreign' Navy, 1896-1914," *CHA Historical Papers* 1972, (class handout) 41.
7. Ibid., 41.
8. Ibid., 36.
9. Ibid., 41.
10. Ibid., 38.
11. Ibid., 37.
12. Bruno Raminex and Michele Del Bolzo, "The Italians of Montreal: From Sojourning to Settlement, 1900-1921," in *Little Italies in North America* (Toronto: Multicultural History Society of Ontario, 1981), 14.
13. John E. Zucchi, "Mining, Railway Building and Street Construction: Italians in Ontario before World War One," in *Polyphony*, Vol. 7 No. 2, Fall/Winter 1985, 8.
14. Robert C. Tucker, *The Marx-Engels Readers, Part II. The Critique of Capitalism*, (New York: W.W. Norton, 1978), 203-443.
15. Avery, 42.
16. Antonio Pucci, "At the Forefront of Militancy: Italians in Canada at the Turn of the Century," *Polyphony*, Vol. 7 No. 2, Fall/Winter 1985 38.
17. Ibid., 38.

BIBLIOGRAPHY

Avery, Donald. "Canadian Immigration Policy and the 'Foreign' Navy, 1896-1914." *CHA Historical Papers* 1972. (Class handout).
Canadian Women's Studies. "Mediterranean Women." Vol. 8 No. 2. Summer 1987. York University.
Centre for Contemporary Cultural Studies. *The Empire Strikes Back: Race and Racism in 70's Britain*. London: Hutchinson and Co., 1972.
Corbett, David C. *Canada's Immigration Policy*. Toronto: University of Toronto Press, 1957.
Harvey, Robert F. & J. Vilenza Scarpaci. *Little Italies in North America*. Toronto: The Multicultural History Society of Ontario, 1981.
Hawkins, Freda. *Canada and Immigration Public Policy and Public Concern*. Montreal: Black Rose Books, 1981.
Law Union. *The Immigrants Handbook*. Montreal: Black Rose Books, 1981.
Panitch, Leo. *The Canadian State, Political Economy and Political Power*. Toronto: University of Toronto Press. 1977.

Polyphony. *Bulletin of the Multicultural History Society of Ontario.* Vol 7 No. 2.
    Fall/Winter 1985.
Smith, Dorothy E. "Women, Class & Family." *Socialist Register.* Summer 1983.
Tucker, Roberts C. *The Marx-Engels Readers. Part II. The Critique of Capitalism.* New
    York: W.W. Norton and Co.

This article was published in *Diva* (A South Asian Women's Journal) January, 1990.

Life is Theatre
(Mary di Michele)

How to Kill Your Father

Mary di Michele

He breaks a promise on the road to Firenze.
You will not speak to him all through
the drive in the Tuscan hills,
the rented Alpha Romeo bitches
but the poplar's got your tongue,
long and green and aloof.

You abandon the car and walk
into a Roman afternoon.
You know how to kill your father,
he knows how to kill you.

The sky is waving white cloud
kerchiefs to wipe away your tears,
to offer a truce, if not the truth
in the family. In the intensifying heat
even the wind begins to wilt, its wings
of feather and wax melting.

You are alone on the highway to the sun.
Your North American education
has taught you how to kill a father
but you are walking down an Italian

via, so you will surrender
and visit him in the hospital
where you will be accused
of wishing his death
in wanting a life
for yourself.

A scorpion's sting darkening
your heart buries July in Italy.

Dan's Gift

Sylvia Fiorita

The voice that resonated throughout the church that morning was a strong, confident one. It was a voice I was unfamiliar with, a voice that had been buried in self-pity and a false assumption of weakness. It was my voice, claiming a victory over the years of feeling powerless over my life, my voice, at my brother's funeral.

The words I so carefully chose to comfort everyone there marked the culmination of a journey for me. It seemed as though I had walked on a pebble-strewn road for so long and I hoped that people would clear the path for me. The least they could do was watch as I limped along.

I was the youngest child of my family, a scrawny, feisty chatterbox. My innate sense of curiosity and adventure were acted upon with a vengeance in childhood. I craved attention from the rest, since my two sisters and one brother were considerably older than me. I had the distinction of being the only member of the family to be born in the New World. My father had immigrated to Canada four years before the rest of the family. My mother and siblings arrived in Halifax Harbour from Italy to discover that the husband and father they remembered was a different man.

My life would be marked by this awkward meeting between my father and his wife and children. I was born into a setting already rife with intolerable tension and anxiety. The principal characters in this family drama were my parents and my sister, Teresa. My mother was pregnant when WW II broke out and my father left for the front. Teresa did not see him until she was nearly six. She had been raised with the help of my paternal grandmother who spoiled her and defended her against my mother's better judgment. Teresa's birth had been a difficult one, my mother nearly died bringing her into this world. From early on my mother knew that Teresa had probably been slightly brain-damaged as a result of her traumatic delivery, with crude forceps. Teresa's behaviour was odd. She was slow to learn things and seemed always very immature, compared to other children her age.

Enter my father, back into the picture following the war. My mother insists that the mystery of my father's rejection of his oldest daughter began then, and continued across the Atlantic Ocean into Canada. Into this volatile triangle the other three of us were thrown. I did not have recollections of this brewing hatred between my parents, or between my father and sister, until I was at least four. I do not remember having any feelings towards Teresa. My

Curaggia

father was a different story. I adored him. I was a naturally affectionate little girl and my favourite times were spent snuggled against his soft, round belly. The rise and fall of his breathing and the beating of his heart soothed me to sleep. He would play with my hair and all was calm.

I never knew the security which comes from an honest explanation of what you see happening around you. I became adept at believing that the insanity going on at home was in my mind only, that I had some magical power to change it if only I could change my mind. Many things are still vague. I do remember my father yelling a lot, blaspheming and often tossing our supper and the dishes all over the place. While Teresa was still home it seemed she was the scapegoat for his temper tantrums. She was in trouble for spending too much money, staying out too late or talking to a young man. He could not tolerate her presence at the table.

Four years after arriving to be with my father, the situation became intolerable for Teresa. She could not understand my father's rejection of her, having heard him complain to my mother repeatedly that she made his life miserable. One night she left, and at least physically, never returned home. That particular evening, she had arrived home late. My father was furious with her and slapped her viciously across the face. He had just had surgery on two of his fingers as a result of a work-related accident. The blow had opened up a stitch or two. I was crying and comforting him. He was crying, too. Teresa escaped through her bedroom window.

After Teresa left, life did not stop sliding toward the edge of insanity. It was also the end of the close, loving relationship I had known with my father. I never felt protected by him again. Instead, I learned to fear his dark, unpredictable moods. His mission from then on was to eradicate all traces of Teresa's existence from our lives. Pictures of her were altered and cut. We were not to speak her name or ever to see her. Now, not only was I trying to pretend that a situation did not exist outside my mind, I was forced to believe that my oldest sister's memory was not real either. Just as my father had used Teresa as the scapegoat for his unhappiness, my mother began to conveniently blame my father for everything that Teresa chose to do with her life. Even after many years passed and we still were no closer to understanding the relationship between father and daughter, my mother never forgave him for his rejection of her. She blamed him for Teresa's three broken marriages, for her abuse and neglect of her own seven children, for her deceptive and fraudulent way of life that was always landing her in one crisis after another.

Ever since I was little, my mother feared that I would be a stool pigeon, and tell my father that she was having secret rendez-vous with my sister. She admonished me never to tell my father, lest he kill us for betraying him. I learned early in life that the person with the penis held the power of life and death over everyone who didn't possess one.

I am now reading an excerpt from my journal to my brother, who is dying of cancer. There are many things I now take the risk of sharing with him. He listens quietly, as I read a section describing a session with a therapist I saw for awhile:

I talked about my family over and over again, about my sister's illnesses, my father's rages, my mother's enjoyment of feeling needed by Teresa. I spoke about my own feelings of guilt for being so powerless to resolve everyone's conflicts and make them all happy. The therapist asked me why I felt that my family should have such control over my sanity? I only felt truly alive and complete when I was away from home. Going home meant leaving normality for insanity, peace for confusion. It was not where my heart was.

I escaped the madness during my teen years by spending Sunday afternoons with my closest friend, Rosa. Her family owned a small restaurant in the heart of "Little Italy" and Rosa was obligated to spend weekends there helping out her aunts. Over bottomless cups of tea and the occasional plate of pasta, Rosa and I commiserated, while patrons needed to be served and catered to. She and I shared a dream that has yet to be realized. We spent hours planning the itinerary of our grand escape to Europe someday. We would explore every nook and cranny of the continent. For awhile we would live glamorous, carefree lives, soaking up the sun of the French Riviera.

Our greatest gift to each other was humour. We often compared the latest histrionics in each other's families. We became giddy over the latest antics of her relatives and mine. Men wandered into the restaurant, leering at these two young, ripe Italian girls who talked speedy English and ignored their flirtations. Rosa's restaurant, as I soon came to call it, was a haven for me in those days.

Now I realize that Rosa had really been that haven. Even in moments of silence, we understood what our hearts were saying to each other. She was one of the few, like myself, who loved being Italian but hated the conflicts that that often presented growing up in a wider, more cosmopolitan world.

Dan was nodding while his eyes were closed. He confides to me that he too wanted to escape the clutches of home. This revelation is only one of many he makes to me while we journey from the day of his diagnosis to the day of his death. They are life-affirming insights from a man I once mistakenly believed to be insulated from acting as one more crutch for my mother to lean on.

Dan reveals what we have always believed in our hearts to be true. He says in a soft, tired voice, "Mommy would have sacrificed our lives for that of Teresa's."

I had become my mother's caretaker, enabling her to care for Teresa by putting my needs and wants on hold. I was persuaded that my brother held

Curaggia

special status by virtue of being a male in an Italian family. My mother treated him preferentially, catering to his every whim. I resented him, not so much for being a male but because he was spared the sordid details of my mother's hatred for my father. I cannot ever remember my mother defending her child against this man she called her husband. I believed the victim role she chose suited her much more. This way, she could draw others into her circle of self-pity and not really feel the need to change anything. She kept her children to her bosom, by feeding them on guilt long after we tried to get on with our lives. By the time I was a young woman, I confronted the reality of the deep gulf between my father and the rest of us, created by a vengeful, angry woman. My brother and I needed to forgive this mother, who could not nurture her other children because of her preoccupation with one child and her hatred of her husband.

I am a mother now. I allow the nurturing, protective instincts that are part of me to shine in Dan's cold, sterile hospital room.I hold his forehead while he vomits repeatedly. I do not allow a single nurse to overlook an item. I chastise doctors who, in my opinion, treat a body and not a person. I have learned that motherhood reaches far beyond the nourishment of the body, to that of your child's spirit as well. I hover, plumping pillows, straightening sheets, and reminding him of childhood stories. He is afraid I resent him. We speak candidly about my parents' favouritism. I do not have the heart to tell him that I remember a time when my father ridiculed his ambitions behind his back. He only took ownership of his son after Dan had accomplished so much.

While he is dying, he wants his parents nearby. They are Mommy and Daddy now. He demands their nurturing and their love. They must see him out of this world just as they saw him in. He panics when my father is out of sight. He finally sees in him the father he has always wanted. Dad is there for him, putting aside a lifetime of hurts and old wounds and thinking only of how to make his son more comfortable. Dad is unselfish and gentle, we know that we have been hostages to the grief of a woman who stood between his children and him. She never gave him credit for mellowing. However, Dan's illness is an opportunity to forgive, to acknowledge finally that we are born to imperfect parents and that each of us makes choices that cannot always be blamed on where we came from.

I have discovered along that pebble-strewn path other people who have loved me. They have helped smooth the way to a place where I now feel safe enough to risk just being me. By the time of Dan's struggle, I knew that my presence would be a gift and not a hindrance to him. I could put my ego and its needs aside for awhile, and concentrate on his ordeal. I had played the victim role, but like a dress two sizes too small, it simply did not fit me. I knew, like the lion in "The Wizard of Oz", that I had a lion's courage and resilience.

I was alone with my brother when he died. It was one of the holiest moments of my life and I can only compare it to the birth of each of my three children. I am filled with a tremendous sense of loss for his presence, his laughter and his affection for my children and me. I also know that this experience for me meant that I gained a sense of greater value for my womanhood. For both Dan and me life after death truly exists.

When my parents walked into his room, they mourned the loss of their beloved son. Minutes later I knew that not much had really changed between them. My mother in her grief, raged at my father, calling him names and blaming him for not telling her that he was dying. My father just hung his head sadly. At that moment, I decided to step in and I admonished them for fighting over their dead son's body. They immediately stopped. This was a victory for me. Secretly, I knew Dan would be proud of me.

I have come a long way since the days I felt like a useless, little girl. One of my journal entries, written while I was taking in the delights of a warm, sunny afternoon all alone, attested to this new me I liked and accepted:

There is a tower of strength in me. The trees remind me that though my life branches out in so many directions, I am rooted deeply and I can only do the work of one person. I cannot do the work of every tree in the forest. I am gentle, too, and vulnerable like the flowers of the field where I sit. They are picked but grow again, not the same one but perhaps one stronger and more beautiful.

I am a giver of life-like the water bubbling over the stones. I have given birth, nourished and nurtured the lives of three children. Like the river I am only a channel. When they are ready, they must choose their own vessels. I love a man who tolerates my weaknesses and encourages me every day to see my life in rainbow colours instead of black and white.

I am like the sky, changing moods from grey to blue and in-between. Sometimes when the burden of dark clouds is too much I open up and weep. Like the birds, I am restless at times, flitting from one project to another, anxious to try new things but not for too long. Every tree looks appealing and inviting, then I am bored.

Mostly what surrounds me reminds me that I can love and be loved, enjoy and be enjoyed.I have made a difference in the lives of many who value me for myself and not only for what I might accomplish.

Before he died, Dan and I were talking about our parents and in particular, my father. I will never forget what he told me. He said, "I tried so hard to try and change him, and when I realized I couldn't do that, I decided to leave him be and change myself."

As I spoke to the mourners gathered in the church to pay respects to my brother, Dan's words stood out in my mind, especially as I gazed at my parents. *"If only we had shared our sorrows and concerns earlier, Dan,'* ' I thought to myself *"I would have gleaned a great deal of wisdom and might have had less pebbles to walk on."*

Domestic Affairs

Diane Raptosh

And here's this photograph of my daughter's father holding her in infancy:
he, like some glad violinist in rest position, face muscles calm; her forehead,
his instrument's beige rib nested in underchin. She is our body, which shall
be given up when the time comes. We go at this from two different homes.
Our fingerpads mesh — gentle as leaves of butter lettuce — when one of us
hands over her clothes for the week. Every step's softly worked through. Then
one of us leaves. My other body is a man who makes his way into air like a
reed. We lift by lemon-scent, his place, what few nights we can. And then
raise our separate children. Where I live, so lives my nephew. And three other
women. A golden lab flows through the human current, nudging and leaning.
Barn swallows quiver out of the blue. Such are the loves I am up against.

Matrimony

Diane Raptosh

I do, I do. I think you are. I think you are married, yes, my five-year-old answers. But not until after a pause long as the body of dream. To whom? I ask, scratching my thumb pad with my front teeth. You are married to Karen. You're a bride to your sister. My daughter's every *s* whistles small births. It's true that my sister does most of the physical work at the house. Hauling the 40-pound bags of coarse salt to soften hard water. Escorting controlled fire round the land's rim. Currying the horses, combing out scurf. She and I hand-weeded half of this five-acre pasture ourselves. With help from our mother. Because weeds were there, because she lives here too. Because she comes from a long line of Sicilian farmers. Because if I want my daughter to inherit *her* wedding ring, six tiny diamonds shaped like a tulip, we might as well, all of us now, get down on our knees, one way or another, and do it.

Common Living

Diane Raptosh

Outside, six willows get in one another's hair; the dog in his pen shares Iams
with magpies. The pine table with leaves to seat twelve looks out on them.
Inside, evenings, the smell of live nightgowns — sweet, bitter cream — rises
and dips. Five bodies. Seven wide beds. The Siamese fighting fish. To find
these, come up the blond stairway built like the one in *Gone With the Wind*.
Going back down, fresh palm prints trellis the handrail; a cobweb of neon
green kite string spins off the front porch. For the Bushmen, a curved branch
leaning sideways, one end embedded in ground, marks *entrance*. The doorway's hearth orders us: *Here ... Lie down ... A teaspoon of honey ... It's time
to go.* The horse's thighs tighten each time I drive in. I'm half a hand's width
— less than breath's kiss — from calling this unity.

Basement Suite

Vivian Zenari

Lina's mother and father say that immigrants used to build their houses with a separate entrance to the basement, so that they could rent out the basement to help pay the mortgage. In those days, people took thrift for granted. Lina's cousins and Italian friends take wealth for granted. Those who don't own their own home and who don't have double attached garages live on the fringe. But in the fifties, when Lina's parents moved to Canada, many people had to live in a basement suite at some point in their lives.

The dilapidated house where her cousin Peter lives is a product of those times, except that the tidy immigrant neighbourhood of forty years ago has decayed into inner city. Lina climbs down a sunken entrance at the side of the house to the basement suite door and rings the doorbell.

Peter opens the door. He seems shocked. But immediately his expression closes.

"Hi." He opens the door wide to let Lina in.

He is, as Lina expects, dressed in torn sweatpants cut off at the calves and a wrinkled and stained T-shirt with a neckline that stretches down past his collarbone. His hair is uncombed, matted like the hair of a child's abandoned doll.

Silently he takes Lina down a lightless corridor to a room glowing blue from the light of the television. Peter motions Lina to the sagging sofa, then drops into the folding chair under the unlit floor lamp. The austerity of the room strikes her — no tables, no pictures on the walls, no furniture besides what they sat in and what did and did not light the room. The television's sound is shut off. It intensifies the feeling of deliberate asceticism.

"I just want to say good-bye, since I'm leaving tomorrow morning."

"Yes, I know."

Lina is going to the University of British Columbia to start a masters' degree in creative writing. Peter must have found out about it from his father. Lina herself hasn't seen or spoken to Peter in three years.

"I've gone to see your dad and everyone already."

"So you're ready to go?"

"Yes. I have my suitcases in the car already. I'm going to drive out early tomorrow."

"Then it's kind of late to go out visiting, isn't it?"

"I wanted to see you before I left."

"After all this time." He draws out a silence. It seems to be a specialty of his now. "Do you want a drink? I have pop and beer."

"Water's fine."

He rises and moves smoothly into the empty doorway that leads to the kitchen. And he returns with that same grace and ease Lina likened to a slender boat floating on the water, its sails full with the wind, traveling with great purpose and faith across the Mediterranean Sea.

"Here." He hands Lina the water in a wet, chipped tumbler. Up close, she can see his handsome face and hard, taut body through his unkempt hair and tattered clothes. His natural beauty would almost be obscured, if it wasn't for his features, which he can't alter. He has always been careless with his appearance. It is as though he flaunts his shabbiness to spite the rest of Lina's family, who, no matter what they wear or paint on their faces, can't ever be beautiful by Canadian standards. The Innocentis have yellowish-green complexions and bulging black eyes like ripe olives. They also share genes that give almost all of them a prominent bump on the bridge of their noses. Lina's high-school Italian teacher once announced to Lina's class that she had a classic Roman nose, a comment that was met with dead silence by the class and with deep mortification by Lina. By contrast, Peter is willowy, golden-haired, with deep gray eyes and delicate features. Peter's mother came from York, and his names, Peter Thorton, like his appearance, derive from his mother's father and grandfather. He is no Pietro.

Lina wonders sometimes how her family dealt with Peter's mother, the only non-Italian in-law. She died when Peter was eight, old enough for him to sense any isolation and mild opprobrium his mother and zio Luigi might have endured. Lina has turned the fact of his English mother over and over in her mind. She has trained herself to believe this explains almost everything about Peter.

Peter sits back in his chair. "I hope you like it in Vancouver."

"I know I will."

"Its a beautiful city, I hear."

"Yes. It has wonderful parks."

He takes some time before he answers. "Yes, it does."

Peter didn't finish high school. Peter and Lina went to the same junior high, though he was one grade above Lina. He was so handsome the boys were jealous of him, a white-skinned angel in a school populated by immigrants from Italy, the Philippines, Eritrea, Argentina. The girls would tease him, stand by his locker and steal his books, or tug at his clothes and run off. The teachers, so Lina has heard, thought Peter had a psychological block that prevented him from doing well academically, since he scored high on diagnostic exams. Something must have happened along the way. It seems to Lina that once he reached adolescence, he became a curiosity, something to be tapped and used for other people's purposes. At church picnics and weddings,

Curaggia

zia Antonina or nonna Teresina would point him out to someone or drag him over for display, saying, "That blond one is ours. He's the blondie in the family." It was as though he legitimized Lina's family to North America, their very own WASP to prove that they were wholehearted adherents to the values of their adopted society.

In the end, though, Peter failed to live up to everyone's expectations. When other boys began to wear tank tops and bicycle shorts because they knew they looked good in them, Peter continued to wear his baggy jeans and oversized T-shirts. And when he dropped out of high school, he didn't work in his father's meat shop like zio Luigi wanted him to. Instead, he worked at the gas station across the street from his old high school, as though to encourage scorn from his friends or to embarrass zio Luigi, which his father accuses him of doing. For the past three years, Peter has been on welfare.

Lina has to admit that she was one of those who had expected more of him.

"I'll be coming back for the holidays. Christmas and reading week for sure. I'll try to come back for part of the summer."

He doesn't answer. Lina says, "I'll write to you. Can you give me your postal code?"

"Yeah."

Lina scrambles in her purse for a pen and notepad. As she withdraws the notepad she accidentally pulls out a handkerchief.

"Did Nonna give you that?" Peter asks.

"Yes. How did you know?"

"Who else buys handkerchiefs these days?" He stops. "Nonna gave me hankies too. Remember that time she told us why handkerchiefs were important?"

"No."

"Because you could use them at weddings or funerals, for laughing or crying. For all the important times in your life."

Lina doesn't remember Nonnas maxim. But she remembers being at Nonna's funeral four years ago, and Peter coming to her while she stood sobbing by the open casket, and saying, "Don't cry because she's dead. Cry because you're glad to be standing here looking at her instead of being in there yourself." It was a harsh thing to say, indicative of where he stood on life.

He never spent as much time as Lina did with the rest of their cousins. He stayed away from the church youth groups, the Italian classes on Saturday mornings, the movies and, when they were older, the nightclubs. Yet Lina felt him more than the others. From the beginning, he took an interest in Lina's poetry. No one else in her family did; she didn't think anyone noticed her interest until she was accepted into the master's program. At her confirmation party, Peter saw the short poem she had pegged up on her bulletin board in her room and said, "Do you have more like that? Do one for me." The Christmas after Peter got his job in the gas station, he gave Lina a little chapbook from a poet she had never heard of. He said, "I don't know if she's any good, but you can tell me."

He never did ask Lina about the book. That was how their relationship was: brief intersections, like two hermits wandering in the desert, occasionally crossing paths and whispering revelations from their latest visions with hoarse, unused voices, then moving apart for another period of solitude.

Lina finds her pen and scribbles down the postal code Peter recites to her But if she sends him a letter next week, will he still be here to receive it? He moves around so much, he is nearly untraceable. Only zio Luigi, who still exercises his parental obligations despite everything, can keep track of Peter's rovings.

Once, during their cousin Maria's twenty-first birthday party, Peter said to Lina, "Why do you go to the clubs and the hall parties so much?"

"What do you mean?"

"You should spend more time writing."

"I can't write all the time. I need a life, too."

"You should devote yourself to it. You're wasting your life, otherwise."

"And what are you doing? Nothing! A high-school drop-out and pumping gas!"

He grew pale. "What do you think I should I do?" he asked quietly.

"Anything!"

"Maybe I will do something right for once," he murmured. He turned away, and he didn't speak to Lina the rest of that evening.

He did do something, Lina thinks. That one thing.

"You dropped your handkerchief," Peter says.

He stands up and comes to the sofa. He sits down next to Lina and picks up the handkerchief. He holds it out to her. "Here."

Lina wants to touch his hand. She wants to touch him.

The week after Maria's birthday party, Peter called Lina at home for the first time in their lives, and he asked her to go cycling with him in the river valley that evening. Lina cancelled her plans to go to the nightclub with her cousins so that she could ride with him.

They rode their bicycles in silence along the paths in the river valley, surrounded by cool dark trees and soft green bushes. As mid-evening approached the sky dimmed, but they continued to ride as the traffic on the paths subsided, until they saw no one else on the paths. They pedalled slowly. They didn't stop or speak for a long time.

Finally Lina asked if they could stop at a rest area to use the bathroom. They pulled off the path at a clearing with a picnic shelter and restrooms. As Lina stepped into the shelter, out of the corner of her eye she saw him standing motionless by the bicycles. When she came out he was in the same position, like a statue. As she walked closer to him the metaphor become more appropriate, because the sun had fully set, the only light a faint blueness over the trees and a half moon in the sky, and in the darkness he looked like an ancient Greek statue, details rubbed smooth by time, strong outlines drawing out more emotion than any colour or detail could.

"It's getting late," Lina said.

"Do you want to go back?"

"No."

He remained silent for a moment. "Do you ever feel," he asked, "that you never want to go back?"

"I don't know." Her throat constricted.

"Aren't you happy?"

"Almost."

"Do you want to be?"

Lina swallowed, and nodded.

They walked their bicycles out of the clearing deep into the trees. When they were far into the forest, they threw down their bicycles and lay down under the trees and made love.

In between love-making he whispered poems he said he had written for her, hoping one day to have the chance to read them to her. He said he could remember the last Christmas he had with his mother. She had made plum pudding, just for the two of them, because she said that everyone else in the family hated it, and they were the only two who would ever eat it. Peter's skin was baby-smooth, and beauty marks peppered down the curve of his back to his buttocks, which were hard and cool like stone under her hands, as she pressed him into her.

Then, when she was feeling gloomy and vulnerable because it was late and dark and cold, and Lina knew she would have to go home to her house, to her parents, she said, "Have we sinned?"

He said, "There's no point in thinking about that now. We've done it." He added, more gently, "We've done what weve wanted. That's what matters."

When Lina got home, she couldn't explain to her parents why she was so late, why her hair was down instead of up when she left, why her shirt was on backwards.

The next morning, Lina called Peter and told him that her parents had guessed what had happened. He said he would come over and explain himself to Linas parents.

When he arrived half an hour later, Lina rushed to the door herself when the bell rang. Peter covered her mouth with his fingers and said, "Let me do it. And promise me you won't contradict what I say."

He kissed her, and when Lina drew back from him in confusion, he wiped his eyes and said, "Please. Promise me. It'll all turn out one day."

He went into the living room, and Lina followed behind him. Lina's mother sat on the sofa, head in her hands, Lina's father sitting next to her, his bushy, greying eyebrows furrowed. Papà lifted his head up when he saw Peter. Peter stopped, opened his mouth, but Papà was faster than Peter.

"What's the matter with you?" Papà said. He was looking at Peter, but he was speaking to both of them.

"It's my fault," Peter said. "Lina won't say this, but it's true. I forced myself on her."

"Peter!" Lina shouted.

There was an empty moment, where nothing seemed to happen. It was like an instant of grace, for everyone. But the moment folded in on itself, and Lina's father was leaping toward Peter, and her father's fist cracked against Peter's head, and Peter fell, noiseless, while her mother screamed, and Lina choked out a scream, but it caught there, and she fell, too.

In retrospect, Lina doesn't know what Peter was thinking. What had he supposed would happen when he sat in the family room and told her parents that hed raped her, and that she was trying to protect him by saying nothing? But the rest of it — what do people expect when they submit to the mercy of others? At best, condescension, paternalism, perhaps even gratitude. At worst, consumption, destruction, so that the fabric of ones life becomes unraveled and woven into that of the conquerors. Thus the Greek gods became the Roman gods. Lina did what she had promised to do: she didnt contradict what Peter had said. Her parents told him never to go near Lina again, and Lina promised. The tragedy of it, and Lina thought it was this, a true tragedy, had been that Lina had believed Peter when he said it would turn out.

It's been three years, Lina thinks, and it hasn't.

It didn't have to be that way. During periods of persecution, the early Christians in Rome lived in catacombs. Eventually, the repentant Romans asked them for forgiveness; and the Christians said that no forgiveness was necessary, for they were sinners, too. They were a family of sinners, and now was the time for reconciliation.

Lina can still feel him under her skin as she drives down the Yellowhead highway in the early morning. Out of the car window she sees the morning prairie sky, blue like the sea.

Lina told her family she wanted to leave in the evening so that she could stay overnight in Calgary with friends. No one knew about her plan to visit Peter. But they will. It has been too long since the Innocentis acknowledged Peter as a member of the family. Now they will have to.

Curaggia

Lina has done it all because of him, her poetry, her education. Once before he tried to stop her from taking his influence to its logical conclusion. This time, Lina has refused to let him.

Peter stirs in the seat next to Lina and falls back asleep. It took all night to persuade him to come with her. But it didnt take much.

In the fifties, when the Italian immigrants wanted to hold Mass in their own language, the English parishioners at their inner-city church only allowed the Italians to hold their Mass in the church basement. When Lina arrives in Vancouver, she will be the foreigner. She will know what her parents and others have known, about having to build and live in basement suites. And how to survive them.

Captivity

The Last Time I Saw Elaine

Theresa Carilli

I met Elaine in a church basement when we were both about seven years old. Having finished my after-catechism prayers, I was heading home with my friend Mary Ellen. At seven, Mary Ellen and I had a firm grasp of politics, though not yet religion, and we would walk home together arguing about John F. Kennedy. Mary Ellen's parents taught her that Kennedy was a saint. My parents assured me he was just another Irish bum, a title they proudly assigned to all Irish-American politicians. This argument insulted Mary Ellen, since she was of Irish descent. So, this particular day, after catechism, we lingered by the altar longer than usual, the last sinners to exit from the church basement that fine October afternoon. From nowhere a dark-haired girl and her male friend accosted us on the stairs. Lunging forward, they demanded we stand still. We had been captured. The girl ordered the boy to encircle us, insuring our captivity.

"You are my prisoners," she said.

Being rather annoyed and eager to get home, I sighed deeply to Mary Ellen, with a look assuring her this would not go on for very much longer. And as if on cue, the door opened and a woman called down the steps in frustration, "Elaine! Elaine! Get over here. Can you hear me? Get over here now!" The door closed and there was a momentary look of embarrassment on the girl's face. "You can go this time," she said, "but next time, I'll get you."

Then she scurried off with an air of fear.

That's how I learned her name. For the rest of my life, Elaine would cause me great anguish.

Now and then I saw Elaine in school, but I never had any interest in knowing her. After all, she had been my first captor. I felt great dis-ease each time I saw her.

My second encounter with Elaine took place six years later. Our gym instructor pitted us against one another in a softball throwing contest. The object was to throw the ball as far as possible. The individual who could throw the ball the farthest would participate in a state competition.

I took a serious look at Elaine. We were about the same size, same dark thick hair, same eye color, though I thought I looked smarter than she. To me, she seemed like an old country type, a guniea, a WOP, a dumb WOP, destined to produce several other dumb guniea children, all of whom would be factory workers. How could someone so dumb-looking even consider holding me hostage? In a fit of nausea and anger, I heaved the ball with all my might. Elaine threw it further. I got the ball again, and concentrating on the strength in my right arm, I threw the ball as far as possible. Still, Elaine threw it further. She had beaten me. She could throw further than I could. It wasn't until high school that we were finally able to settle our differences, and put our inauspicious first meetings behind us. I would inherit Elaine, much as I had inherited my ethnicity and my family. She would represent my struggle for freedom from the old country.

We became friends on the basketball court. Elaine was very subdued, though her physical strength and precision with a basketball were uncanny. I was quick and coordinated but overrun by emotion. I would easily lose concentration, while Elaine was steady, always steady. After missing a shot or a rebound, I would spiral down into frustration. Elaine would take pity on me, offer encouragment, and remind me that basketball said nothing about a person's future successes or failures.

I loved her. I hated her. I felt nothing for her except I knew she was in my life. She took to calling me by my last name, which made me feel athletic and important.

Often after basketball practice, we would spend time together, listening to America, Paul Simon, or Neil Young albums. We developed a unique understanding of one another, especially after learning that her father and all our grandparents had come from the same town in Sicily. Elaine spoke the Sicilian dialect. I knew a few words and I knew the gestures. This was, after all, my parent's native language, though they would not share it with me. For them, it represented shame, poverty, and illiteracy. Yet, contact with the older relatives required some ability to communicate. While I felt cheated by my lack of knowledge, Elaine used the language selectively, as though it were a secret. As we grew older, she would never disclose this knowledge to anyone, much as she had not told me of the relationship between our grandmothers.

I learned about this relationship the first time I met her grandmother.

We were at Elaine's house one day after practice when the old Sicilian woman walked into the kitchen unexpectedly. Elaine had not known she was there. The old woman caught my eye, swallowed hard and swore repeatedly. "Son a'ma bitch, son a'ma bitch." Elaine told her grandmother to be silent, and she looked down. In a fury, her grandmother left the room. "Why is she swearing at me?" I asked. Elaine looked down and waited for her mother to intervene.

"Honey," her mother spoke, "your grandmother, your father's mother..."

"I never met her, you know," I said, "she was dead before I was born."

"I know," her mother spoke slowly, "your grandmother..."

She hesitated again, calling me "honey" repeatedly, to soften the blow about to come.

"Uh," she began, " he kept her like a prisoner. You know what I mean?'

"Yeah." I looked down at my sneakers, and realized that I needed new shoe laces. At this point, Elaine's grandmother blurted out impatiently,

"Every day. He beat her every day."

I had heard only one story of my grandmother's beatings and thought it was just a one-time incident. My father described a childhood remembrance of how he hid under his bed, watching his mother get beaten and thrown across the room. I had little sympathy for my father. He had taken up the same sport, holding me and my sisters as captive audience to his wild displays of rage, which often resulted in broken or damaged furniture and threats of suicide or homicide. I didn't want Elaine to know about the agonizing history, which I faced and which faced me, in my day-to-day adolescence. I wanted to share only what felt hopeful and inspiring, what put me a step further away from an excruciating existence of witnessing rage. But Elaine knew the terrible secrets and this daunting history.

Filled with embarrassment, I bit my lip, listening to their words as though someone held a microphone on my heart. The vibrating fear was no longer my very own secret of captivity.

Elaine's mother explained, "My mother, Elaine's grandmother, took care of your grandmother after she had been beaten. She washed her off, kept her away. She hates your grandfather."

At this point, Elaine's grandmother chimed in, "May your grandfather rot in hell."

I nodded at the old woman as she cried, "Your grandmother, beautiful person."

From then on, the old woman became my friend. She taught me to play cut throat poker and often she would shed a tear upon seeing me. But she never spoke to me about my grandmother again.

Now I was bound to Elaine by more than just a love for basketball, Paul Simon, Neil Young, and America. She was meant to be in my life, a sister I was supposed to have, a mother, a friend, a soulmate of sorts. She was my mirror of ethnicity and assimilation. She represented my struggle for freedom. Born ten days apart, we came out together and shared the secrets of our broken love affairs, drawn to women who were culturally dissimilar, who kept us at a distance. We worshipped these lovers much as we worshipped the Sicilian matriarchal figures in our lives. We were drawn to the emotionless punishment inflicted upon us by our lovers, just as we had been drawn to the fear of our mother's voices. Throughout our lives, we would be separated and reunited, torn by our lovers, professions, and ideologies. Together, we would suffer illnesses and surgeries. I would leave home while

Curaggia

she would remain. We would never discuss the secrets between our ⸦.
mothers. We thought we had evolved far beyond the expectations of ⸦
families and our ethnicity.

The last time I saw Elaine, she was living down the street from her
parents in a home that her grandmother, still very much alive, had purchased
for her. I was visiting my parents and looked forward to seeing Elaine. But,
this was the visit that would separate us. Thirty years after our first meeting
in the church basement, we would take a boat trip to Long Island where she
would conduct business. We would talk for hours about how much we needed
one another. But after all was said, there was this silence between us.

A few days later, as the silence began to eat away at me, I met with Elaine.
I cried for all the miserable years I had spent living in that neighborhood.
She listened with a coldness but an understanding. Her body was rigid and
she looked at me, ashamed of my vulnerability. We were strong women after
all, from sacrificial stock. To cry was to break the code of sacrificial silence.

And suddenly it occurred to me that Elaine was being held captive living
down the street from her family. She was truly imprisoned though she could
act as an American women who had great freedom. I, instead, take the
historical legacy with me from coast to coast, searching for the way out, for
a sense of home.

Once we had been strong and steady and innocent. We were sisters and
friends and soulmates of sorts. We cared deeply for one another. The grandchildren of immigrants, the children of people who thought self-denial was
a virtue. We had worked through two generations of guilt and suffering and
sorrow. What had we really become? Weren't we still prisoners of the values
we had inherited, captives of estrangement from our history, our homes,
ourselves?

That night, I left Elaine knowing I would never see her again. For her, I
would always be a remembrance of who she was and where she came from.
For me, she would always be the reminder of a captivity, a silence, I could
never break.

Theatre

or

O to Be Italian in Toronto
Drinking Cappuccino on Bloor Street
at Bersani & Carlevale's

Mary di Michele

Back then you couldn't have imagined
yourself openly savouring a cappuccino,
you were too ashamed that your dinners
were in a language you couldn't share
with your friends: their pot roasts,
their turnips, their recipes for Kraft
dinners you glimpsed in TV commercials -
the mysteries of macaroni with marshmallows!
You needed an illustrated dictionary
to translate your meals, looking to the glossary
of vegetables, *melanzane* became eggplant,
African, with the dark sensuality of liver.
But for them even eggplants were exotic
or alien, their purple skins from outer space.

Through the glass oven door
you would watch it bubbling in Pyrex,
layered with tomato sauce and cheese,
melanzane alla parmigiana,
the other-worldliness viewed as if
through a microscope
like photosynthesis in a leaf.

                    *

Educated in a largely Jewish high school
you were Catholic. Among doctors' daughters,
the child of a truck driver for la Chiquita banana.
You became known as Miraculous Mary,
announced along with jokes about virgin mothers.

You were as popular as pork on Passover.

You discovered insomnia, migraine headaches,
menstruation, that betrayal of the female
self to the species. You discovered despair.
Only children and the middle aged are consolable.
You were afraid of that millionth part difference
in yourself which might just be character.
What you had was rare and seemed to weigh
you down as if it were composed of plutonium.
What you wanted was to be like everybody else.
What you wanted was to be liked.
You were in love with that Polish boy
with yellow hair everybody thought
looked like Paul Newman.
All the girls wanted to marry him.
There was not much hope for
a fat girl with good grades.

                    *

But tonight you are sitting in an Italian cafe
with a man you dated a few times and fondled
fondly until the romance went as flat as the froth
under the domed plastic lid of a cappuccino ordered
to-go. And because you, at least, are committed
to appearing mature as well as urbane
in public you shift easily into the nevertheless doubtful relationship of coffee to conversation.

He insists he remembers you as vividly
as Joan Crawford upstaging Garbo in *Grande Hotel*.
You're so melodramatic, he said, *Marriage*
to you would be like living in an Italian opera!
Being in love with someone who doesn't love you
is like being nominated for an Oscar and losing,
a truly great performance gone to waste.
Still you balanced your espresso expertly
throughout a heated speech without spilling a single
tear into the drink. Then you left him to pay the bill.
For you, Italians! he ran out shouting after you,
life is theatre!

Life is Theatre

Nonno

Maria Maziotti Gillan

I never met you.
I saw you only in an old photograph
in an oval mahogany frame.
In the photograph that follows us
to all our tenement apartments,
you are young and handsome and very serious.
Your forehead's high, like mine;
my father said high foreheads were signs of intelligence.
Blue letters come from Italy from my grandmother.
None from you.
"He is dead," my father told me,
and that's all I knew,
except that you lived in Argentina
and were a journalist and when I asked
for more, my father pretended not to hear.

It is only now, when you are more than 50 years dead, that I learn
that you left my grandmother and your seven children in Italy,
found a new woman in Buenos Aires,
and had a son with her.
At first you sent money to Italy for Nonna and the children,
letters filled with love, then silence.
If I had met you. I would have called you Nonno.
but for me you are a flat figure,
in a coloring book.
I cannot find the details to fill you in.
My father does not carry bitterness
in his heart against you, he
forgives you, though he, too,
barely knew you. And if he can
forgive you, surely I can,
but even forgiveness requires
more knowledge than I have.
How else were we alike?
Grandfather, Nonno, stranger

in a black suitcoat and stiff high-necked shirt,
step out of that mahogany frame,
tell me what happened,
why you left your wife,
why you never went back?
What shame did you carry
in your heart, that first wife
those seven children?
How did you turn your mind and heart
against them? Nonno, tell me, I will listen.
Let me know, so I can hear myself in you,
those pieces that are part of me,
and of my father and of my children,
pieces of you I carry in my blood
and that I need to know come to us from you.
Nonna, step out of your frame and speak to me.

͵ on Aging

Gianna Patriarca

i am middle aged now
something I thought
would only happen
to others
has happened to me

*

i sometimes think
i have been old all my life
Italian women are born old
they carry the weight
right from the womb
old with fear
old with responsibility
the first beat of the heart
pounding out
fear fear fear
like the eleventh
commandment

*

lately it seems
all words are about
loss
always about leaving

*

what to write about
my life
always in the past
the days become history
so quickly
i cannot write the future

*

i am lost without dreams
when did they stop

such a dreamer i was
such fantasies
such possibilities
but all around me there is
pain
dreams have stopped
just like the candle light
at a quick breath
no warning
even my pen is heavy to lift

*

i am looking for a reason
to write about snow
looking for a muse
in the cracks of my life
looking for a landscape
to tickle my heart
but i am sad
my steps are timid
in the winter night
awkward
how i miss running
how i miss the laughter
in my mother's house
where she lives alone
how i miss the length
of my hair
it's black sheen
faded
i miss my father's anger
how strange this
aging

*

i will leave my poems
somewhere
in time they will be
stumbled upon
and my father's name
will live on
without sons

*

i want to write
about my dying aunt
i hate the word
dying
she isn't dead yet
who am i to think
death must be the next
visitor
but the blood clots
are heavy and thick
like rocks
throughout her lungs
her right arm and leg
no longer move
her chest heaves
painfully
with each struggling breath
i bend to kiss her brow
her skin smells clean
sweet with talcum powder
i caress sparse white curls
little bundles of pure silk
i lift her still hand
to my lips
with a silent kiss
comes a prayer
asking for a miracle
all that is left
to believe in
but miracles don't happen
to old women
in Scarborough hospitals
in Canadian winters

*

i am nothing
she is nothing
we are nothing
but a breath
a moment
a sunrise
a storm

Curaggia

a silence

*

she asks me how i am
is my husband well
and my child, is she
growing strong and tall
"go home" she tells me
the weather is bad
the road is long
between home and
here

*

there is a slow tearing
in my heart
like a last love letter
another wound to heal
soon another gravestone
to visit
another voice in my life
silenced
another January
with its sharp icicles
plunged into my soul

*

forty years
eighty years
a long time
a short time
when is death
less tragic

*

it is life we lose
each time
and we are less
for it

*

in my culture
middle aged poets
are not highly regarded
unlike doctors or lawyers

Life is Theatre

and land developers
poets hold no position
you cannot measure
their worth
in real estate
my aunt
will not know
i write poems for her
life without metaphors
only the rhythm of
a broken language
she never acquired
thirty years spent
in airless factories
my dying aunt
will never hear my poems
but i know her life
helped me write them

*

my heart is strong
my mother's lineage
in my father's family
the hearts were weak
my aunt hangs on
that muscle
broken over and over again
will not give up
women's hearts grow stronger
with each rupture
maybe
women's hearts never die
my aunt, my mother
my sister, my daughter
my nieces, me
one heart, forever stronger
infinite.

Curaggia

Contemplations

Gabriella Micallef and Dora Timperio

I met Dora many years ago and have spent many hours in her kitchen drinking espressos and listening to stories. When she started painting I noticed a difference in her. As if she was uplifted. She seemed calm, peaceful and began to tell her stories through her paintings.

Dora recalls: I started painting in 1996. It was through the hospital. I have a lot of health problems, so the hospital visits have been a regular thing with me. At the urging of hospital staff, I joined the art program. I painted some pictures, but I didn't see anything nice in what I had painted. Then on December 12th, 1997, I dreamt of my father. My father is dead now, God bless him. My father said to me in my dream, "Dora come help me to work the field." I replied, "Ok papa, I coming." I went to the fields to meet my father who immediately disappeared for fifteen minutes or so. When he came back, he brought me a little statue of the Virgin Mary and he said to me, "Dora, here it is, it's for you."

The next day I went to the hospital to go on the machine. Later that night, I went to bed but I couldn't sleep. I tossed and turned, opening and closing my eyes. Then I saw an image of the Madonna. It came right to the front of my eyes and swung back and forth, back and forth. It was so clear and the image remained in front of my eyes for sometime and I thought, this is something I could do, why don't I paint the Madonna? So I go to the kitchen and I take a pencil and I draw the Virgin Mary. I remember afterwards going back to bed and sleeping so easily.

After that, I start to have this thing in my head, so why I don't paint? So I think from somewhere, my father came to my dream with the Virgin Mary to tell me I have something inside me and it still won't come out. So between the dream and the Virgin Mary, I started painting.

Then my birthday rolled along and the group at the hospital gave me a little party. I brought my pictures. The art guy and the doctor, they said that they liked my pictures. The doctor, he was so proud of me. So I thought, there's something here, they like my paintings. I was so happy. I was the most happy lady in the world that day. You know I was never happy, no matter how many crochet or whatever else I gave to people, on one ever said, oh you do a nice job. So that day everybody make me happy. Just to hear that. You know at least somebody appreciates something I did.

I felt something inside me that day. I felt good. Now when I go to the hospital, I bring my pictures to let everybody see. Everybody is proud. Everybody knows I paint now.

I love this picture of the boat and I loved painting it. The first time I travelled, it was on a boat like this. I stayed twenty-two days. I was on my way to Buenas Aries. I really enjoyed it. I have never been on a boat since then, my fantasy now is that someday I can go on a boat again.

When I was young, I used to climb trees. I used to go on the top of the tree and I see myself at the top of this tree. I felt happy when I painted that. It feels as though it's inside of me. I never knew I could do this.

This one is like the house I used to live in. The cow, no, no, it's a donkey. It's like I'm in there too. All my picture's have a little piece of me inside.

We used to have the mountain in front of us, then the valley, then the wheat. And I cut a lot of wheat.

Curaggia

I grew up with birds, lots of birds. I love birds. I used to watch them eat. I could even touch them. And the flowers. Wherever I used to go, walk here, walk there, you know, you see flowers. Flowers and butterflies. I used to run with the butterflies, wondering where they would go.

Curaggia

I went to school, up to grade three, you know, and that's it. The teacher had the books I used to love to look at. They made me want to draw and paint. My brother was in the military at the time and he noticed how I loved the pictures in the magazines he used to bring me. Soon he was bringing me colours and paints. I used to paint the Madonna and Jesus.

I used to do a lot of things because when we were little we didn't have a television. What we used to do is sew and embroider, lots of things like that. But when I left for Argentina, I left all that behind and didn't pick it up again for thirty-eight years. Now I can do it. I can do anything. It's passionate to do that work.

After I finish painting I stay away from it for about five minutes. Then I go back and I really enjoy my painting. It's something inside me, when I'm happy inside I can relax. You see I have pain and there's no pills to take for it. When I paint, I forget all about my pain. This is one nice therapy. This is the nicest therapy God could give me.

When I paint I go into the dream of the painting, everything is gone for me, the bad things and the good things. Everything is gone. It's so good.

My father used to say to me "someday we can have a treasure," but you know he never saw it. I feel like he came in my dream to give me a treasure. Maybe this was his dream, to have a treasure one day, to give me.

The Origins of Milk

Daniela Gioseffi

Faces explode old family albums
with sighs that shatter gravestones.
I'm torn up for confetti and showered
on the celebration winding in the streets below.
Another grey man is elected to rule the flow of milk.

I look for my mother copulating among the sheep
in a dream field. A haze floats over her
as she disappears on a long cold shore of sand.

I ask a genie waiting to be born
in blue smoke from my navel
if he's heard my magic words
and knows that I, too, wish to see into the lamp.

The frenzy I've offered as love
has rusted my heart values.
All the telephone booths are out of order
in the traffic of the city. Strange voices,
shells from unknown seas sound in my ears.
Stray children wander in gutters, hungry dogs nip
as their toes. Abandoned fathers sit on curbs.
Panhandlers replace clowns on every corner.
They do not smile or dance, but simply ask
for money to be dropped in empty cups.
I ponder newsprint, terrorist bombs, genocide, ethnic hate,
false hair, surgical faces, plastic breasts, strontium 90,
plutonium, acid rain, Stranded in a society of barbaric,
mathematical men who live by market competition,
I want to create symbiotic symphonies
of economic cooperation as an antidote to greed and hate.

I'm made of primal customs practiced in varied
languages. I gather water, try to commune with you
among the flower boxes where fumes clog my throat;

Life is Theatre

machines follow me down the street, grinding gears
against flesh. Grey dials turn in me. I try to call
you, whom I met by the accuracy of chance.

The telephone receiver is gone. It's stuck to my mouth
and my eyes are dimes caught in my hair.
Blood I once left on your sheets came from moons of change
once hidden in my belly. When we parted, were you still there?
Were we still lovers as we were?
Curdling time gave us up to undecided decisions.
Now, kettles whistle for morning coffee,
and we mourn our dreams as visions of what we hoped.

I want to bottle the wind and drink it for cola.
But, I lost you among strange hands, open mouths,
umbrellas. I would have been what you were searching for
with sheer will, if you could decide what sleeper you resemble,
and which of your dreams struggles behind your eyelids.

I can't bear the hollow music of a half-lived life.
Birds in my inner ear batter wings to get out.
I call them by their exotic names to my open windows.
The artful lover lacks artless feelings.

I knew when you touched me where your thoughts were.
I can't be fooled into orgasm, but women know how to pretend.
Into my chest, I follow birds, trying to sing
proper notes to the moon, mirroring the sun,
to the darkness in me, nothing without your love.

Perhaps, the finest language is silence in its glory.
I long to be an apple tree blossoming in your garden.

Curaggia

Inheritances

Kathryn Nocerino

From my father, what they call
Attitude,
And a tendency to lead with the mind;
From my mother:
Loyalty, Slavic gloom,
And the music of languages;
From my father,
The ability, beyond reason,
To squeeze optimism from the hard nut of disaster;
From my mother,
A hungry eye;
From my father,
Attitude;
From the two of them, really,
When I think of it,
A constitutional distaste for moderation;
From my father,
A polite anticlericalism;
From my mother, Polish catholicism
With its scapulars, its miracle-working icons,
And its gaze, unblinking as a child's
Upon eternity.
(Although, last week,
My mother called the sitting Pope
"That stupid Polack")
From my father,
Attitude.

Florence, 1975

Claudia Giordano

In Which Music
is a Dominant Factor

Michelle Alfano

This piece is an excerpt from a work-in-progress entitled Opera *about three children Lilla, Joey and Clara infected by their Italian-born mother's love of opera. The Pentangeli family lives on a lot behind a giant billboard in Hamilton, Ontario, under which all forms of entertainment take place.*

Opera n. A form of drama in which music is a dominant factor, made up of arias, recitatives, choruses, etc... with orchestral accompaniment, scenery, acting, and sometimes dance.

On Saturday night, Clara, Joey and I favored the assembled crowd of aunts, uncles and children with a different scene from an opera. These scenes reminded me of the stories Mama had told us of Sicily where all the villagers gathered at the cinema or watched the marionette show in the town square, calling out to each figure, berating or warning them with each plot turn.

Some nights were devoted to dance; we re-enacted the Dance of the Moorish Slaves in *Aida*, the Gypsy Song in *La Traviata* or the Dance of the Furies in *Orpheus and Eurydice*. On another night, we mimicked love arias from the romantic scenes in operas: Lauretta's love aria in *Gianni Schicchi*, Alfredo's arias to Violetta, Nedda's Bird Song in *Pagliacci*. On this night, we were to enact famous death scenes to a running commentary of abuse or praise from our parents, aunts and uncles.

In the giant lights reflected from the billboard, we competed as to who could kill or die the most dramatically and elicit the greatest praise from the crowd. The adults sat on identical, backless stools on the driveway, facing the billboard in an eager semi-circle. They balanced glasses of red wine or beer on one knee and small plastic plates of food on the other. The younger children, including some of the neighbourhood kids, sat on the grass in front of them, throwing food or fighting amongst themselves. The older boy cousins leaned coolly along the brick wall of the house searching for females that may have wandered by. The portable stereo was placed outside, with a stack of well used L.P.'s gathered from the record collections of my mother and all her sisters.

In this world, I was the undisputed diva. That night, I chose to play Manon's death scene in the final act. For some bizarre and unknown reason, Puccini contrives to send Manon and her lover to America to die. Manon is sentenced to life as a convict in the French colony of Louisiana after being labeled a prostitute by her older lover, a wealthy cuckold. The whole messy affair could have been quickly and efficiently disposed of at the port of their departing ship with a quick murder or two, but no... Puccini had to have them drag their pitiful carcasses into a desert outside of New Orleans and *then* die. Puccini's cruelty towards his heroines knew no bounds, my mother often said.

I knew Manon to be vain and affected so I borrowed one of Mama's long black wigs and powdered my face, drawing large and uneven bow-shaped pink lips over my pinched round ones. The floor length pink dress from my confirmation served as my impromptu gown, together with pale pink ballet slippers. In my short life, I had never known a soprano to die in anything other than full makeup and a sumptuous gown.

I motioned for Joey to put on the last *duetto* in the final act. He sprung, in full clown outfit (he was to play Canio in *Pagliacci* after me) to the stereo and put on the record. He walked to the front of the group and intoned solemnly: *"La ultima scena di Manon Lescaut!"* The crowd clapped politely between eating their slabs of pizza and cracking small mountains of walnuts. The silver tongs of the nutcrackers glinted in the reflected light of the billboard as the day slipped away, chased by the blue black night sky. I saw some of the younger cousins trying to crack the walnuts with their shoes until one of the aunts noticed and started yelling at them.

I began at the perimeter of the billboard on the far side and placed one weary hand on an iron post, the other to my brow. I concentrated hard, imagining the weeds on the lot as cactus and the wooden posts on the edge of the lot as mirages in this dry, arid desert.

"All that trouble just to kill off an unfaithful woman!" I could hear one uncle snort, puffing heavily on his Rothman's cigarette. He stabbed it into a cut glass ashtray. Each uncle seated in the semi-circle held one in his left hand and smoked elegantly with his right. Some of the boy cousins had slipped away and were nervously lighting discarded butts with Bic lighters around the corner. But only I could see them from my vantage point center stage.

One aunt, the most religious of the group, yelled to the assembled crowd: "See? This is what happens to bad girls!" Mariangela shook one admonishing finger, wrinkled from too many buttons sewn on in half light, at the female cousins who flinched under her gaze and then giggled amongst themselves. Several flicked their dark brown hair behind their shoulders and looked longingly at the cigarette smoke snaking its way upward from the now sputtering group of boys, just out of view, gagging on their first cigarettes.

"*Settiti Mariangela! Settiti!*" they ordered my aunt to sit. She was blocking their view.

I staggered, a mop impersonating my lover Des Grieux in one hand, towards some unknown destination in the horizon. I saw the strands of the mop's head as the sweet tendrils of my faithful lover and pretended to kiss each one passionately.

"Now why did Puccini have to send them all the way to America to die?" another aunt inquired loudly, echoing my thoughts. She was ssshhed by my mother.

"She's lucky she wasn't murdered by the old man on the spot!" retorted another knowingly, as she stuffed some mild provolone into her mouth.

"*Ci hanno fatto i corni buoni!*" yelled an aunt and pointed two fingers at me, her index and pinkie, to symbolize the cuckold. *They have made him a cuckold.*

I clung to the broom's bony frame, all the while crying that I was "Alone! Lost ! Abandoned!" Then I collapsed in a heap of sweat and simulated tears in front of the adults. My generous lip gloss smeared the summer grass with a pink dew.

"*Aaah, ch'e' carina!*" they murmured approvingly. Adulterous females were fine as long as they ended up *alone, lost, abandoned* and preferably *dead.*

"*Brava! Brava!*" another uncle cried out, standing and whistling with two fingers. "*Ancora! Ancora!*" I could have given them more, perhaps the madrigal from Act 2, but I didn't want to monopolize the stage, particularly as this night was to be Clara's solo debut.

I sprang up, bowed as elegantly as I could and helped Joey prepare the stage for his scene. As we were doing this, two boys from Our Lady drove by on one of those bikes with banana seats that could ride two kids.

"Hey Joey, what are ya, a girl in that makeup? Jo-ey-'s a fag-got!" They yelled in sing song voices, hooting with laughter.

The last word came in a long, slowly receding cry that half the neighborhood probably heard. Joey turned red and almost left at this point but I grabbed him by the collar. I was still taller than him but just barely. I tightened my grip around his small brown neck and shoved him in the direction of the billboard lights. He stumbled, fell, then righted himself as he heard the familiar ominous tones of the last scene of Pagliacci where Canio murders his wife Nedda for her infidelity.

Joey's costume consisted of white makeup and an oversized ring of red lipstick around his mouth and two more of blue eyeshadow around his eyes. A pair of Papa's old white striped pajamas were tied off at the ankles and wrists with rubber bands creating a harlequin effect. The silver letter opener served as a dagger. One of Clara's toys was to play the unfortunate Silvio, Nedda's lover.

We had been told by Mama that Leoncavallo had based *Pagliacci* on a true event. As a child in Calabria, he had been brought by a servant to see a troop of traveling players. This servant was caught fooling around with the *pagliaccio's* wife. The jealous husband had stabbed both of them there and then, and the performance ended with his arrest.

In *Pagliacci,* Canio kills Nedda because he suspects that she is unfaithful after he has been poisoned by the gossip of a fellow player who also desires Nedda. During a performance, as she enacts a scene of betrayal and infidelity, Canio confuses her on-stage persona with her off-stage infidelity and stabs her. When her real life lover Silvio leaps on the stage, Canio stabs him too.

Joey and I had propped up two dolls at Clara's little white table. Two discarded beauties with fatal flaws were to act as Nedda and Tonio who are acting on stage (in their roles as Columbina and Taddeo) when Nedda is killed. I started the music.

Joey listened to the two voices of Nedda and Tonio, one hand cupped dramatically over his ear. Enraged at Nedda, he leapt forward and stabbed her (actually a one eyed doll with red hair that Clara had discarded years ago). Some of the children covered their eyes and the women started to shriek. At this point, the aunts started to vehemently interject:

"But it's not fair! She never loved you, Canio! She loves Silvio. Let her be with Silvio!" as if by the vehemence of their cries they could change the course of the opera and the world of men and women as well.

Then Joey stabbed Silvio, a plastic inflated clown with a round bottom that kept bouncing back as Joey furiously and repeatedly plunged the letter opener into its soft, plastic underbelly.

"Poor orphan!" the aunts wailed of the parentless Nedda who had been found and adopted by the older Canio. "What would she do with a broken down old man like you? Bah!" They waved their hands dismissively towards Joey. "Let her be with her true love you old fool!'

"Why don't you kill yourself instead?" They yelled, almost in unison. Joey started getting nervous, seeing how angry the aunts were getting. The uncles sat silently, trying to be unobtrusive and avoiding the wrath of the women.

"*La commedia é finita!*" he yelped and ran out of the lights of the billboard. I dragged him back and made him do a proper bow and then shoved him out of the way. I was trying to get ready for Clara's scene, the death of Mimi in *La Boheme.* This was one of Clara's favourites. In her play-acting she often cried "Let's be *Bohems.*" I sometimes had to forcibly restrain her from wandering around to the neighbours in her costumes, inappropriately expiring on their front step. Some of the older folks had received quite a shock from her morbid play-acting and half-undressed scenes.

"No Clara," I said, correcting her time and time again, "The opera is *La Boheme* but the people are *bohemians.*"

"Whatever," Clara had said, in her petulant six-year-old voice, as if she cared.

All day she was busy constructing her wardrobe for her performance from bits of clothing around the house. She wrapped a shawl around her head and powdered her face with Mama's pale face powder, her fairy dust. Of course, she applied too much and the pink granules coalesced on her soft, smooth cheeks and brow in an oddly appealing way. One of my long skirts secured with a belt around her plump waist had been her floor length, tattered gown. She asked me to apply some smudges of black mascara under her eyes to give her fresh skin the appropriately haggard appearance of the consumptive seamstress. With her little white face and plump cheeks she looked a great deal more like Lillian Gish in the silent movie when she played Mimi, than any opera singer.

Yet Clara did have something of Mimi's dreamy quality about her. She too loved "April's first kiss," the perfumed petals of flowers and all things "... that have gentle magic,
that talk of love, of spring
that talk of dreams and fancies —
the things called poetry..."

But, whereas, Mimi was small with delicate hands and a pale face, Clara was brown and sturdy with rounded cheeks, flushed red from passion. As much as Clara played out Mimi's death from consumption in *La Boheme* , she couldn't be robbed of her shining face and strong arms toasted brown by the sun to a colour of pale cafe au lait.

We could not hope to duplicate Puccini's Latin Quarter of 1830's Paris with its oranges, chestnuts, crosses and candles; its flowers, cream pies, larks and fish or its coconut milk and carrots, or, its barrow of toys from a street vendor laden with horns, tambourines and drums. But a garret, yes! We could simulate a garret with its bluish hues of death, the torn, blemished clothes of the poor bohemians and the weak flames of the dying candle light before the billboard.

Mama was in the kitchen preparing more platters of food for the family and missed our preparations and the opening section of Clara's piece. Prior to this night, Clara had always served as a silent extra, never a star, never the soprano.

Clara posed forlornly at the bottom of the stairs leading to the house, just as Mimi had, while she waited for Musetta to tell Rodolfo that she was there. On cue, Joey, as Rodolfo, picked her up and carried her to the bed of blankets in front of the billboard. Clara coughed weakly as the tinny stereo played out the last scene.

As Musetta, I took off a pair of gaudy earrings, puckered with rhinestones, that I had stolen from Woolworth's, and held them upraised before the crowd. I mimed my departure to sell the earrings and bring back medicine

Life is Theatre   345

for the ailing Mimi. I returned with a large blue bottle of Milk of Magnesia which glowed brightly in the light and pretended to feed Mimi with it. Joey knelt stalwardly by her side as Mimi tossed and turned, slowly expiring, with long sweet gasps. I exited, then brought Mimi a muff to warm her hands (actually a roll of toilet paper wrapped in cloth which easily slipped over her hands). Gently, Joey and I resumed our vigil by the makeshift bed. I covertly pinched Joey so that he would not block the audience's view of me. He mouthed a silent "Ow!" and moved accordingly.

Clara raised herself weakly, clutching the famous pink bonnet that Rodolpho had bought for her, in this case, Joey's black woolen toque emblazoned with the Hamilton Tiger Cats logo in a lurid yellow.

"Brava! Brava Mimi!" the aunts murmured as they gently stirred their last cups of espresso with small spoons.

At this moment, Mama came out, platter in hand, stood at the top of the verandah and glanced at the scene being enacted below. With her encyclopedic knowledge of opera, she quickly deduced which scene it was and promptly started shrieking. The platter dropped, spilling pepper cheese slices, prosciutto and olives over the graying heads of the aunts and uncles sitting below on the driveway.

"*Ma che faccete?*" she implored desperately. Mama looked towards Clara, still playing dead on her bed of blankets, bathed in the white light tinged a ghostly blue. Joey and I leapt up. A special knowledge seemed to fill Mama's eyes and informed the corners of her down turned mouth. She glanced worriedly at my father, who merely continued smoking his Rothmans thoughtfully with downcast eyes.

"But this is very bad luck!" she said to no one in particular. "Clara is too young to play this game!" Finally, Clara opened her date brown eyes, frightened by my mother's tone.

"Do you understand? You are not to play this game with Clara." She picked up her youngest child and walked with her hurriedly into the house. The aunts slowly rose and began to clear the plastic plates and unfinished glasses of red wine. The uncles continued to smoke together quietly. Very sheepishly, Joey and I began to put our props away and clear the stage.

Curaggia

The Second Aria

Michelle Alfano

"The Second Aria" is another excerpt from Opera.

Opera n. A form of drama in which music is a dominant factor, made up of arias, recitatives, choruses, etc... with orchestral accompaniment, scenery, acting, and sometimes dance.

My little sister Clara was an incorrigible nudist. She loved two things: being naked and music, preferably, both at the same time.

She fought valiantly for her right to be naked. We sometimes found her on the sidewalk in front of the billboard clad only in her pink rubber boots penning an elaborate chalk creation involving flowers, butterflies, forests, angels and small animals, or so she said, because we could not be sure what these fantastic lines of cobalt, turquoise and butter yellow really represented. Like most young artists of that age, she inclined towards the modern and the abstract. A small AM/FM radio that I had won in a contest from Kellogg's Corn Flakes sat on the sidewalk beside her tuned to the classical station. Sometimes, the pink boots were accompanied by a short dress as colourful as her creation, but not often.

Clara insisted on bathing naked in the kiddie pool at Gage Park until a few disgruntled matrons insisted she be clothed and an embarrassed life guard had to ask my parents to have Clara keep her frilly tulip green bathing suit with its imprinted yellow ducklings on. We would often find her running in the backyard, amongst the plants, with a mere red towel wrapped around her neck. In her four year old mind, it may have represented either the cape of some unknown hero or perhaps an angel's wings. She danced naked to tangos, polkas and pop tunes, with or without music, clambering up upon the furniture and encouraging other neighborhood children to do so as well. She established quite a reputation amongst the mothers in the neighborhood.

My parents had varied responses to her garden forays. This behavior mortified Papa because she laid waste to the *cuccuzza*, a kind of Italian eggplant that grew in long, light green, oblong shapes that had to be "married" (have it's vines tied together in order to produce fruit) once a year *and* he was horrified that she would display herself so liberally. But Mama thought Clara had much of *her* romantic side. If Mama had been born wealthy

I could imagine her jumping naked into the fountain of Trevi in Rome or swimming topless on the Riviera. Clara would have followed suit of course.

Or Clara sat in her little pink chair in front of the house on the sidewalk, observing the people passing by, the cars and all matter of wonderful things. She had a habit of running inside and informing us of her daily discoveries as in "I just saw a bird!" or "Tommy Campbell got a new bike!" to which we would nod enthusiastically and then shoo her away.

Clara at four years of age: round cheeks, long dark brown hair the colour of freshly watered earth, almost black, and held up in ponytails, poised like question marks, above her small head. A sometimes mournful face, large brown eyes and four crooked front teeth, two above and two below, pushed in, my father insisted, by her kissing the many dolls from her rather large collection too, too passionately.

Even though *La Traviata* was Mama's favourite opera, her favourite aria was from a one act comic opera called *Gianni Schicchi* by Puccini. It was one of a trio of short operas, a *trittico* or triptych. And, as I mentioned, it was one of Clara's favourites. It was the one, Mama claimed, she had sung to Clara when she was pregnant with her. Mama was a great believer in the efficacy of opera music claiming it could heal both physical and emotional ailments. During her pregnancy with Clara, Mama had often sat in the garden, portable stereo on her left and basket of sewing on her right. She would occasionally stroke the growing oval mound absentmindedly, as if caressing her future child and she would sing.

The grape vines overhead cast intermittent shadows over her face and torso, like disappearing pieces of a puzzle. And I felt a pang of something, of jealousy, of love, that I would lose one more piece of my mother — the first to Joey and now to this unborn child. To Clara, who would claim the largest, and finest, part of her soul.

One day Mama was washing the kitchen floor and Clara was sitting at the little white table dusted with pink stars and the pink chair that Mama had bought for Clara to work on her puzzle of Canada. Clara would lay the puzzle on the table and slowly piece together the country after school. Ontario was blue, Quebec was pink, Alberta green, Saskatchewan yellow, the Yukon white, etc... Then she would separate all the provinces and start again.

Mama put on *Gianni Schicchi* with Victoria De Los Angelos as Lauretta. It had been recorded at the Opera House in Rome. She pointed to the black & white photo of De Los Angelos. With her broad face, flashing eyes and shapely lips she even resembled Mama or so I thought. But come to think of it, to me, Mama often resembled any or all of the soprano heroines she

Curaggia

idolized in her operas: Solange Michel, Renata Tebaldi, Guilietta Simionato, Leontyne Price and most of all Callas, whether they played English queens, courtesans, geishas, Ethiopian princesses or peasants' daughters.

"*De Los Angelos,*" she repeated the Spanish name and stared at he LP cover. "Of the angels," she translated. "And she sounds that way doesn't she?" she murmured dreamily.

Mama always said that the characters in *Gianni Schicchi* reminded her of some distant cousins in our village back in western Sicily. The village was set in the mountains and was rife with bandits and goats, as Papa would say. In the photographs that we were shown, the houses and buildings were the colour of the sun. Their stuccoed surfaces bore a warm, golden rose colour with peeling surfaces which appeared as if they might crumble at your touch. Each layer of colour spoke of a previous generation or time. I traced one finger over the surfaces imagining their roughness under my finger. From the nearby hills, the town resembled a labyrinthine of snakelike alleyways with no discernible order except for the long rectangular strip known as the *piazza*.

The *piazza* had a fountain which rarely functioned and several cafes where only men drank bitter *tazze* of espresso and the women remained at home to complain of the men. The balconies of wrought iron faced the piazza where one could gossip with or abuse one's neighbor and the passersby. Seven Grecian temples had dotted the fields of yellow wildflowers outside the village where now only two still stand after the ravages of the war and earthquakes.

She told Clara that our family back in the old country made the opera's characters look like lambs. Only one daughter escaped the avarice that consumed this family. She put on the recording and began to tell the story of the opera.

As it begins, a Fiorentine family of a wealthy, but now dead, man hover over his body. They ransack the room searching for his will because it's rumored he has willed everything to the monastery. Rinuccio, a young nephew, finds it and makes his aunt promise that, as a reward, he may marry Lauretta, the daughter of a Florentine peasant named Gianni Schicchi. In a frenzy of greed, the family agrees because they feel that they will soon be very wealthy. When it is determined from the will that, after all, the estate *will* go to the monks, the family changes its mind. Rinuccio is deemed too good for that peasant's daughter. Mama stuck her nose in the air doing her impersonation of the rich and greedy family.

Gianni is outraged that this family thinks they are too fine for his daughter and refuses to let *her* marry. Lauretta implores her father in the love aria, also known as Rinuccio and Lauretta's aria. For his daughter's sake, Schicchi pretends that he will help alter the will by impersonating the dead man and calling three witnesses to his bedside. He feigns the old man's last dying wishes. To the witnesses, he dictates a will parceling out the estate to the family but finally giving the best of it to his friend… Gianni Schicchi. The family listens in horror but realizes it's either what Schicchi has given them or all of the estate will go to the monks. In the end, the dead man's family ransacks the house leaving the lovers alone and happy with the knowledge that they will marry and that one day this grand house will be theirs because of Gianni's clever trick.

"But how are our cousins like these people?" Clara asked, a piece of the puzzle suspended in her hand, I think it was Whitehorse.

"Just listen," she said, and propped up the mop she held against a counter. She sat on the small pink chair next to Clara and moved closer. "They all had faces like horses and forked tongues like snakes."

"Forked?"

"*Sì!* One tongue spoke Sicilian and the other the devil's *lingua*. They lived on a grand estate with many servants."

"And these people were our family?" Clara asked, somewhat incredulously as she looked around our house. We lived on the first floor and rented the other two out. The five of us squeezed into five rooms which included the kitchen and living room. I had a room. Joey and Clara, the two youngest, shared another.

My mother followed Clara's gaze and then said, "I said they were *distant* cousins." She resumed her story. "The old mother and father both grew sick. First the mother died and then the father was on his deathbed. The old man had always loved opera. They said that he had been a friend of Puccini's and even thought of becoming a librettist before he went into *lu biziness*. He had oil portraits of Puccini and Verdi in his house. There was a rumor that he had even —" Here Mama made a shoving motion with her closed fist back and forth towards Clara — "with one or two sopranos while his wife was sick. (Clara gave a puzzled look but Mama continued.) At the end, the only music he could bear to listen to was that of Puccini's.

"All the sons had married and that left only one daughter Arianna unmarried. As the only girl, most of the responsibility fell to her while the old couple was sick because they considered it women's work. *Ogni cosa difficili la lasciano per la donna!* The smart girl that she was, Arianna asked that, in exchange for her dedication and because she was unmarried, she be left the house. Well, eventually the old woman died and on the day of the funeral, the brothers and Arianna gathered at the house. They were trying to decide the old man's fate.

"It was determined that the old man must go to a nursing home of some kind very shortly. Arianna wanted to care for her father but the brothers were afraid of her influence, and, in their greed, assumed that she wanted to turn the father against the sons. On the day of the funeral, each brother quietly began to remove precious objects from the house. One took the photographs of the family and their ancestors in their gilded frames, another searched

Curaggia

through the father's wardrobe for his rings, gold pocket watch and expensively hand carved pipes. A third hunted for his father's collection of antique pistols and his mother's jewellery. Meanwhile Arianna fumed, followed each brother around the house and sometimes tried to pull a piece of jewellery or take back an old photograph. She screamed that her brothers were destroying the house that she would have married in! The brothers dropped everything. *Jesu Christo!*" Mama let the imaginary plunder drop from her hands in mock horror. Clara drew closer, leaning two small elbows on unfinished portions of Newfoundland and New Brunswick.

"*Maritata!* As far as *they* knew, there were no suitors for their sister. What did she mean by this? It turned out it was a boy she knew from Palermo, a penniless soldier. They dragged Arianna before their father…" Here Mama pulled one of Clara's dolls by one limp arm and propped it on the small white table with pink stars. "They demanded that she renounce the boy and her engagement. The father was weak and ill, unsure of himself. His sons hung over his deathbed, yelling at Arianna and then at each other, complaining that one had taken too much of this or that. They accused Arianna of thievery and greed and much more!"

"Like what?"

"Things too horrible to repeat! The same things that some men accuse women of. With the confusion, the old man bent to their greed and his fear that she would leave him. 'You must choose between your new husband or this house — not both,' he said. 'Either care for me until I die and inherit or leave here as you are and go with him.' She was given only a few moments to think it over. Arianna went to sit in the library where her father's music and gramophone were. It was the music that he had loved all of his life.

"When she came back, her only response to her father and her three brothers was to sing the love aria from *Gianni Schicchi*." Here my mother sang Lauretta's aria:

O mio babbino caro,	*Oh dear father,*
Mi piace, e bello, bello,	*I love him, he's beautiful, beautiful,*
Vo' andare in Porta Rossa	*I'm going to Porta Rossa*
a compreer l'anello!	*to buy a ring!*
Si, si, ci voglio andare!	*Yes, yes, I want to go!*
E se l'amassi inadarno	*And if you still say no*
Andrei sul Ponte Vecchio	*I'll go to the Ponte Vecchio*
Ma per buttarmi in Arno!	*But to throw myself in the Arno!*
Mi struggo e mi tormento	*I struggle and I am in torment,*
O Dio! Vorrei morir!	*Oh God! I want to die!*
Babbo, pieta! Pieta!	*Father, pity me! Pity me!*

"The old man was so moved that he willed not only his house but all that he possessed to his only daughter. In a fury, the sons ran through the house tearing precious paintings and family heirlooms from the walls. They even stole their mother's silverware with the family crest!" She showed me the crest in *Famigli Nobili Siciliani*, a book of the crests of Sicilian nobility. It featured two swords crossed over a golden chalice."

"They did?" Clara asked, her puzzle forgotten now.

"*Ma certo!* And do you know what happened? She cared for her father with her new husband until the end of his life and lived to prosper even more. Her brothers all died in poverty — one as soldier in Ethiopia, one in a drunken fight in the *piazza* and the third shot himself over a woman. And what does this tell you?"

"Family comes first," Clara said, almost by rote. This was *our* family motto. *This* should have been carved on some dusty old crest somewhere.

"*Si! Sempre la famiglia prima!*" she repeated and with that wrung out the mop and tossed the dirty water into the backyard as if purging herself of the unpleasantness of her story.

Contributors

Michelle Alfano is a Toronto writer and the Fiction Editor of the literary journal *B & A: New Fiction*. Her fiction has been published in many Canadian literary journals including the 1995 *Journey Prize* anthology. Her fiction and non-fiction work has been published in Prentice Hall's anthology *Contemporary Canada*, *eyetalian* magazine, *Canadian Fiction Magazine*, *The Capilano Review* and *Paragraph*. She is currently at work on her first novel.

Maria Barile was born in San-Giovanni in Fiore, Cosenza, Italy and immigrated to Canada in 1963. She has a B.S.W. and M.S.W., with a minor in Women's Studies, from McGill University. She currently works as a research assistant with the Disability and Integration research team at Dawson College. A long time feminist and disability rights activist, Maria writes, lectures, and conducts action research in the areas of disability rights, NRGT, health, and violence against women. She is particularly interested in the role of modern eugenic practices in the lives of persons with disability and society more generally, and; with the promotion of disability culture in Canada.

Laura Scaccia Beagle: I am a guitarist, singer, songwriter, strega, drummer, writer and I teach English as a Second Language classes to adult women. I've lived in the Chicago area most of my life. My soul "repatriated" to Italy for six weeks in 1995. I fell completely in love with the country of my foremothers. I vow to return again soon. My body craves her earth, air, mountains, sun, food, and wine, I feel most alive there. I am grateful to the ancestors for getting me here, giving me the stories and to my friend Maria Fama' for her vigilant and gracious support.

Boa. She's young and she's bossy, she kicks and she strips, and she hopes to join a circus in the next six months.

Anna Camilleri is a queer femme writer, video artist and performer, currently living in Toronto. She is a member of *Taste This*, an interdisciplinary performance troupe which toured the West Coast extensively and has produced a collection of fiction. *Boys Like Her* will be released internationally in October 1998 by Press Gang Publishers. Anna looks forward to her first book tour in November! She recently completed her first play, *Red Luna* and is working on/ dreaming up her next fiction collection and film. Anna dreams in colour of places where there is one season: summer.

Giovanna (Janet) Capone is a lesbian poet and fiction writer. She was raised in an Italian American neighborhood in New York, whose strong Napoletan' influence still resonates in her life. Her writing has appeared in various books, including *Unsettling America: a Multicultural Poetry Anthology*, *The Voices We Carry: Recent Italian American Women's Fiction*, *Bless Me Father: Stories of Catholic Childhood*, and *Fuori: Essays by Italian/American Lesbians and Gays*. She recently edited a book of writings by gay men and lesbians of Italian heritage, with Tommi Avicolli Mecca and Denise Nico Leto, forthcoming from Guernica Editions in Toronto. She is also completing her first novel: *Olive and Lavender*. Giovanna lives in Oakland, California, where she teaches poetry workshops to children through California Poets in the Schools.

Rosette Capotorto was born and raised in the Bronx. She lives in Hoboken, NJ with her daughter, Sophia, and their two cats. Her fiction and poetry has been published in *The Paterson Literary Review*, the *girlSpeak journals* and *VIA: Voices in Italian Americana*. Her book of poetry *Bronx Italian*, is forthcoming. Capotorto has run a poetry workshop for persons with Alzheimer's and for Project Read in the NYC public schools. She swears she will keep her Bronx accent for life.

Theresa Carilli (Ph.D., Southern Illinois University) is an Associate Professor of Communication and Creative Arts at Purdue University Calumet. Her work includes a book of plays, *Women As* Lovers (Guernica, 1996), a co-edited anthology, *Cultural Diversity* and the U.S. Media (SUNY, 1998), a guest edited theater issue of *Voices in Italian Americana* (1998) and a variety of performance pieces and essays in various publications. She resides near Chicago.

Anna Maria Carlevaris lives in Montreal and is a sessional lecturer in the Faculty of Fine Arts at Concordia University. Her writings on art have appeared in exhibition catalogues and art journals such as *C Magazine*, *History of Photography*, and *Poliester*. She is currently working on an exhibition project on contemporary art by Italian-Canadians.

Nancy Caronia is a native New Yorker who now resides on the Lower East Side. In 1997 she co-founded girlSpeak, an on-going reading series, and published the girlSpeak journals under her own Women's Words Press banner. Caronia has been a guest lecturer and workshop leader at Jersey City State College and has read her work at the Cornelia Street Cafe, the Nuyorican Poets Cafe, La Mama Galleria, the Knitting Factory and Barnes & Noble Astor Place. Caronia received an Honorable Mention in the 1997 New Millennium Writings Awards IV for *Go To Hell* and an Honorable Mention in the 1996 Allen Ginsberg Poetry Awards. Her work is published in *Footwork: The Paterson Literary Review* and *phati'tude Literary Magazine*. Caronia is a freelance writer, teaches workshops on memoir writing, teaches tai chi and sees private clients as an advanced reiki practitioner.

Nzula A. Ciatu is a sister, writer, feminist, actor, performer, agitator of Sicilian mixed-race origin. Her work has been published in several journals and anthologies, and reflects on race politics, ethnic identity, class consciousness, sexuality and gender. She has recently changed her name to honour her mother, grandmother, and aunt, women she holds dear to her heart. With the publishing of this anthology, she celebrates the strength of these — and other kick-ass Southern Italian — women.

Laura D'Alessandro was born in 1970 in 'Little Italy,' Cleveland, Ohio. During her many years of all-girl Catholic schooling, she acquired the desire to do photography and — with the help of the journals she has kept since the age of nine — a sense of what the issues/content of her work would be. She attended college at the Cleveland Institute of Art (with a major in photography and a minor in creative writing), and completed her graduate studies at the School of Visual Arts, New York City. She has had numerous gallery exhibits in Ohio, New York, and one in Firenze, Italy. Laura currently lives in Cleveland with her husband (a graduate student in immigration history) and her extended family. She does photo freelance work, teaches photography, and continues to write short stories.

Rita DeBellis is a first-generation Italian-American, born and raised in the Bronx. She is a graphic artist and photographer and, with her husband, co-owns Fermata Creative Services in Austin, Texas. Rita speaks a fluent and wildly irregular Central Italian dialect which she is endeavoring to teach to her son, Rudy.

Domenica Dileo was born in Calabria, Italy. She has been a citizen of Toronto since 1969. Domenica has completed a B.A. in Anthropology from York University and is working on a M.A. in Sociology at the Ontario Institute for Studies in Education at the University of Toronto. She worked over a decade in the area of violence against women and children. Domenica is engaged in feminist writing and publishing. She has been involved with

Women's Press, *Fireweed* and *Effe* — an Italian feminist publication. Domenica is a member of Avanti — an Italian Lesbian and Gay social support group and Voce Alternativa — an Italian feminist group. Domenica lives with her partner Teresa Rodriguez and Doggy Gucci. Domenica is continuously working on understanding how the social aspect of life gets transformed both locally and at the global level; and how race, class, gender, ableism and sexual orientation impact on these issues. She is fascinated with the issue of "family" and "community" and how they affect her Italian heritage. Domenica's published articles include: *The Politics of Social Services* and *Power The Invisible Issue of Feminist Collectives.* Her published poetry includes *Gay Pride Day* and *Cigars & Cigarettes.*

Mary Russo Demetrick is an assistant director of publications at Syracuse University. She is a Sicilian, Neapolitan, Rusyn American who explores the heritage and art of each of these cultures. To nurture her soul, she travels as much as possible, paints in watercolour, knits with real wool, and does eastern European-style cross stitch. She has two collections of poems (Hale Mary Press): *First Pressing (1994)* and *Italian Notebook (1995)* co-written with Maria Famà. Publications where her poetry and fiction have appeared include *Plainswoman; Word of Mouth: Short Short Writings by Women; Voices in Italian Americana; Sinister Wisdom; Paterson Literary Review; poeti italo-americani (Italian American Poets)* published in Italy; *Asheville Poetry Review, Vivace,* and *Malachite and Agate.*

Francesca di Cuore: I am a born and bred Torontonian who is a rebel living a mere four kilometres from her family — a family just waiting for her to marry and become *sistemata!* Meanwhile...

Giovanna Di Lena, from Laterza, Taranto, Italy, has recently published *Bambino tra Grande* and *Come un Girotondo,* two collections of her poetry. Translator Laura L. Ferry, from Hoboken, New Jersey, USA, began her study of Italian in order to communicate with her family in Laterza, and for singing.

Mary di Michele is the author of eight books of poetry, including *Debriefing the Rose* (House of Anansi, 1998) and *Stranger in You, Poems Selected and New* (Oxford University Press, 1995) as well as the novel, *Under My Skin* (Quarry Press, 1994). Her poetry has been translated into French, Italian, Spanish and Dutch. Born in Italy and raised in Toronto, she currently teaches in the English department of Concordia University in Montreal.

Toni Ellwand is an actor, writer, producer, mother and wife. She has been a professional actress since 1984. As well as performing across the country in other peoples' works, she has also written, produced and acted in two of her own plays; *La Donna Immobile* and *Cause Unknown.* Toni has three beautiful daughters and one great husband.

Maria Fama is a writer of Sicilian descent. Her work has been published in numerous journals and anthologies. She is the author of three books of poetry, co-founder of a video production company, and was named a finalist in the 1994, 1995, and 1998 Allen Ginsberg Poetry Awards. Fama has read her work on National Public Radio.

Dr. Maryann Feola is an Associate Professor of English at the College of Staten Island, City University of New York, where she is Coordinator of the Program in Science, Letters, and Society. She has published articles on ethnography, pedagogy, and early-modern English poets and politicians. Her *George Bishop: Seventeenth-Century Soldier Turned Quaker* was published in 1996 by the Ebor Press, York, England. Her current research focuses on the English ambivalence towards Huguenot refugees that can be found in the plays of Christopher Marlowe and his contemporaries. Born and raised in New York City, Maryann Feola lives on Staten Island and is the mother of a twenty-year old son, Mathew, and two feminist cats, Mrs. Aphra Behn and Colette.

Sylvia Fiorita was born in Montréal, Québec, and was raised in the multi-ethnic community of *Park Extension*. Her parents are originally from the Southern Italian region of Calabria. She is married to a Canadian of English descent and has three children. She works in the educational field, but writing is her main passion. This first publication is dedicated to the memory of her brother, Dan, whose life and death were both gifts of love.

Kathy Freeperson is a second generation Italian American political poet activist who 'genre-hops.' She has published and performed her work extensively since 1970 in the United States and internationally. Ms. Freeperson was a member of, directed and produced the Tampa Feminist Guerrilla Theatre Troupe. Past publications include: *The Dream Book*, edited by Helen Barolini; *If I Had A Hammer, Woman And Work; Poeti Italiani Y Canadesi; and Via Magazine's* Italian American Women's issue. She was recognized for her work by the Chesterfield Competition. Ms. Freeperson lives with two dogs, Angelina Grimke and Red Skye at Morning.

Maria Mazziotti Gillan is the author of seven books of poetry, including *The Weather of Old Seasons* (Cross-Cultural Communications), *Where I Come From: New and Selected Poems* (Guernica) and *Things My Mother Told Me* (Guernica). She is the Director of the Poetry Center at Passaic County Community College and the editor of the *Paterson Literary Review*. Along with her daughter, Jennifer Gillan, she edited *Unsettling America: An Anthology of Contemporary Multicultural Poetry* (Viking/Penguin) and *Identity Lessons* (Penguin/Putnam).

Claudia F. Giordano is a MFA in Painting. She teaches art, travels frequently, and writes. She lives in New York City.

Daniela Gioseffi, born in 1941 in the Northeastern U.S., is one of very few Italian American women to have been widely published in the U.S. literary mainstream since the early 1970s. Her poems, stories, criticism and essays have appeared in leading periodicals such as *Ms.*, *The Nation, The Paris Review, The American Book Review, Hungry Mind Review,* and *Prairie Schooner.* Her book of poems, *Eggs in the Lake* and her comic feminist novel *The Great American Belly* [Doubleday/ Dell: NY & New English Library, London, 1979-80] were widely praised in the United States and abroad. Her poetic plays, *Care of the Body* and *The Golden Daffodil Dwarf*, produced in New York City received poetry awards from The New York State Council on the Arts, 1970-77. Her anthology, *Women on War; Global Voices for the Nuclear Age,* won the 1990 *American Book Award* and became a women's studies classic. [It contained many Canadian feminists as well.] Her 1993 Anchor/Doubleday compendium *On Prejudice: A Global Perspective,* won a Ploughshares World Peace Award. Her 1995 book of poems, *Word Wounds and Water Flowers* was published by VIA Folios, Bordighera, the premier Italian American press at Purdue University, IN. She has taught intercultural communications and creative writing, lecturing widely at universities throughout the U.S. and Europe. She has published literary criticism in leading periodicals and is a member of The National Book Critics Circle. In 1990, her fiction, "Daffodil Dollars," was aired on National Public Radio as winner of The PEN Syndicated Fiction Award. She has presented her work for NPR, the BBC and CBC. *In Bed with the Exotic Enemy*, stories & novella, were published in 1997 by Avisson Press, N.C. and tell of her life as a journalist and Civil Rights Activist, in 1961, in the days of the *Freedom Riders* — when she helped to integrate Deep South television in Selma, Alabama.

Edvige Giunta is assistant professor of English at New Jersey City University. She has edited a special issue of *VIA: Voices in Italian Americana* on Italian American women authors and co-edited *A Tavola: Food Tradition and Community Among Italian Americans.*

Curaggia

She has written the Afterword for the reprints of Tina De Rosa's *Paper Fish* and Helen Barolini's *Umbertina* published by The Feminist Press.

Joanna Clapps Herman teaches at The Center for Worker Education, at City College. She has published in *Voices in Italian Americana, Italian Americana, Massachusetts Review, Kalliope, Critic, Crescent Review, Forkroads, Sing Heavenly Muse, Earth's Daughters, Slackwater Review, Fan, Woman's Day and Paterson Literary Review*, as well as in other journals.

Laura: I am a lesbian feminist whose mother is from Calabria and father from Molise. I am quickly approaching my 30's and have spent the latter half of my life as an activist working in anti-violence and anti-oppression movements. I love and live in Toronto and have learned much about staying true to what I believe and fighting for what's right. Spending time with my nephew, mom, family — extended, chosen and otherwise — is where you'll find me most often.

Deb LeRose grew up in a small town in British Columbia, surrounded by a large extended family of Italian immigrants. Besides her day job, she's an immigration activist and volunteers her time with LEGIT, the Lesbian & Gay Immigration Task Force. Deb lives in Vancouver with her loving partner. This is her first published work of fiction.

Denise Nico Leto is a San Francisco Bay Area poet, writer, and editor. She co-edited, with Giovanna Capone, *il viaggio delle donne: Italian American Women Reach Shore* for the journal *Sinister Wisdom*. She is also co-editor *of Angie Loves Mary, Vinny Loves Sal: Writings by Lesbians and Gay Men of Italian & Sicilian Descent* due out by Guernica in 1999.

Maria Lisella has been working as a staff writer for 25 years reporting on women's politics, health, labor and travel. Her work has been published in *Travel & Leisure* and the *Newark Star Ledger*. She is senior editor-Europe at the premier travel trade weekly *Travel Agent*, and is a columnist for *Diversion* magazine. Lisella has studied in Italy, visits annually and lectures on the subject of Italian Americans and their journeys. She speaks Calabrese and Italian.

Darlene Madott is a Toronto lawyer and writer. Her call to the Ontario Bar in 1985 coincided with the publication of a collection of short stories, *Bottled Roses*, Oberon. Prior to entering law school, she worked on the editorial staffs of *Saturday Night* and *Toronto Life* magazines. Her short stories have appeared in a variety of literary periodicals across Canada. Her most recent work is a film script, *Mazilli's Shoes*. A mother of one son, she continues to write and practice, primarily in the area of matrimonial law.

Francesca Maniaci was born on December 9th, 1965 in Windsor, Ontario. She studied at the University of Windsor in the fine arts department and at Concordia University in Montreal. She received her bachelor of fine arts in 1991 from Concordia University. She has participated in numerous group exhibits and has had several solo exhibits of her art work.

Gabriella Micallef. I am the daughter of a Sicilian mother and a Maltese father. I am feminist, lesbian, mother of two girl children. I emigrated to North America with my family in the early nineteen sixties. After growing up on the west coast with little contact with an identified Italian community, I moved east to Toronto in my early twenties where I became immersed in a large, identifiable, vibrant Italo-Canadian community. I am a film and video director/producer who is extremely active in anti-oppression work and in community development. Working on this anthology is an extension of my political activist work. Reading and bringing together the works, experiences and thoughts of so many of my Italian sisters has been joyful and humbling. I live in Toronto with my partner Debbie and our two daughters Siobhan and Kalia.

Carol Mottola-Knox is a new author who was born in Winnipeg, Manitoba and studied at York University's Glendon College, in Toronto, majoring in Philosophy. She has lived in Calgary, Toronto, and Los Angeles, and travelled extensively. Ms. Mottola-Knox has enjoyed writing poetry and short fiction for many years, but only recently began submitting her work for publication. She is currently working on a novel. She resides in Winnipeg with her two sons and foster-daughter. When not writing, she enjoys travelling, gardening, films, and a spectrum of music and books. Ms. Mottola-Knox has worked at a variety of jobs including Administrative Assistant with Toronto Public Libraries Learning Resources Centre, Children's' Aide Society in Toronto; and presently with Child and Family Services of Winnipeg as permanent foster mother to children with disabilities.

Anna Nobile is a writer and journalist living in Vancouver. Her work has appeared in such journals as *the eyetalian*, *effe*, and *The Antigonish Review*, as well as the anthology of erotic short fiction, *Hot and Bothered*. A former editor of *Prism international*, she now sits on the editorial board for the Federation of BC Writers. She is currently at work on a book of fiction.

Kathryn Nocerino has three books of poetry in print: *Death of the Plankton Bar & Grill* (St. Paul, MN: New Rivers Press, 1987); *Candies in the Daytime* (West Orange, NJ: Warthog Press, 1986); and *Wax Lips* (New Rivers Press, 1980). Two of her short stories are forthcoming in anthologies from Penguin Books in 1998. She has been widely represented in magazines and anthologies, including *The Dream Book* (Barolini: Schocken Books, 1985).

Mary di Paola is a freelance designer/illustrator who resides in Montréal with her cat Witkacy, her dog Emma, and her partner Allan.

Rose Palazzolo grew up in Grosse Pointe, Michigan and received a BFA in Journalism from Wayne State University in Detroit. She moved to Chicago and worked as a crime reporter and an editor. She then moved to New York City and received a MFA in Creative Writing from Sarah Lawrence College. Now living in Brooklyn, New York Rose works as an editor and freelance writer. She has been published in *Italian Americana*. "The First Italian" explores the idea that all our stories are mere reminders of the truth. She is currently working on a novel set in Detroit.

Ann Pardo has been a therapist for twenty years and a Sicilian for forty six. Happily married, living with cats in a Chicago house that is yellow inside and out, she writes for pleasure and gardens for balance. Family, mental illness, food and tragedy are resilient themes in her writing. Her future holds more therapy, more cats, more gardens and perhaps a screenplay or two. Ann is a recipient of the Illinois Arts Council Screenwriting Fellowship and a frequent lecturer on the topic of grief.

Gianna Patriarca was born in 1951 in Ceprano, Frosinone Italy in the central region of Lazio. She emigrated to Canada with her mother and sister in 1960 to join her father who had emigrated in 1956. She completed a BA and a B.Ed in 1975 from York University, and has since been teaching elementary school for the Metro Separate School Board. Gianna began writing at age nine after leaving Italy for a new land. She published her first poem in 1978 and her work has appeared in *Jewish Dialogue*, *Fireweed*, *Poetry Canada Review*, *The Worker*, *Quaderni Canadesi*, *League of Poets Newsletter*, *VIA* (Voices in Italian Americana), *Perdue University*, *Fra Noi* (Chicago), *Patterson Literary Review*

(New Jersey); and has been performed on CFMT TV, TELELATINO, and CIUT Radio Toronto. Gianna Patriarca was runner-up to the Milton Acorn's People's Poetry award in 1995 for *Italian Women and Other Tragedies* and recipient of the Scarborough Italfest recognition award for 1997. Her second book *Daughters for Sale* was published in 1997 by Guernica Editions.

Susan Raffo is a writer and community organizer from Cleveland, Ohio currently living in Minneapolis, Minnesota. She is the editor of the anthology, *Queery Classed: Gay Men and Lesbians Write about Class* (Boston: South End Press, 1997).

Diane Raptosh is of Czech and Italian descent, and was raised in Idaho. She received her MFA in creative writing from the University of Michigan. Having lived in a number of places, ranging from Chicago to Laramie, Wyoming, she returned to Idaho in 1990 to teach literature and creative writing at Albertson College. She is currently co-chair of the English Department there. Her first book of poetry, *Just West of Now,* was published in 1992 by Guernica Editions of Toronto. Her second poetry collection, *Labor Songs,* will be published by Guernica in 1999. She has published widely in journals and anthologies in the U.S. and Canada. She is the mother of one daughter, Keats.

Vittoria repetto is a native downtown lesbian New Yorker and a second generation Italian American. She has been published in Mudfish, The Paterson Literary Review, Italian Americana, Excursus and *Unsettling America: An Anthology of Contemporary Multicultural Poetry* among others. She has a poetry chapbook entitled *Head For The Van Wyck.* She was a finalist in the 1994/1997/1998 Allen Ginsberg Poetry Awards. In 1995, she was selected for the In Our Own Write Emerging Poets Reading series. Vittoria repetto is the vice-president and press contact person for the Italian American Writers Association. Her poetry chapbook will soon be available via www.amazon.com.

Francesca Roccaforte was born in 1956 in Brooklyn, N.Y. She is second generation Napolitana and Siciliana, and currently resides in the San Francisco Bay Area, California. Francesca has over twenty years of photography, writing, film, video, art, and healing arts experience. She has been recognized as one of America's leading emerging artists (1991-1992), and she has exhibited and published her work throughout the U.S., Canada, and Europe. She has won photography competitions and scholarships including Kodak/KTSF as Most Innovative photography. Her graduate thesis work and book in progress on Bay Area Italian American Women has been published in *Voices of Italian America* and in the forthcoming anthology *Mary loves Angie,Vinnie loves Sal, Writings by Italian Descended Lesbians and Gays,* Capone, Leto, Avocolli-Meca. For further information about my project and about B.A.S.I.L please contact me at P.O. Box 1219 Alameda, California. USA 94501, email: rocknfranny@juno.com or rocknfranny@hotmail.com

Francesca Schembri immigrated to Canada from her native Italy by way of South America. She is married with three children. Francesca is a researcher, teacher as well as writer and poet; some of her poems were published by *Soleil* Inc. in 1996. Her passion for theatre has encouraged her to enjoy many years in acting and directing. She also enjoys traveling, reading and the study of folk culture with emphasis on Sicilians in North America. Francesca is the Co-Founder of the Sicilian cultural Society of Canada and ItalTheatre Association. Francesca values your comments and suggestions and she can be contacted through Women's Press or by e-mail frans@ idirect.com. Finally, Francesca thanks her husband and children for their endless support. Her appreciation goes to her friend Jennifer for her advice and to the Sicilians who have shared their experiences with her to further her research.

Vita Orlando Sinopoli is a freelance writer living on Cape Cod. She was raised and attended school in Boston. Her writing career began in 1989 as co-author of a column "Remembering The North End," Post-Gazette of Massachusetts, Boston, MA. In 1995, she won first prize in Cape Cod Times Legacies Contest, Hyannis, MA. Her article received an Honorable Mentions Award in the 1996 National Legacies Contest, N.Y, N.Y. She has been published in *Green Mountain Trading Post,* VT; *Senior Forum of Cape Cod*; *Reader's Page and Prime Time Magazine of Cape Cod Times*; *Regional Review,* Boston; and *Good Old Days Magazine.* Vita, growing up in Boston's "Little Italy" during the 30's and 40's, is completing a book entitled "From My Bakery Perch."

Adriana Suriano is currently pursuing a Master of Arts in Women's Studies at The George Washington University, Washington, DC. Her poetry has been published in *Voices in Italian Americana, Footwork: The Paterson Literary Review,* and *Feminista.* She often writes about her experience as a first generation Italian-American and how her culture clashes with her feminist ideology. She is a staunch feminist, vegetarian, and lover of her mother and nonna's great Italian cooking. She owes her development as a poet to Dr. Toni Libro.

Dora Timperio. I'm so proud of myself. I believe it's never too late to learn. I keep learning everyday from my life. I was married and I have kids but my grandson is who I adore. So terribly. He will stay in my heart forever. You can tell the world that I am a happy lady. Although I'm separated from my husband, we have remained friends. I'm the kind of person who talks to everybody. I like life. I like to be happy. No matter what has happened in my life, I am still a happy lady. Yeah, I think now I'm at peace. I found my peace. It's with my painting.

Elisabetta Palombella Vallone. Born in Hoboken, New Jersey of Molfettese parents, Elisabetta Palombella Vallone was graduated from Montclair State College and Long Island University with a B.A. and M.S. respectively. Mrs. Vallone is a foreign language teacher, counselor and free lance writer. Together with her husband of 23 years and two children, she lives in Rockland County, New York. Mrs. Vallone is one of the founding members of the organization, Rockland County Women Promoting Italian Culture.

Stefania Vani. I was born in 1965 in Lachine, Quebec. I graduated from Concordia University with a Bachelor of Fine Arts in 1991. I have worked in a variety of media from painting to video. All of my work revolves around my upbringing as the daughter of Italian immigrant parents. In the past most of my art has laid some blame for my sense of alienation in Canada on my parents, especially my mother. It is only recently that I came to realize that all of my triumphs are the result of their endless support. I am honoured to participate in this anthology. It is my hope that my participation will also honour my wonderful parents.

Vivian Zenari. My father was born in Calvene, Veneto, and my mother was born in Campobasso, Molise. I was born and raised in Edmonton, and I am employed with an Edmonton aviation company as an electronic publishing specialist. My work has appeared in *The Quarterly, Zygote,* CBC Alberta Radio's "Alberta Anthology," *Transversions, Blood & Aphorisms,* and the *Toronto Review of Contemporary Writing Abroad.*

Curaggia